HERMIT IN PARIS

HERMIT IN PARIS

Autobiographical Writings

ITALO CALVINO

Translated from the Italian by Martin McLaughlin

Pantheon Books, New York

CALVINO
ITALO

All rights reserved under International and Pan-American Copy-
right Conventions. Published in the United States by Pantheon
Books, a division of Random House, Inc., New York. Originally
published in Italy as Eremita a Parigi by Arnoldo Mondadori
Editore, Milan, in 1994. This translation originally published in
Great Britain by Jonathan Cape, London, in 2003.

Pantheon Books and colophon are registered trademarks of
Random House, Inc.

Library of Congress Cataloging-in-Publication Data
[Eremita a Parigi. English]
Hermit in Paris : autobiographical writings / Italo Calvino ;
translated from the Italian by Martin McLaughlin.
p. cm.
ISBN 0-375-42184-X
1. Calvino, Italo. 2. Calvino, Italo--Homes and haunts--Paris,
France. 3. Italy--Intellectual life--20th century. 4. Paris (France)--
Intellectual life--20th century. 5. Authors, Italian--20th century--
Biography. I. Title.
PQ4809.A45 Z465 2003   853'914--dc21   2002075965

www.pantheonbooks.com
Printed in the United States of America
First American Edition
2 4 6 8 9 7 5 3 1

Preface

The bulk of this volume consists of twelve items published by Italo Calvino in different books, one unpublished piece 'American Diary' and one work that was never published in Italy but was printed in Lugano in a limited edition, *Hermit in Paris*.

In August 1985, a month before he was due to leave for Harvard University, Calvino was tired and worried. He would have liked to have finished the six lectures that he was preparing before arriving in the USA, but he could not do so. He would make corrections, change the order, fiddle about, and then would leave everything as before, or almost. He was making no progress.

I thought that a possible solution was to persuade him to move on to something else, to concentrate on another of the many projects he had in mind. To my question: 'Why don't you leave the lectures and finish *The Road to San Giovanni*?' he replied, 'Because that's my biography, and my biography is not yet . . .' He did not finish the sentence. Was he about to say 'is not yet finished'? Or maybe he was thinking, 'That book is not *all* of my autobiography'?

Years later I came across a folder entitled *Autobiographical Pieces* containing a series of texts with notes already written by him about their first publication. There was, then, another autobiographical project, quite different from the one hinted at in *The Road to San Giovanni*. It is difficult, not to say impossible, to understand how Calvino would have presented these works, which he left in chronological order. There is no doubt that they refer to the most important aspects of his life, with the explicit intention of explaining precisely his political, literary and existential choices, of informing us about how, why and when they happened. The *when* was very important: in the note accompanying 'Political Autobiography of a Young Man', Calvino writes: 'As for the convictions expressed . . . they − like every other work in this collection − are only the testimony of what I believed at that particular time and not necessarily afterwards.'

The material prepared by Calvino for this book goes up to December 1980. It is by the express will of the author that three of these fourteen pieces appear in two successive versions. I added the last five texts because they are strictly autobiographical and because they seem to me to complete the others.

Looking at this collection of texts it appeared to me that some of them lacked that sense of immediacy that one expects from an autobiography. It is not just for this reason that I thought of including 'American Diary 1959–1960'. Calvino talked and wrote on several occasions of the importance that journey had in his life. And yet he decided, when it was already at the stage of second proofs, not to publish *An Optimist in America*, the book inspired by that trip. The explanation for this brusque change of mind is to be found in a letter to Luca Baranelli of 24 January 1985: 'I decided not to publish the book because rereading it at proof stage I felt it was too slight as a work of literature and not original enough to be a work of journalistic reportage. Was I right? Who knows? If it had been published then, the book would at least have been a document of its time, and of one stage in my journey . . .'

'American Diary', however, is nothing but a series of letters sent regularly to his friend Daniele Ponchiroli at Einaudi, but meant also for all his colleagues at the Turin publishing house and even, as Calvino says, for anyone who wants to know about his impressions and experiences in America.

As an autobiographical document – and not as a piece of literature – it seems to me to be absolutely essential; as a self-portrait, it is the most spontaneous and direct one we have. The sense of this collection, then, could be: to effect a closer relationship between the author and his readers, and to deepen it by means of these writings. Calvino believed that 'what counts is what we are, and the way we deepen our relationship with the world and with others, a relationship that can be one both of love for all that exists and of desire for its transformation.'

Esther Calvino

I should like to thank Luca Baranelli for his incalculable support in this and in other matters, and for his equally precious friendship.

E. C.

Translator's Note

I should like to acknowledge the valuable help given by the following: Luca Baranelli; Christopher Brooke; Giovanni Capoccia; Alan Divack and the reference librarian of the Ford Foundation; Cathy McLaughlin; Francesca Miotto; Oliver Ready; Neelam Srivastava; Emmanuela Tandello; Diego Zancani.

Contents

HERMIT IN PARIS

Stranger in Turin

I do not think that those of us who – in the field of literature
– are Turinese by adoption are very numerous. I know plenty
who are Milanese by adoption – no wonder: almost all the writers in Milan are not native; the number of adopted Roman authors
continues to grow; Florentines by adoption there still are, though
less than before; but as for Turin, one feels that one has to be
born there, or to have come down there from the valleys of
Piedmont following the natural movement of the rivers that flow
into the Po. In my case, however, Turin was actually the result of
a deliberate choice. I come from a region, Liguria, which has
only fragments or hints of a literary tradition, so that everyone
can – luckily! – discover or invent his own tradition. Liguria is
a region which has no clearly defined cultural capital, so the
Ligurian writer – a rare bird, to tell the truth – is also a migrat-
ing bird.

Turin possessed certain qualities that attracted me that were
not unlike those of my own region, and were ones I preferred:
absence of romantic froth, reliance above all on one's own work,
an innate diffidence and reserve; and in addition the sure sense
that one was part of the big world of action, not the closed
provincial world, a pleasure in living that was tempered with
irony, and a rational, clarifying intelligence. So it was Turin's moral,
civic image, not its literary dimension, that attracted me. It was
the lure of the Turin of thirty years earlier, which had been
perceived and evoked by another adoptive Turinese, the Sardinian

3

Antonio Gramsci, and which had been defined in certain passages that are still so stimulating today, written by a Turin intellectual – this time of genuine extraction – Piero Gobetti.* This was the Turin of the revolutionary workers who in the aftermath of the First World War had organized themselves into the city's ruling class, the Turin of the anti-Fascist intellectuals who had refused to compromise. Is this Turin still alive today? Does it make its presence felt in today's Italy? I believe that it possesses the virtue of retaining its strength like a fire beneath the ashes, and that it continues to survive even when it least seems so. The Turin that was for me a world of literature was identified with one single person, to whom I had been lucky enough to be close for a number of years but whom all too soon I lost: a man about whom much is written these days, and often in a way that makes it difficult to recognize him. The fact is that his own writings are not capable of giving us a full picture of him: for it was his example of productivity that was fundamental, witnessing how the culture of the man of letters and the sensitivity of the poet were transformed into productive work, into values that were put at the service of his neighbours, into the organization and commerce of ideas, into practice and into a school of all the techniques of which a modern cultural civilization consists.

I am talking of Cesare Pavese. And I can add that for me, as for others who knew and saw him regularly, what Turin taught us amounted to what Pavese taught us. My life in Turin is deeply marked by his example; he was the first to read every page I wrote; if I have a profession it is because he was the one who taught me it, introducing me to that world of publishing for which Turin is today still a cultural centre of more than just national importance; lastly, it was he who taught me to see his city, to appreciate its subtle beauty walking along its streets and in its hills.

---

* Piero Gobetti (1901–26), influential Turinese intellectual, founder of the anti-Fascist journal *La rivoluzione liberale*, which was forced to cease publication in 1925. Gobetti died in exile in Paris from the after-effects of Fascist beatings.

Stranger in Turin

Here I really ought to change topic and say how a stranger like myself manages to fit in with this landscape, how I have settled in, I who am more a rockfish or woodland bird who has been transplanted here among these colonnades, to sniff the mists and the sub-Alpine chills. But that would be a long story. I would need to attempt a definition of the secret interplay of motifs which links the spare geometry of these grid-plan streets with the spare geometry of the dry-stone walls of my own countryside. And explain too the particular relationship between civilization and the world of nature in Turin: which is such that all it takes is the re-emergence of green leaves along the boulevards, the glimmer of the river Po, the warm proximity of the hills, and suddenly one's heart is open again to landscapes that had never really been forgotten, and you rethink your position within the vast world of nature, in short you taste the flavour of being alive.

['L'Approdo', *Rivista trimestrale di lettere ed arti*, II.1 (January–March, 1953).]

The Writer and the City

If one admits that a writer's work can be influenced by the environment in which it is produced, by the elements of the surrounding scenery, then one has to admit that Turin is the ideal city in which to be a writer. I do not understand how one could manage to write in one of those cities where images of the present are so overwhelming and powerful that they leave the writer no margin of space or silence. Here in Turin you can write because past and future have greater prominence than the present, the force of past history and the anticipation of the future give a concreteness and sense to the discrete, ordered images of today. Turin is a city which entices the writer towards vigour, linearity, style. It encourages logic, and through logic it opens the way towards madness.

[Unpublished note on Turin from 1960.]

Questionnaire, 1956

Italo Calvino's Replies to a Survey by *Il Caffè*

Bio-bibliographical details

I was born on 15 October 1923 in Santiago de Las Vegas, a village near Havana, where my agronomist father, a Ligurian from San Remo, was the director of an experimental agriculture institute, and my mother, who was Sardinian and a botanist, was his assistant. Unfortunately, I cannot remember anything about Cuba, because by 1925 I was already in Italy, in San Remo, where my father had returned with my mother to take charge of an experimental floriculture institute. My birth overseas now boils down to an unusual detail on official forms, a bundle of family memories, and a first name which was inspired by the *pietas* of émigrés towards their own household gods, but which back in their homeland sounded brazen and pompously patriotic like Carducci's poetry. I lived with my parents in San Remo until I was twenty, in a garden full of rare and exotic plants, and in the woods of the hinterland behind San Remo with my father, an old and indefatigable hunter. When I was old enough to go to university, I enrolled in the Agriculture Faculty because of this family tradition and with no real vocation, but my head was already full of literature. In the meantime the German occupation took place and, fulfilling political ideals I had held for some time, I fought with the Garibaldini partisans in the same woods that my father had taught me to know as a boy. After the Liberation I enrolled in the Arts Faculty, in Turin, and I graduated, far too quickly, in

1947, with a thesis on Joseph Conrad. My initiation into the world of literature came about towards the end of 1945, in the ambience of Vittorini* and his journal *Il Politecnico*, which published one of my first short stories. But by then my very first short story had been read by Pavese who recommended it to Muscetta's *Aretusa* which published it. My development as a writer was primarily due to Pavese's teaching: I worked closely with him on a daily basis in the last years of his life. I have been living in Turin since 1945, always in the ambit of the Einaudi publishing house, for which I started to work by selling books on hire purchase, and it is in their editorial offices that I still work today. In the past ten years I have written only a fraction of the things I would have liked to write, and I have published only a small proportion of what I have written, in the four books that have been printed so far.

Which critic has been most supportive of you? And which most hostile?
They have all been far too generous about my books, right from the outset, from the most authoritative names to the young critics of my own generation: among the former I am delighted to mention here De Robertis, who has followed my work closely from my first book onwards, and Cecchi† for what he wrote about *The Cloven Viscount*, not to mention Bo, Bocelli, Pampaloni, Falqui and also poor old Cajumi who was my first ever reviewer. The few critics who have been unfavourable are those who intrigue me most, the ones from whom I expect more: however, I have not been lucky enough to have received a negative critique

---

* Elio Vittorini (1908–66), novelist, journalist, translator (particularly of American literature in the 1930s and 40s) and leading cultural figure in post-war Italy. Initially a Fascist, he switched to anti-Fascism after the Spanish Civil War and in the Second World War fought with the partisans in Milan. His most famous novel was *Conversazione in Sicilia* (*Conversation in Sicily*) (1938–39), defined by Calvino as 'a one-off Guernica of a novel'.
† Emilio Cecchi (1884–1966), influential critic, expert on English and American literature, and author of two major travelogues, *Mexico* (1932) and *L'America amara* (*Bitter America*) (1940).

which is both serious and in-depth, one which teaches me useful things. I did receive an article by Enzo Giachino, when *The Path to the Spiders' Nests* came out, a total, absolute dismissal of the book, a real hatchet-job, but also extremely witty, which is perhaps one of the best articles written about my books, one of the few which every so often I like to reread, but not even that taught me anything really: it attacked only external aspects of the novel, which I could have improved by myself.

Could you tell us briefly something about the aesthetic canon that you subscribe to?

I expounded some general ideas of mine on literature in a lecture last February, entitled '*Il midollo del leone*' ['The Lion's Marrow'] and recently published in a journal. At present I would not want to add anything to that. But bear in mind that I am far from claiming that I succeed in putting into practice what I go around preaching. I write as well as I can on each occasion.

From what background, and from what characters and situations, do you like to derive the themes of your books?

I still don't really know, and this is perhaps why I change tack so frequently. In nearly all my most successful works there is the backdrop of the Riviera, and they are therefore often connected to the world of my childhood and adolescence. From the point of view of fidelity to one's own themes, my moving away from the town of my childhood and my ancestors deprived me of a certain source of inspiration, but on the other hand one cannot write about something one is still inside. For a long time now I have been trying to write something about Turin, which is for many profound reasons my adopted city, but it never works out properly. Perhaps I need to leave Turin to manage it. As for social classes, I cannot say that I write about one rather than another. As long as I was writing about partisans I was certain that it worked well: I had understood lots of things about the partisans, and through them I had become familiar with several social strata,

including those on the very fringes of society. I am very interested in working-class people, but I still cannot write about them
convincingly: it is one thing to be interested in something, it is
quite another knowing how to represent it successfully. I am not
really discouraged by this: I will learn to do it, sooner or later. I
do not have very strong roots in my class, the bourgeoisie, since
I was born into a nonconformist family, which was very far from
traditional ways of thinking and behaving; and I should say that
the middle class do not interest me very much, not even for
polemical purposes. I am going into all this detail because I set
out to reply to the question, not because these are problems that
disrupt my sleep. The stories that I am interested in narrating are
always stories about a search for human completeness, integration,
to be achieved through trials that are both practical and moral at
the same time, and that constitute something above and beyond
all the alienation and division that is imposed on contemporary
man. This is where any poetic and moral unity in my work should
be sought.

*Who is your favourite contemporary Italian novelist? And which of the
younger writers interests you most?*
I think that Pavese remains the most important, most complex and
the densest Italian writer of our time. Whatever problem you set
yourself, you cannot but refer back to him, both as a literary expert
and as a writer. Vittorini, too, with the literary discourse he initiated, influenced my development strongly. I say 'initiated', because
today we have the impression that it was a discourse left half-
finished, which we are waiting to take up again. Later on, once
we had got beyond the phase of a predominant interest in new
experiments with language, I moved closer to Moravia, who is the
only writer in Italy who is an author in a way that I would call
'institutional': that is, he produces at regular intervals works which
each time chart the moral definitions of our times, definitions
which deal with the way we behave, the way society is developing, and general trends in the way we think. My penchant for

Questionnaire, 1956

Stendhal makes me feel I have much in common with Tobino,* though I cannot forgive him his affected glorying in being provincial and, what's more, Tuscan. I have a particular predilection for and indeed friendship with Carlo Levi,† first and foremost because of his anti-romantic polemics, and secondly because his non-fiction narratives represent the most serious way forward for a literature that deals with society in a problematic manner; however, I do not go along with his claim that today this kind of narrative must replace the novel, which, as far as I am concerned, serves other purposes.

Turning to younger writers, in the small group of authors born around 1915, Cassola‡ and Bassani§ have set about studying certain fractures in the Italian middle-class conscience, and theirs are the most interesting stories that one can read nowadays; but in Cassola I would criticize a certain superficiality of reactions in the way his works deal with human relationships, and in Bassani the hint of preciosity that makes you think of the Crepuscular poets in Italy. Among those of us who are even younger and who began by working with story-formats that were tough, set among workers, full of action, the one who has gone furthest down that road is Rea.¶ Now there is Pasolini, one of the foremost exponents of

---

* Mario Tobino (1910–91), prolific Tuscan novelist and also psychiatrist, whose early works, *Il figlio del farmacista (The Chemist's Son)* (1942) and *Il deserto della Libia (The Libyan Desert)* (1950), were largely autobiographical.

† Carlo Levi (1902–75), Turinese medical graduate, painter and writer. Imprisoned then exiled to Basilicata for anti-Fascist activities in 1935, he based his most famous book on that experience, *Cristo si è fermato a Eboli (Christ Stopped at Eboli)* (1945).

‡ Carlo Cassola (1917–87), novelist. His novels of sub-Flaubertian realism, set in provincial Tuscany, were successful in the 1950s but were increasingly the target of more experimental writers such as Calvino. His most famous work is *Il taglio del bosco (The Cutting of the Woods)* (1949).

§ Giorgio Bassani (1916–2000), famous novelist and poet whose works are nostalgically evocative of Jewish life in his home-town of Ferrara. Largely responsible for ensuring that Lampedusa's *Il gattopardo (The Leopard)* (1958) was published after being turned down by several publishers, his own most famous novel is *Il giardino dei Finzi-Contini (The Garden of the Finzi-Continis)* (1962).

¶ Domenico Rea (1921–94), important Southern neo-realist writer whose novels and short stories depict life in Naples both during and after the war.

his generation both as poet and as a literary expert: he has written a novel about which I feel many reservations as regards its 'poetics', but the more one thinks about it, the more you feel it is something which is well-finished and which will last.

Which is your favourite contemporary foreign novelist?
I wrote an article about a year ago on what Hemingway meant for me when I started out as a writer. Once I realized that Hemingway was not enough for me, I cannot say that his place has been taken by any other contemporary author. For the last five or six years, like everyone else, I have been making inroads into Thomas Mann, and I am more and more impressed by the richness of his subject matter. However, I continue to believe that nowadays we have to write in a different way. I am freer in my relationships with writers of the past and I indulge in limitless enthusiasms; in the eighteenth and nineteenth centuries I have a whole host of models and writers I regard as friends whom I never tire of going back to.

How have your books been received outside Italy?
It is too soon to say. *The Cloven Viscount* is just coming out in France, and will come out shortly in Germany. *The Path to the Spiders' Nests* will be published in Britain in the spring, to be followed six months later by *Adam, One Afternoon*.

What are you working on now?
I never count my chickens until they're hatched.

Do you think writers should be involved in politics? And how should they do so? To what political tendency do you belong?
I believe that all men should be involved in politics. And writers too, inasmuch as they are men. I believe that our civic and moral conscience should influence the man first and then the writer. It is a long road, but there is no other. And I believe that the writer must keep open a discourse which in its implications

cannot but be political as well. I have remained faithful to these principles, and in the nearly twelve years of my membership of the Communist Party, my conscience as a Communist and my conscience as a writer have not entered into those agonizing conflicts which have tormented many of my friends, making them believe that it was necessary to opt for either one conscience or the other. Everything that forces us to give up a part of ourselves is negative. I participate in politics and literature in different ways, according to my abilities, but both things interest me as forming one and the same discourse about humanity.

[*Il Caffè*, IV.1 (January 1956) introduced Italo Calvino under the rubric '*La nuova letteratura*' (*New Writing*) with a short story ('*Un viaggio con le mucche*' ('A Journey with the Cows'), later included in *Marcovaldo*) preceded by his replies to a questionnaire set by G. B. Vicari. The same text, with a few variants, is found in Elio Filippo Accrocca, *Ritratti su misura (Personal Portraits)* (Venice: Sodalizio del Libro, 1960) and appears below.]

Personal Portrait

I am the son of scientists: my father was an agronomist, my mother a botanist; both were university professors. Among my family and relations only scientific subjects were held in any honour; one maternal uncle was a university professor of chemistry married to another chemist (in fact I had two uncles who were chemists married to two women chemists); my brother is a university lecturer in geology. I am the black sheep of the family, the only one to have studied literature. My father was Ligurian, from an old San Remo family; my mother is Sardinian. My father lived for about twenty years in Mexico, in charge of various institutes of experimental agronomy, then Cuba; he took my mother to Cuba: they had got to know each other through exchanging scientific papers, and they were married during a whirlwind visit to Italy; I was born in a village near Havana, Santiago de Las Vegas, on 15 October 1923. Unfortunately I do not remember anything about Cuba, because before I was even two I was already in Italy, in San Remo, to which my father had returned, along with my mother, to be director of the experimental floriculture institute. All I retain of my birth overseas is a complicated detail on my birth certificate (which in brief biographical notes I replace with the more *accurate* one: born in San Remo), a certain amount of family memories, and my first name, which my mother, thinking that I was going to grow up in a foreign land, decided to give me so that I would not forget my ancestors' homeland, but which in Italy sounds belligerently nationalist. I lived with my parents in San Remo until I was twenty, in a garden full of rare and exotic plants, and in the woods of the Ligurian pre-Alps, along with my father who was a tireless old hunter. After secondary school I made some attempts to follow the family's scientific tradition, but my head was already full of literature and I gave up. In the meantime the German occupation had taken place and, following political feelings I had held since adolescence, I fought with the partisans, in the Garibaldi Brigades. The partisan war took place in the same woods which my father had taught me to know since childhood; I deepened my identification with that landscape, and in it I made my first discovery of the pain of the human world.

It was that experience which, some months later, in the autumn of 1945, gave birth to my first short stories. The first one was sent to a friend, who was in Rome at the time; Pavese thought it was good and passed it on to Muscetta, editor of the journal *Aretusa*. That issue of *Aretusa* came out very late, the following year. Meanwhile Vittorini had read another story of mine and had published it in the weekly *Il Politecnico*, in December 1945.

By then I had enrolled in the Literature Faculty of Turin University, going straight into the third year, as a result of the exemptions given to war returnees. During 1946 I took all the examinations that the four-year course required, and I even obtained some good marks. In '47 I graduated with a thesis on the Opera Omnia of Joseph Conrad. I went through university too quickly, and I regret it; but then my mind was on other things: on politics, in which I got involved passionately; on journalism, because I was writing pieces on a wide range of topics for *l'Unità*; on creative literature because in those years I wrote very many short stories and one novel (in twenty days in December '46), entitled *The Path to the Spiders' Nests*: that was how that world of poetics evolved from which, like it or not, I have never substantially departed. From 1945, and especially from when Pavese returned to Turin in '46, I had started to gravitate around the Einaudi publishing house, for whom I began working by going round selling books on hire purchase: I became an editor there in 1947, and am still working for them. But I also felt the lure and influence of Milan and Vittorini, right from the time of *Il Politecnico*. As for Rome, I have a relationship of both polemical rejection and attraction to the city, attracted by the presence of Carlo Levi and other critics such as Alberto Moravia, Elsa Morante, Natalia Ginzburg.

I have travelled through Europe, both on this side and on the other side of the Iron Curtain; but travels are not events of much importance.

As for work involving a considerable amount of scholarship and bibliographical research, I produced the edition of *Italian Folktales* (1956); it took two years of total commitment and I enjoyed it; but afterwards I abandoned the career of the scholar; I am more interested in being a writer, and that already causes me enough sweat.

[E. F. Accrocca, *Ritratti su misura (Personal Portraits)* (Venice: Sodalizio del Libro, 1960).]

American Diary 1959–1960

Dear Daniele* and friends,

      For me boredom has now taken on the image of this transatlantic liner. Why did I ever decide not to take the plane? I would have arrived in America buzzing with the rhythm of the world of big business and high politics, instead I will arrive weighed down by an already heavy dose of American boredom, American old age, American lack of vital resources. Thankfully I only have one more evening to spend on the steamer, after four evenings of desperate tedium. The *'belle époque'* flavour of liners no longer manages to conjure up a single image. That hint of a memory of past times that you can get from Monte Carlo or the spa at San Pellegrino Terme does not happen here, because a liner is modern: it may be something 'old-world' in concept but they are built pretentiously now, and populated by people that are antiquated, old and ugly. The only thing that you can glean from it is a definition of boredom as being somehow out of phase with history, a feeling of being cut off but with the consciousness that everything else is still going on: the boredom of Leopardi's Recanati, just like that of *The Three Sisters*, is no different from the boredom of a journey in a transatlantic liner.

    Long live Socialism.

    Long live Aviation.

---

* Daniele Ponchiroli (1924–79), then chief editor at Einaudi.

My Travelling Companions (Young Creative Writers)

There are only three of them because the German Günther [*sic*] Grass failed the medical examination and, thanks to the barbaric law that you have to have sound lungs to enter America, he has had to give up the scholarship.*

There is a fourth writer who is going tourist (third) class because he is bringing with him, at his own expense, his wife and young son, so we have only seen him once. He is Alfred Tomlinson, an English poet, a typical example of a British university type.† He is thirty-two but could be fifty-two.

The other three are:

Claude Ollier, French, thirty-seven years old, a *Nouveau Roman* writer: to date he has only written one book.‡ He wanted to take advantage of the voyage finally to read Proust but the ship's travelling library only extends as far as Cronin.

Fernando Arrabal, Spanish, twenty-seven years old, small, baby-faced with a beard under his chin and a little fringe.§ He has lived in Paris for years. He has written works for the theatre which no one has ever wanted to put on and also a novel published by Julliard. He is desperately poor. He does not know any Spanish writers, and he hates them all because they call him a traitor and would like him to do Socialist Realism and write against Franco and he refuses to write against Franco, he doesn't even know who Franco is, but in Spain you cannot publish anything or win

---

* Calvino and the other writers mentioned were all visiting the USA on a Ford Foundation Scholarship.

† Alfred Charles Tomlinson (1927–), poet and artist, the visual qualities of whose verse are evident in *Relations and Contraries* (1951) and *Seeing is Believing* (1958).

‡ Claude Ollier (1920–), novelist. He won the Prix Médicis for his novel *La Mise en scène* (1958), which turned out to be the first of a cycle of eight novels in the *Nouveau Roman* style.

§ Fernando Arrabal (1932–), playwright and director. He was exiled from Franco's Spain in 1955 and settled in France. His plays, such as *Cimetière des voitures* (1958), are often unconventional and evocative of ritual.

17

literary prizes unless you are against Franco because the person who runs everything is [Juan] Goytisolo who forces everyone to do Socialist Realism, i.e. Hemingway-Dos Passos, but he hasn't read Hemingway-Dos Passos, and hasn't even read Goytisolo because he cannot stand reading Socialist Realism, and apart from Ionesco and Ezra Pound he does not like very much else. He is extremely aggressive, and jokes in an obsessive and lugubrious way, constantly bombarding me with questions about how on earth I can be interested in politics, and also about what exactly one does with women. There are two targets for his attacks: politics and sex. He and the French Teddy Boys, for whom he acts as interpreter, cannot even conceive of people who find politics or sex interesting. He is only interested in cinema (especially Cinemascope, Technicolor and gangsters), and pinball. Since leaving the seminary (he studied to be a Jesuit, in Spain) he has not had any sexual relations, apparently not even with his wife (they have been married three years), and has never had any desire to have any, and the same goes for politics. He says that the French Teddy Boys who are coming on to the scene now are even more remote than he is from politics and sex. He does not speak a word of English, and writes in French.

Hugo Claus, a Flemish Belgian, thirty-two years old, he began publishing at nineteen and since then he has written an enormous quantity of things, and for the new generation he is the most famous writer, playwright and poet of the Flemish-Dutch-speaking area.* Much of this stuff he himself says is worthless, including the novel which has been translated and published in France and America, but he is anything but stupid and unpleasant: he is a big, fair-haired guy with a stunning wife who is an actress (whom I got to know as she was saying goodbye to him at the quay), and he is the only one of these three who has read

---

* Hugo Claus (1929–), major Belgian novelist, poet and playwright. His first novel, *De Metsiers* (*Duck's Game*) (1950), which Calvino refers to, embodied both Flemish traditions and American influences.

a lot and whose judgments are reliable. Four hours after the launch of the first sputnik he had already written a poem about it, which was published instantly on the front page of a Belgian daily paper.

My new and, I think, definitive address for all the time I will be in New York, i.e. up to around 5 January, is:

Grosvenor Hotel
35 Fifth Avenue
New York

From the Diary of the Early Days in New York

9 November 1959

Arrival

The boredom of the voyage is handsomely compensated for by the emotions stirred up on arrival at New York, the most spectacular sight that anyone can see on this earth. The skyscrapers appear grey in the sky which has just cleared and they seem like the ruins of some monstrous New York abandoned three thousand years in the future. Then gradually you make out the colours which are different from any idea you had of them, and a complicated pattern of shapes. Everything is silent and deserted, then the car traffic starts to flow. The massive, grey, fin-de-siècle look of the buildings gives New York, as Ollier immediately pointed out, the appearance of a German city.

Lettunich

Mateo Lettunich, Head of the Arts Division of the Institute of International Education (IIE) (his family were originally from Dubrovnik), who has an obsession with saving money, did not want me to get a porter for my stuff. The Van Rensselaer hotel where he has arranged for us to have rooms is filthy, down-at-heel, stinking, a dump. If we ask him about a restaurant, he always recommends the worst one in the area. He has the worried, frightened look of those Soviet interpreters who accompany delegations, though he has none of the phlegmatic *savoir-faire* with which Victor V., the functionary who was the son of aristocrats, accompanied our delegation of young city and country workers. Those of us who have been spoiled by the hospitality of socialist countries are made to feel ill at ease by the awkward tentativeness with which the land of capitalism manages the millions of the Ford Foundation. But the fact is that here you do not travel as a delegation, and once you have cleared a few formalities, everyone goes off on his own and does what he wants and I won't see Mateo again. He is a writer of avant-garde plays which have never been performed.

Hotels

The next day I go around Greenwich Village looking for a hotel and they are all the same: old, filthy, smelly, with threadbare carpets, even though none of them has the suicidal view of my room at the Van R. with its filthy, rusty, iron fire-escape stairs in front of the window and its view over a blind courtyard on which the sun never shines. But I make for the Grosvenor which is the Village's elegant hotel, old but clean; I have a beautiful room in quintessentially Henry James style (it is just a short walk away from Washington Square, which has stayed mostly as it was in his time), and I pay seven dollars a day as long as I guarantee to stay two months and pay a month in advance.

New York Is Not Exactly America

This phrase, which I had read in all the books on New York, is repeated to us ten times a day, and it's true, but what does it matter? It's New York, a place which is neither exactly America nor exactly Europe, which gives you a burst of extraordinary energy, which you immediately feel you know like the back of your hand, as though you had always lived here, and at certain times, especially uptown where you can feel the busy life of the big offices and factories of ready-made clothes, it lands on top of you as though to crush you. Naturally, the minute you land here, you think of anything except turning back.

The Village

Maybe I'm wrong to stay in the Village. It is so unlike the rest of New York, even though it's in the centre of the city. It is so like Paris, but deep down you realize that this is an unwitting similarity which does everything to make you believe it's deliberate. There are three different social strata in the Village: the respectable middle-class residents, particularly in the new apartment blocks which are rising up even here; the native Italians who try to resist the influx of artists (which began in the 1910s because it cost less here) and who often fight with them (the riots and mass arrests of last spring has meant fewer Sunday tourists, who are mostly New Yorkers from other districts), but at the same time it is thanks to the bohemians and the bohemian atmosphere that the Italians survive and their shops make money; and the bohemians themselves who are all now known popularly as 'beatniks' and who are more dirty and unpleasant than any of their Parisian confrères. Meanwhile, the way the area looks is threatened by property speculation which plants skyscrapers even here. I signed a petition to save the Village, for a young female activist collecting signatures on the corner of Sixth Avenue. We Village people are very attached to our own area. We also have two newspapers just for ourselves: the *Villager* and the *Village Voice*.

A Small World

I am right opposite Orion Press, Mischa* lives a block away, Grove

---

* Ugo Stille, New York correspondent of the *Corriere della sera*, and a personal friend of Calvino and the Einaudi publishing house.

Press is just round the corner, and from my window I can see Macmillan's huge building.

The Cars

The most amusing thing when you arrive is seeing that in America *all* the cars are enormous. It is not that there are small ones and big ones, they are all huge, sometimes almost laughably so: the cars we consider only for major tourist trips are normal for them, and even the taxis have really long tailfins. Among my friends, the only New Yorker with a small car is Barney Rosset, ever the nonconformist: he has one of those tiny little cars, a red Isetta.

I am very tempted to hire immediately an enormous car, not even to drive it, just for the psychological sense of being in control of the city. But if you park in the street, you have to go down at 7 a.m. to move it to the other side of the street, since the parking restrictions alternate between the two sides of the street.

And a garage costs a fortune.

The Most Beautiful Image of New York by Night

At the bottom of the Rockefeller Centre there is an ice-rink with young boys and girls skating on it, right in the heart of New York by night, between Broadway and Fifth Avenue.

Chinatown

The poor immigrants in their neighbourhoods are rather depressing: the Italians in particular look sinister. But not the Chinese: Chinatown, for all its tourist exploitation, exudes an air of civilized, hard-working well-being and genuine happiness unknown in the other 'typical' neighbourhoods in New York. At Bo-bo's the Chinese cuisine is amazing.

My First Sunday New York Times

Although I had read and heard about it, going to the newsagent to take delivery of a bundle of paper you can hardly carry in your two arms, all for twenty-five cents, leaves you stunned. Amid the various sections and supplements I manage to find the *NYT Book Review* which we are used to thinking of as a separate journal, whereas it is just one of the many inserts in the Sunday edition of the paper.

My Ford Grant Colleagues

In New York we came across the English poet who was travelling in tourist class and who now instantly wants away because he cannot settle here and he prefers to live in the country; and the Israeli scholar and essayist on politics and religion, Meged,* who is also the author of a novel which has never been translated into any European language. He is a serious character, quite different from the others, and not very pleasant; I do not really understand him, and I don't think I'll see him again, because he also wants to go and stay in a small university town. The place of Günther Grass (poor Grass didn't know he was tubercular: he only discovered it when he went for the medical for the visa, and now he is in a sanatorium) will be taken not by a German but by another Frenchman, Robert Pinget, the person who wrote *Le Fiston* (he has now finished another novel).†

The Press Conference

The IIE is organizing a press conference with the six of us. In

---

* Aharon Meged (1920–), Israeli novelist and leading figure on the Israeli left. His *The Living on the Dead* was considered the best Israeli novel of the 1960s. The novel Calvino refers to was probably *Fortunes of a Fool* (English translation 1962).
† Robert Pinget (1919–97), novelist. His parodic novel *Le Fiston* (1959) explores the possibilities and limits of language. The other novel referred to is *Clope au dossier* (1961).

the biographical notes distributed to those present, the item about me that struck everyone was that I was recommended by Princess Caetani, who has such a high opinion of me. The press conference has the same amateurish and rather forced air that you find in Eastern-bloc democracies, the same kind of people, young girls, silly questions. Arrabal, who speaks no English and replies in a whisper, failed to cause a stir. 'Which American writers do you want to meet?' He replies: 'Eisenhower', but does so very quietly, and Lettunich, who acts as interpreter, does not want to repeat it. Ollier dryly points out (replying to the question of whether we are pessimists or optimists) that he holds a materialist conception of the world. I say that I believe in history and that I am against the ideologies and religions that want man to be passive. At these words, the President of the IIE gets up from the Chairman's table, leaves the room and never reappears.

Alcoholic

I will become very shortly, if I start drinking at 11 in the morning and continue until 2 a.m. the next night. After the first few days in New York, what is necessary is a strict regime of energy conservation.

Is my book [*The Baron in the Trees*] displayed in the bookshops, either in the window or on the shelves?

No. Never. Not in one single bookshop.

Random House

The real pain is that the managing editor, Hiram Haydn, after sponsoring *The Baron* has left Random House to found Atheneum, and Mr [Donald] Klopfer, the owner and founder, has no faith in the commercial possibilities of my book, talking to me in the same way

as Cerati* does to Ottiero Ottieri.† Every bookshop received four or
five copies of my book and whether they sold them or not, they don't
restock: what can the publisher do in these circumstances? The
Americans don't appreciate fantasy, it's all very well getting good reviews
(there was a wonderful one in Saturday's *Saturday Review*), even the
bookshop owner reads them and ought to know what to do. I manage
to wring a promise from him to send Cerati to talk to the bookshop
owners, but I don't believe it will happen. However, I am having lunch
with him on Thursday. I have learnt from the girls (I am always very
impressed by them: in terms of its editorial department, Random House
is one of the most serious publishers) that there have been mix-ups in
distribution because of the IBM machines that Random House has
just installed in its sales department: two machines had faults and so
tiny bookstores in villages in Nebraska have received dozens of copies
of *The Baron*, while major bookshops in Fifth Avenue have not received
a single one. But the basic point is that the publicity budget for my
book was only 500 dollars, which is nothing: to launch a book you
have to spend half a million dollars, otherwise you will not achieve
anything. The fact is that the big commercial publishers are fine when
the book is a natural best-seller, but they are not interested in promoting the kind of book which first has to do well in terms of the literary élite: all they want is the prestige of having published it. At present
they have three best-sellers: the new Faulkner, the new Penn Warren,
and *Hawaii* by a commercial writer called [James Michener], and those
are the ones they sell.

Orion Publishers

consists of two tiny rooms. This [Howard] Greenfeld is a bright,
rich boy, but it's difficult to understand what they want to achieve.
However, since they only do very few books, they look after the

---

* Marketing manager at Einaudi.
† Ottiero Ottieri (1924–), intellectual and writer. He was particularly interested
in the ways in which literature can reflect the industrial world.

commercial side, also as a kind of public relations exercise, and the *Italian Folktales* are everywhere, also because they come under children's books even though Orion has done nothing to push the book in the children's literature direction. On Sunday there was a review of it in the *New York Times Book Review*, very flattering as far as the Italian original was concerned but rightly critical of the translation.

Horch

She seems a woman who is on the ball, a fearsome old bird, but very warm and kind. She does not want to give *The Cloven Viscount* to Random House, who now want it, and I agree with her in keeping it for the smallest but most prestigious publishing house. So she will give it to Atheneum which will start publishing soon and it will certainly be a publishing event of tremendous importance since these are three highly prestigious editors who have got together: one is Haydn who used to be manager of Random House, another is Michael Bessie from Harper's and the third is Knopf's son [Pat]. I have already made a bit of a mess of things because I made a promise to Grove who are sticking close to me, and indeed Grove books you find everywhere: they are the most fashionable books in avant-garde circles. Actually they did have an oral promise from Horch, but she wants to give the book to Haydn, and I also believe that Atheneum will be important.

10 November

Rosset

The cocktail party at Barney Rosset's of Grove was the most interesting party to have brightened up my days here so far, and also the one that had the widest variety of people. It confirmed the verdict we reached on Rosset at Frankfurt: daringly and very classily avant-garde but lacking in historical and moral backbone.

Rosset (and his partner Dick Seaver, who was also at Frankfurt, and who lives with a French wife in a hovel at the top end of Manhattan, which has nevertheless been adapted internally into an elegant intellectual's house) has to be understood mostly by seeing him in the Village: he has the spirit of the Village intellectual's eternal (and unproductive) protest against the even more eternal conformism of America. Consequently he gives credit to the beatniks because he says they are useful in waking up young Americans from their TV-watching; he gives credit indiscriminately to everything that Europe does in terms of avant-gardism, because it is useful for waking up America.

The Beat Generation

Allen Ginsberg came to Rosset's party, with his disgusting black straggly beard, a white T-shirt beneath a dark, double-breasted suit, and tennis shoes. With him there was a whole crowd of beatniks who were even more bearded and filthy. They have all moved from San Francisco to New York, including Kerouac, who did not come tonight, however.

Arrabal's Adventure

The beatniks naturally fraternize with Arrabal, who is also bearded (his Parisian under-the-chin beard and their unkempt beatnik beards), and invite him to their house to listen to his poetry readings. Ginsberg lives with another bearded man as man and wife and would like Arrabal to be present at their bearded couplings. When I got back to the hotel, I found Arrabal looking frightened and scandalized because they wanted to seduce him. This Teddy Boy who had come to America to scandalize others is totally terrified at his first encounter with the American avantgarde and suddenly is revealed as the poor little Spanish boy who up until a few years ago was still studying to become a priest.

He says that at home the beatniks are very clean, they have a beautiful house complete with fridge and television, and they live as a quiet bourgeois ménage and dress up in dirty clothes only to go out.

A Broadway Première

Hugo Claus went to the première of a new play by [Paddy] Chayefski [*sic*]. He says that after the show he went to dinner at Sardi's, where all the playwrights and theatre people dine. Everyone awaits the appearance of the next day's papers in a state of great anxiety, because one hour after the end of the show, around 1 a.m., the *New York Times* and the *Herald* are already out with their reviews (the reviews are written then, not at the dress rehearsal). The papers arrive. Amid a total silence one of the actors reads the review. As soon as they hear that the critic liked the show, they all applaud, embrace each other and order champagne. The play will be on for two years; if the notices had been unfavourable it would have been taken off after a few days. Immediately the impresarios and agents come forward, the world-wide rights to the show are sold, people rush off to the telephones, and in the space of an hour the fate of the show for the foreseeable future has been decided, with an instant turnover of millions.

The Jews

Seventy-five per cent of the publishing world here is Jewish. Ninety per cent of the theatre is Jewish. The ready-to-wear clothes industry, New York's major industry, is almost exclusively Jewish. Banks, however, are completely closed to Jews, as are the universities. The few Jewish doctors are regarded as the best because such difficulties are put in the way of Jews trying to get into university and to pass exams that those who do succeed in graduating in medicine have to be of extraordinary brilliance.

The Women

Very attractive women are rare. On the whole they are *petite-bourgeois*. Whichever way you look at it, it's basically like Turin.

Adventure of an Italian

In order to familiarize himself with the big city, the Italian newcomer spent the evenings going to one party after another, following people he did not know into houses owned by people he knew even less. Thanks to a very witty and intelligent actress, he ends up in the house of a beautiful singer from television, amid a rather commercial crowd of theatre people, impresarios, etc. He meets a young fellow-Italian who is an airplane steward who spends half his week in Rome, the other half in NY. When the Italian newcomer is about to take the actress back to her home, the steward suggests they form a foursome, and persuades the actress to invite along a rather pretty girl who is a cinema actress. The girl quickly agrees, the two Italians are already rubbing their hands as if everything was signed and sealed, and all they had to do was to decide on who takes which girl. But in the actress's house the conversation turns to culture and progressive politics. By this stage it is clear that there will be no action. The girls are anything but stupid, even the Hollywood actress who at first seemed the usual starlet. It turns out that both are Russian and both Jewish. In the end the two Italians leave and the Hollywood actress stays to sleep with her friend. It turns out that they are both lesbians. The two Italians go out into the deserted, drizzling streets of New York at 5 in the morning.

The Situation

My desire to discover something new taking shape in this America which has emerged from the Cold War has not found anything promising so far. It seems that there are no other groups like the

New Deal people emerging on the horizon, and the current climate – although everyone agrees it is enormously improved – seems to hold no promise of any change among the country's leaders. The country continues to prosper and the relaxed mood strengthens the internal status quo.

Corruption

Everyone's conversation these days is about American corruption, the corruption and greed for money in the institutions of power, the newspapers, etc., which they say has never been so rife. The TV scandal concerning Van Doren,* which is the main topic in the papers, is seen as a symbol of the universal acceptance of deceit. In certain quarters (for instance, in the theatre world) Van Doren is defended as being just a scapegoat for a situation which prevails everywhere.

The Third Sex

is even more widespread than in Rome. Especially here in the Village. The unwitting tourist goes into any outlet to have breakfast and suddenly notices that everyone in the place, customers, waiters, chefs, are all clearly of that persuasion.

A Small World

The European visitor was really happy with his first American girlfriend. He certainly could not have wished to find anyone better, any girl more joyfully enthusiastic and problem-free. But the thing which he liked best of all was that she was so totally American, devoid of any contact with Europe. She had only spent a few weeks in Europe some years ago. After a few days of contented love, he

---

* Charles Van Doren, a Columbia professor, had in 1957 won over $100,000 on a popular quiz show by having answers fed to him. He confessed to taking part in the fraud in November 1959.

discovered that when in Europe she had been the girlfriend of his friend X whose ex-girlfriend Z had also been his girlfriend.

Mischa

I have only seen him once, out at lunch, because at home his children have got 'flu. But we will see each other a lot. He is the person who says the most intelligent things and gives the most valuable pointers on America. Elizabeth I have only met in the street; she has not written again because she was waiting for Giulio to write.* Now we will work out how to organize the work.

Jacqueline

Wonderful creature. I spent yesterday evening with her. But being with her is difficult for me since her extreme irritability transmits a certain uneasiness (though I've noticed that as you speak to her this gradually diminishes), and it is not very useful because I can't get anything out of her either as regards publishing (her qualities are neither literary nor editorial), nor socially (being a pessimist and a misanthrope, she stays very much inside her shell). She represents the other side of America, the negative, painful one. And as such, she too will be an inevitable point of reference for me, precisely because she is the one American woman I have met so far with whom you cannot instantly establish a naturally cordial relationship.

How Random House Works

Editorial Department: every editor (whether Senior or Junior) knows the author personally. A writer such as Faulkner has his own editor with whom he is in continual correspondence for all

---

* Elizabeth is the wife of Ugo Stille (Mischa); Giulio is Giulio Einaudi the publisher.

matters editorial. (Administrative issues are not part of the picture: these are dealt with between the author's agent and the publisher's legal department.) The editor works with the author on the book; it is common practice for him to make the author correct his manuscript until there is nothing left that he is unhappy with. The editor is usually the person who has sponsored the book's publication, in the case of a new author; if the author has long been on the publisher's books, his editor is the person who has always dealt with him and knows how to approach him. The editor, they tell me, has to ensure that a character who has dark hair in the first chapter does not have fair hair in chapter ten. But in reality the person who deals with these minutiae is the copy-editor who works under the editor: he reads and rereads the proofs finding things to correct, though he is not the person who corrects typographical errors, because they work in the printers and have nothing to do with the publisher. (Random House does not have its own printers.) The person who is responsible in the publisher's eyes for the book coming out, for how long it takes to get published, etc. was called the managing editor while Haydn was there, but now Albrecht Erskine has arrived he is called the executive editor. (Erskine is, moreover, Faulkner's editor.)

The *Art Department* deals with the cover, the binding, the illustrations.

The *Production Department* is what we call the technical office.

The *Publicity Department* is not to be confused with the *Advertising Department*. The latter deals with publicity that is to be paid for. Random House has no such department because it has a contract with an advertising firm that deals with publicity for the books, operating on a budget for every book that is decided by the publisher. This firm also prepares the wording of fliers and sends them directly to the publisher for approval. Instead the Publicity Department deals only with the papers, with relationships with reviewers (and when possible with radio and TV), and it all revolves round public relations and lunch invitations, and is always carried out in fact by female staff. Even very small publishers like Orion concentrate their efforts in this area.

The *Promotions Department* works on mail-order sales, using advertisements with order forms in newspapers and sending out postcards to various addresses depending on the kind of book. This is a very important department with around ten staff in it.

The *Sales Department* is run by machines, as I have explained already and as my book has discovered.

The *Juvenile Department*: Random House has one of the largest outputs of children's literature and this is looked after by a separate editorial department.

The *College Department* is for school texts. The Modern Library series was initially under the College Department, but is now under the Editorial Department.

The *Legal Department* deals with the question of rights.

From what I have been able to work out, the structure of Macmillan's is no different, apart from the enormous importance of university editions and differences in nomenclature (they do not know what a Promotions Department is, and sales by mail-order come under the Business Department).

The Most Important Young Writers in America

According to Mr Dompier, the critic of the *Herald Tribune*, with whom I had a lunch interview yesterday, organized by Orion, the main writers of the new generation, which in his view is an extraordinary generation, are (in this order):

> Peter Fiebelman (*A Place without Twilights*)
> Philip Roth
> William Humphrey
> Bernard Malamud
> Grace Paley
> H. E. Humes
> Herbert Gold
> Harvey Swados

Systematic Editorial Work,

of course, I have not been able to begin yet. In the coming week I have several important publishing engagements. But above all I need to organize my days in such a way as to have time to read and get my ideas in order. In the meantime, therefore, I can only transcribe for your benefit some scattered notes from my notebook.

People talk well also of James Yaffe, who has already written four books, one of which – *What's the Big Thing?* – is published by Little Brown.

I have heard positive comments about an English novel (published by Heinemann): A. E. Ellis, *The Rack*.

I cannot remember if William Styron has already signed up for a publisher in Italy. Random House will publish his new novel around March: *Set This House on Fire.*

Grove are very keen on a new novelist they will launch in spring, and whom they introduced to me: Alexander Trucchi [*sic*], *Cain's Book*.

In the bookshops I have seen a very beautiful *abstract* book for children: Leo Lionni, *Little Blue and Little Yellow* (an Astor book published by McDowell).

Random House has had great success with children's books by a writer who signs himself as Dr Seuss, and who specializes in books for 5–6 year olds which are written using only 300 words.

Instructions for Use

Daniele, this is a kind of journal for use by my friends in Italy. Einaudi receives a private copy of it at home, but this copy is public, except for the strictly publishing details which you can cut out and pass on to Foà;* the rest of it you can keep in a folder, for consultation by all colleagues, and also by friends and

---

* Luciano Foà, in charge of the Rights Office, would shortly leave Einaudi to found the Adelphi publishing house.

visitors who want to read it, so that this hoard of experiences that I am accumulating becomes part of the heritage of the nation.

The Emigrant's Desires

The emigrant needs someone to write to him, to be kept in touch with the land of his birth, otherwise soon his letters will become fewer and fewer, and he will forget his native tongue. He has not received any post so far, not even from his mother, nor from any of the women he has loved, nor even from the *Eco della Stampa* for which he took out a subscription before leaving. When he travels into the city centre he goes to Times Square to buy the odd issue of *La Stampa* to read the local news pages, about motorway accidents, pensioners asphyxiated by gas, etc. But this is not enough.

A Nightmare

After four days in New York I dream that I have come straight back to Italy. I cannot remember why I have come back: for some reason or other I wanted to return on the spur of the moment, and here I am once more in Italy and I don't know what I have come back for. But I feel an urgent need to return instantly to America. In Italy the fact that I have been in America or that I have now come back is of no interest to anyone. I am seized by a mad sense of despair at not being in America, a terrifying sense of anguish, a desire for the USA that is not connected to any particular image but it is as though I had been snatched out of my normal existence. I have never felt such all-encompassing despair. I wake up trembling: finding myself back in the squalid little room in my first American hotel is like finding myself back home.

Yesterday a Day Full of Publishers

With Mr [Victor] Weybright from the New American Library,

an old friend from Frankfurt. He recommends two novels just about to appear:

Irving Wallace, *The Chapman Report*, to be published by Simon & Schuster and then by the NAL. The film rights have been sold to Zanuck-Fox for $300,000. The plot is very funny: a group of university professors carry out a survey along the lines of the Kinsey Report, only it is in a club for ladies of high society and a whole series of complications ensues.

Peter Zilman (or Tilman – I can't read W's handwriting very well), *American novel*, published by Coward McCann-NAL; the film rights have gone to Columbia. He says that it is like Alec Waugh's *Island in the Sun* which was a huge best-seller.

I am not sure how reliable W's recommendations are. Signet Books' fiction is on the whole disappointing (and he cannot decide whether to take *The Baron!*), but he is very kind and wants me to choose from the Mentor Books list whatever might be useful to us. As far as I can see, we have already seen all the titles of any interest. I await instructions.

At Knopf: Mr Pick, whom I met at Frankfurt, has been scouting me, and will certainly take the next long novel by Bassani; I will scout Mr Kushland another day. All the Knopf team is very friendly. I await instructions.

Cocktail party at [Kyrill] Schabert's (from Pantheon) attended solely by publishers. Mr Schabert met Einaudi in Vienna and is very friendly, but as the publisher of *Dr Zhivago* and *The Leopard*, Schabert is becoming an American branch of GGF.* I will see him next week. I await instructions. Old Knopf was there too, as was [James] Laughlin from New Directions, Haydn from Atheneum with whom I am dining this evening, and Mrs Van Doren from *Publishers' Weekly*: she is the aunt of the man involved in the scandal.

The book most talked about this week is Norman Mailer's

---

* Giangiacomo Feltrinelli.

Advertisements for Myself (Putnam), which contains essays, auto-biographical pieces and unfinished fictions.

Colour Television

Yesterday evening I saw some colour television. Perry Como's show was interrupted every so often by advertisements for a firm that makes food products, and for ten minutes you saw plates of spaghetti with a hand pouring sauce over them, all in colour, and plates of meat and salad, with explanations about how to prepare it all. Wonderful. It should be introduced as soon as possible into underdeveloped countries.

I was with friends of a woman who is an avant-garde choreographer: she was presenting some scenes from one of her ballets on the *Perry Como Show*. But the ballets were terrible. Shortly afterwards, they telephone her. She was already at home, in despair, crying: she ran out of the studios before the end of the programme, and wants to kill herself as a protest against the outrage inflicted by television on her art.

20 November

The UNO

The most interesting thing to do is to go to see the United Nations building with Ruggero Orlando who as soon as he found out that I was in New York often invites me to explore this world which he knows like nobody else. I think that in terms of architecture and interior furnishings the UN building is the great monument of our century; even the meeting rooms are wonderful, apart from the one where the Security Council sits. And the atmosphere one breathes at the UN is also magnificent because you feel the spirit of the United Nations at work in a way that you no longer can in America or Europe, and this is certainly also to the credit of Le Corbusier, because ambience counts, and how. Yesterday evening I was present at the vote on atomic experiments which saw France (and Afghanistan) isolated. Everyone votes by saying 'Yes' except the Latin American delegates who say '*Si*', I think out of anti-American nationalism. Later at a party held by the Morocco delegation, I meet: Soboleff who congratulates me on my 'very good timing' when I tell him that *Italian Folktales* is coming out at the same time in the USA and the USSR; Alí Khan (head of the Pakistan delegation) who congratulates me on the two beautiful girls I am with; the Algerian foreign minister, from the National Liberation Front (here as an observer; they are not optimistic in the short term about the possibility of negotiating), whom I ask to write a book for Einaudi; the only woman who is head of a delegation (Sweden), a beautiful and witty woman; the current president of the UN, old Professor Belaunde from Peru, who in order to please me articulates his admiration for Fogazzaro,[*] Ada Negri,[†] and Papini;[‡] Ortona[§] who never misses a party; the Afghan who explains that he voted against the resolution because the motion was too weak; the reverend[¶] who is fighting against racial discrimination in South Africa and is here as an observer (he has been expelled from South Africa); Mr Mezrick from the American Cooperative Movement who publishes a Bulletin of UN documents and who has now been reported by Senator Eastman to the Committee on Un-American Activities because he 'publishes a Communist pamphlet' (the Bulletin publishes all the speeches,

---

[*] Antonio Fogazzaro (1842–1911), late Romantic novelist, whose most famous novels, *Piccolo mondo antico* (1895) and *Piccolo mondo moderno* (1901), mix Romantic and decadentist traits.
[†] Ada Negri (1870–1945), poet and novelist whose works were popular in the first two decades of the twentieth century.
[‡] Giovanni Papini (1881–1956), iconoclastic intellectual and writer. He co-founded the important literary journals *Il Leonardo* (in 1904), and *Lacerba* in (1913), but later became a representative of Fascist Catholicism.
[§] Egidio Ortona (1910–95). A major Italian diplomat at the UN, he went on to become Italian Ambassador to the USA (1967–75) and a major architect of Italian foreign policy.
[¶] Gap in the typescript.

even the Russian ones): he will now have major problems (financial above all: he will have to pay a top lawyer to prove, etc.), but in truth Eastman, who is a Southerner, wants to attack his wife who is from the League for the Emancipation of Colored Peoples.

Sunday in the Country

Last Sunday I went for the first time into the country, or rather the wooded hills north of the Bronx, along the wonderful motorways; first to lunch at the house of relations of the woman who was accompanying me, who is from a family of bankers who own all the estates in the area, in one of the few surviving eighteenth-century wooden villas. There was an atmosphere of great refinement, though because it was Sunday the maid was not there; but everything was so well organized that you did not notice. Then to see Giancarlo Menotti* who had invited me to his house at Mount Kisco: he lives (with Samuel Barber, but he was not there) in a really beautiful chalet in the woods, which is however full of the bad taste of that kind of building: their real moral defect is the lack of any distinction between the beautiful and the horrible: plates with the photograph of a woman, a magic lantern, a chamber of horrors. Menotti complains that the fame of the Spoleto music festival prevents him from receiving funds from American foundations. Sunset in an American wood is something that is totally unreal. As is the sky in New York at night.

19 November

Wall Street

Naturally the first thing I want to see is Wall Street and the Stock Exchange. I arrange for a visit to Merrill Lynch, Pierce, Fenner & Smith, which is the biggest stockbroker firm there. They have

---

* Giancarlo Menotti (1911–), composer. He taught in Philadelphia's Curtis Institute, and later founded the Spoleto Arts Festival. His most famous opera at this time was *The Consul* (1950).

girls who act as guides and accompany visitors and those hoping to invest to see round all the offices and explain how everything works. A pretty girl explains everything to me in great detail. I do not understand a thing, but at the same time I am full of admiration and also suffering enormously because this New York stock market is the first thing that I have felt is bigger than me and that I will not be able to get my head round. Merrill Lynch, Pierce, Fenner & Smith operates entirely electronically. Linked to the Stock Exchange, all its offices have the tape with all the stock values printing out continually, and it receives all the requests to buy and sell by telephone and telex from its branches in every city in America, and in Europe too, and every second, with their calculators, they can work out dividends, securities and commodities and all the data recorded and transmitted to the Stock Exchange, and then there are the calculations for the over-the-counter market which are very complex, and from all the offices and the machines in this enormous skyscraper which houses Merrill Lynch, Pierce, Fenner & Smith, all the data end up on the top floor where the huge IBM 705 machine sits, which in one minute can perform 504,000 additions or subtractions, 75,000 multiplications, 33,000 divisions and can take 1,764,000 logical decisions and in three minutes can read all of *Gone With the Wind* and copy it on to a tape as wide as your little finger, because everything ends up on this tape, all written in little dashes, and on an inch of this there are 543 characters. I have also seen the 705's memory which is like a piece of cloth you would wipe with, all made up of tiny threads. I also went to the Stock Exchange and it is certainly a grand sight but one which we already know well from the cinema. But this Merrill Lynch, Pierce, Fenner & Smith is some place: it is a pity I am now too old, but something your children should do first thing is to work with them for a while to learn the trade (there is an enormous students' office): send them for an apprenticeship with Merrill Lynch, Pierce, Fenner & Smith, then they can learn philosophy, music, and all the rest, but first of all a man has to know how to work Wall Street. They also do a huge amount of propaganda for investments, with brochures based on the principle that money breeds money, with maxims about money by the great philosophers, and this propaganda for the cult of money is constant in America: if by chance a generation grows up that does not put money above all else, America will go up in smoke.

Now, however, at Columbia University I have met Mario Salvadori, scientist and mathematician, who was with Fermi in the team that worked on the atom bomb: he seems a first-class person, and he says that that 705 is nothing and he will take me to see real electronic brains.

New York Diary

24 Nov.

The Girls' College

Yesterday I was invited by Mark Slonim (the most famous expert on Russian literature in America, and he also teaches Italian: I had met him in Rome) to the Sarah Lawrence College in Bronxville where he teaches comparative literature. Sarah Lawrence College is a very chic girls' college, where each girl chooses the course she wants, there are no lectures just discussions, no exams, in short everyone has a great time dealing with pleasant and varied cultural topics. Girls in trousers and big socks and multicoloured jerseys, just like in films about college life, flutter down from the buildings where they have their faculty rooms and dormitories. Lunch is very meagre because in any case the girls want to keep their figure (while the starving tutors protest). The students of Italian are waiting for me in the cafeteria: there are about twenty-five of them, of whom at least a couple are very good-looking. Their teacher tells me that they have prepared a surprise for me: they want to sing me a song; one has a guitar; I think it will be the predictable Neapolitan song or something Italian they have heard on the radio; instead they actually sing '*Sul verde fiume Po*'.* My surprise is beyond all their expectations. (I later learn that a record brought by the Momiglianos to America had ended up there.) The teacher explains that the song is very useful for learning verbs. The girls ask me questions about my short stories which they know off by heart. Then I go to the seminar on comparative literature: today we are discussing Alesha Karamazov. The girls give their opinion of Alesha, then Slonim intervenes, raising questions and directing the discussion, with great finesse and pedagogical effectiveness, but these young girls are surely as far from Dostoevsky as the moon. Seeing Dostoevsky and Russian religious and revolutionary thought skimming over that gathering of young heiresses in Westchester brings on the kind of astonishment and enthusiasm that would be provoked by a collision of planets. Then I go to the Italian lesson: today the girls have to do *La sera fiesolana*. They translate D'Annunzio's lines with terrifying ease. The discussion turns to St Francis. And the teacher asks me to read his poem 'Brother Sun, Sister Moon'. I read, translate and give a commentary on St Francis to the various Beths, Virginias, Joans. And since their teacher has dropped a timid hint that she prefers D'Annunzio, I rebel and produce a lengthy eulogy putting St Francis above all other poets. I realize that this is the first time since coming to America that I have explained anything or defended an idea. And it had to be St Francis. Very appropriate.

The Guggenheim Museum

In the last few weeks the obligatory topic of every New York conversation is the new museum designed by Frank Lloyd Wright to house Solomon Guggenheim's art collection. It has just been opened. Everyone criticizes it; I am a fanatical supporter of it, but I find myself nearly always on my own in this. The building is a kind of spiral tower, a continuous ascending ramp without steps,

---

* A satirical song written by Calvino in 1958, set to music by Fiorenzo Carpi.

with a glass cupola. As you go up and look out you always have a different view with perfect proportions, since there is a semicircular outcrop that offsets the spiral, and down below there is a small slice of elliptical flower-bed and a window with a tiny glimpse of a garden, and these elements, changing at whatever height you are now at, are an example of architecture in movement of unique precision and imagination. Everyone claims that the architecture dominates the paintings and it is true (apparently Wright hated painters), but what does it matter? You go there primarily to see the architecture, and then you see the paintings always well and uniformly illuminated, which is the main thing. There is the problem of the permanently sloping floor which poses the conundrum of how to get the picture straight. They solved the problem by hanging the pictures not on the wall but on iron spars that stick out from the wall to the centre of the painting. In reality the Guggenheim collection is not extraordinary, apart from the powerful collection of Kandinskys which we have already seen in Rome, and there are many pieces that are second-rate. (Unlike the Museum of Modern Art, which is not enormous, but everything it houses is a breathtaking masterpiece; or the beautiful rooms of modern painting in the Metropolitan, spoiled unfortunately by a horrendous Dalí which people queue in order to see.) Everyone is in agreement in criticizing the exterior of the Guggenheim Museum, but even that I like too: it is a kind of screw or like a lathe driveshaft, totally in harmony with the interior.

Laughing at Death

Much has been said about the Americans' lack of a sense of mortality. The other evening in Harlem, in a night-spot called Baby Grand where jazz is played, a very famous black comic started his piece by joking about the death of Errol Flynn, amid widespread sniggering; then he told a crude joke about Flynn's death and the funeral, again amid general hilarity. Another continual topic for the black comic's satire and humour is the racial question, the fight against the segregationists.

Olivetti

Adriano Olivetti has been to New York in the last few days and bought Underwood, which had been in trouble for some time. From now on Olivetti will produce goods in America using the Underwood name, thus avoiding customs problems. Underwood's shares are not quoted on the Stock Exchange at present but now it seems as though they will come back on to the list. That idiot Segni,* when he was here at the press conference, an American journalist asked him what he thought about the infiltration of Olivetti into Underwood's shares, and he replied: 'A big firm like Underwood will certainly not have anything to fear from a small concern like our own Olivetti!'

At Prezzolini's

23 Nov.

At dinner chez Prezzolini† who had invited me when I was still in Italy to come to his little cell on the sixteenth floor, already described many times, to enjoy his famous skills as cook and host. Also present is Mrs [Sheila] Cudahy, widow of the Marquis Pellegrini, a Catholic and Vice President of Farrar Straus, and a Hungarian count, Arady, if I caught the name right, author of a biography of Pius XI. After days and days of meeting only Jews, this mixing with reactionary Catholics is a not unpleasant distraction. Naturally, alongside Prezzolini, the Hungarian count, who is a Catholic liberal, admirer of the moderate Lombard aristocracy

---

* Antonio Segni (1891–1972), major Christian Democrat politician. He was Prime Minister of Italy from 1955–57 and 1959–60, before becoming President from 1962–64.
† Giuseppe Prezzolini (1882–1982), writer and critic. Founder, in the early twentieth century, along with Giovanni Papini, of influential cultural journals such as *Leonardo*, and editor of *La Voce* (1908–14), he later moved to the USA. A conservative critic of Italian culture, he also wrote about his life in America.

of the nineteenth century, actually seems more like a comrade to me. Extremely interesting conversation in which the count proves the continuity of the line going from Pius XI to John XXIII, a line which however has still not managed to win because Pius XII's party is still strong. Everyone attacks America's Irish clergy and Cardinal Spellman, but I notice that their reasons are the opposite of the usual criticisms of the Church's authoritarian, hierarchical spirit: here they criticize their lack of formality, their 'democratic' offhandedness, their ignorance of Latin. Everyone is scandalized here by the fact that they have placed a glass case in St Patrick's cathedral with a coloured wax statue of Pius XII, of natural size, with hair and everything just like in Madame Tussaud's; they cannot understand how the Vatican has not intervened against this act of sacrilege, which was surely engineered by Spellman in order to spite Pope John XXIII. They are full of praise for Mencken as the great destroyer of American democratic myths. And the Hungarian in turn is full of praise for Karl Kraus (now adored by Cases,* just as Mencken played the role of master to all of America's left wing). The way they extol *The Leopard* (which they have no hesitation in putting on the same level as Manzoni), solely for reactionary reasons, confirms – as far as I'm concerned – the enormous importance of this book in the West's current ideological involution. Many of these discussions were clearly inspired by my presence in their midst, with minimal polemical effort on my part, naturally: I am absolutely fine with those who openly declare themselves to be reactionary, I am on friendly terms with Prezzolini, while with the count and the marchioness (whom I will see later at a business lunch) we have common ground in our knowledge of Bordighera and its society.

N.B. Opinions on [James] Purdy and particularly on *Malcolm* are negative even in the Farrar Straus environment. I have not

---

* Cesare Cases (1920–), literary critic, expert on German as well as Italian literature, and the first to introduce into Italy the work of the Marxist critic György Lukács.

found anyone who had a good word to say about Purdy (whom I shall meet soon); on the other hand, yesterday evening they were all unanimous in lauding Malamud as the great new writer; an interesting verdict coming from Catholics. Consequently, in this year's planning, I would say to promote Malamud more than Purdy.

How a Big Bookshop Works

(From the conversation I had with the manageress of Brentano's.) The American bookshop is more complicated than an Italian one for the simple fact that the number of books published is so great that nobody, on the sales side, thinks it is possible to be on top of all of it. Brentano's is organized very well: it is a huge bookstore with separate tables for new fiction, history, poetry, and so on, and even including sections for paperbacks (which are usually handled not by a bookseller but by the local drugstore or newsagent or separate paperback shop), periodicals, and of course a Juveniles section which you find in every bookshop. They do not buy on the one-free-copy-per-dozen system; the bookseller receives a discount of 40 per cent; on rare occasions the publisher provides one free copy in every ten. Orders are taken when the publisher's agent makes his monthly call. The staff are just shop assistants as in tie-shops and would not dream of knowing anything about books. The public are not in the habit of visiting bookshops; if for example a mother reads a review of a book on child-rearing she maybe telephones or writes to the publisher asking what she has to do to buy it, but she is not in the habit of going to the bookseller. In short, it is not really interesting: it is exactly as it is in Italy. Now the bookshops are full of small reproductions of famous classical or modern statues, which must be the latest discovery by those engaged in mass reproduction of works of art, after the reproduction of paintings (in other words it is a practice as old as can be). However, it is ugly stuff.

Tail-lights

A study of the American psyche could be carried out by examining in particular the enormous tailfins of their cars and the great variety and elegance of the shapes of their tail-lights, which seem to embody all the myths of American society. Apart from the enormous round lights, which one often sees even in Italy and which evoke chases of cops and robbers, there are those shaped like missiles, like skyscraper pinnacles, like film-actresses' eyes, and the full repertoire of Freudian symbols.

New York, 7 December 1959

This time I am not going to write much. For the last week I have been living a rather secluded life, writing up my lecture. It's a real bore because here they know nothing at all about Italy, so you have to start from first principles and explain absolutely everything. I mean you have to construct a whole ethical-political-literary discourse, the kind of thing you would no longer dream of doing in Italy; and even so they will not understand a thing here, since the Italophiles are always the least intelligent. However, when one sees how inadequate the official organs for the spreading of Italian culture are, one feels duty bound to try to compensate as best one can; and this lecture, unless I immediately get bored with it and ditch it completely, might be one of the more important purposes of my journey, if for no other reason than the fact that someone will have travelled throughout the USA explaining who was Gramsci, Montale, Pavese, Danilo Dolci, Gadda, Leopardi. So I have not gone on with the American diary, but it also happens that I have fewer things to say, because New York is no longer a new city to me, and although initially everyone I saw in the street was the occasion for me to offer some particular observation, now the crowd is just the usual New York crowd you see every day, and the people I meet and the way I spend my day all fall under the category of the predictable.

47

However, I have accumulated a number of observations which I will work through gradually, and I have plunged into a more active existence now that I have finished the lecture and handed it in to be translated. I should also be able to find the time to read some books, though this is still in the future and the little wall of books on my dressing-table is by now covering up the mirror without me being able to begin dismantling it.

So, for now, just a few points about publishers.

Fruttero:* I've bought the Modern Library anthology of horror stories and I will put it in the post tomorrow (the post offices are shut on Saturday and Sunday). What size of shoes do you wear?

James Purdy

I've been to see Purdy, who lives in Brooklyn but in the more residential part. He received me in the rented room he shares with a professor. The kitchen and a double bedroom are all in the one room. Having left his job, Purdy is living for a year on a grant from the Guggenheim Foundation and this has allowed him to finish his novel, *The Nephew*, which he delivered to his publisher today: it is something more like his short stories than like *Malcolm*. Purdy is a very pathetic character, middle-aged, big and fat and gentle, fair and reddish in complexion, and clean-shaven: he dresses soberly, and is like Gadda without the hysteria, and exudes sweetness. If he is homosexual, he is so with great tact and melancholy. At the foot of his bed is weight-lifting equipment; above it, a nineteenth-century English print of a boxer. There is a reproduction of a Crucifixion by Rouault†, and scattered all around are theology books. We discuss the sad state of American literature, which is stifled by commercial demands: if you don't write as the *New Yorker* demands, you don't get published. Purdy published his first book of short stories at his own expense, then he was

---

* Carlo Fruttero was at the time one of the editors at Einaudi.
† Georges Rouault (1871–1958), French painter, subjects include biblical characters.

discovered in England by Edith Sitwell, and subsequently Farrar Straus published his work, but he does not even know Mrs Cudahy, and the critics don't understand him, though the book is, very slowly, managing to sell. There are no magazines that publish short stories, no groups of writers, or at least he does not belong to any group. He gives me a list of good novels, but they are nearly all unpublished works which have not been able to find a publisher. Good literature in America is clandestine, lies in unknown authors' drawers, and only occasionally someone emerges from the gloom breaking through the leaden cloak of commercial production. I would like to talk about capitalism and socialism, but Purdy certainly would not understand me; no one here knows or even suspects that socialism exists, capitalism wraps itself round and permeates everything, and its antithesis is nothing but a meagre, childish claim to a spiritual dimension, devoid of any coherent line or prospects. Unlike Soviet society, where the totalitarian unity of society is totally based on the constant awareness of its enemies, of its antithesis, here we are in a totalitarian structure of a medieval kind, based on the fact that no alternative exists nor even any awareness of the possibility of an alternative other than that of individualist escapism.

I ASK EVERYONE ABOUT SALINGER AND EVERYONE TELLS ME ABOUT THIS SAD CASE: THE MOST IMPORTANT WRITER OF THE GENERATION BETWEEN US, WHO NO LONGER WRITES, HAS BEEN TAKEN TO A PSYCHIATRIC INSTITUTION, AND THE LATEST THINGS HE HAS WRITTEN ARE STORIES FOR THE *NEW YORKER*. IT IS RATHER LIKE WHAT HAPPENED TO FITZGERALD IN THE SECOND HALF OF THE CENTURY. I THINK WE SHOULD DO THE OTHER BOOK BY SALINGER AS WELL, AS SOON AS POSSIBLE, NAMELY *NINE STORIES* (LITTLE BROWN, AND REPRINTED BY THE MODERN LIBRARY). SALINGER IS BY NOW A KIND OF CLASSIC IN AMERICA.

All writers here have the chance to say that they have to write a book and have to stay at home for a year and can obtain a grant for it.

Grants

For professors grants are easy because they usually don't teach for more than two years in succession before finding a way of securing a grant for a year or two, without having to be accountable to anyone. However if they then want another grant, they have to somehow write a book, so there is this inflation of academic books which are maybe pointless but at least they are books, whereas in Italy publications for university posts are maybe pointless but they are not even books, and you certainly cannot live off them.

Sweezy

Dear Raniero,* I wrote to Sweezy† in order to see him, but he had Leo Hubermann telephone me to say that he is now at Cornell University for a few days, then he is going to his house in the country (here everyone disappears at Christmas), and that I should write to him. But since we have to contact him, it is of course better if you do so: you can explain your plan in detail. If then he wants to reply through me, I am at his disposal. But bear in mind that I will be staying in New York only until early January then I shall be leaving for California and will not be back in NY until mid-March.

Styron

I have the proofs of Styron's new novel;‡ from the early pages I have read it seems good. Will I ever find the time to read? I don't

---

* Raniero Panzieri (1921–64), editor at Einaudi, dealt in particular with books on politics and sociology.

† Paul M. Sweezy (1910–), Marxist economist, author of *The Theory of Capitalist Development* (1942) and (with Leo Hubermann) *Cuba: Anatomy of a Revolution* (1960).

‡ *Set This House on Fire*, which Einaudi would publish in 1964 as *E questa casa diede alle fiamme*.

know (that is, I always think I have something better to do than read) and if I see that I can't manage to read on I'll send the proofs to you.

The Lecture

I gave my lecture at the Casa Italiana of Columbia University, and there was quite a big audience despite it being Christmas, and so I have begun to carry out my role as ambassador for Italian opposition culture, which when one arrives here one feels one has to do, even though it is a bore to stand there and explain Italian Resistance literature and post-war culture down to the present day and to launch into a discourse which will include all the forbidden names; however, the fact is that here nobody has said these things, and I believe that I have accomplished at least one initial achievement regarding Italian cultural policy in America, just by saying all the things that Prezzolini does not want said and showing Donini (who runs the Embassy's Italian Cultural Institute: he is Ambrogio's brother, almost as much a conformist as his brother but on the opposite side; he is not stupid, and what's more has a complex about having a brother who is a Communist) how to do his job. They were all there and they took it on the chin, Prezzolini did not object: on the contrary, he said he agreed with me in many respects and they all congratulated me 'on that part of the lecture in which [I] spoke about Ludovico Ariosto' (namely, the final part where I was only speaking about my own position in order to cheer the audience up and where I ended with a profession of loyalty to Ariosto) but not on the rest. And the few clear-thinking Italians in that ambience felt slightly cheered. I do not know what impression it made on the Americans, as American Italophiles are never very bright. And the truth is that Italian culture has little to say, these days even less than ever, even in a world as refractory to ideas as this one.

Christmas

I will spare you the description of the phantasmagoria that is Christmas in this city, because you have read about it a hundred thousand times and all I could add is my guarantee that it is even more excessive than you can imagine, and nowhere could you see a festival permeate the life of a city more: it's not a city any more, it's Christmas. Christmas in this consumerist civilization has become the ultimate celebration of consumerism; the ubiquitous Santa Claus (Father Christmas) you see in human form at the door of every shop holding his little bell, and depicted on every poster, in every shop-window, while at every shop-door the unremitting God of consumption imposes on everyone happiness and well-being, cost what it may.

Prospects for the Election

The cult of Stevenson* among the majority of intellectuals, as though he were some sort of saint, is not likely to have any effect this time either, on the decision of the mass of voters. Stevenson probably will not even be his own party's candidate after being ousted last time, and there is a great danger that the Democratic candidate will be the Catholic Kennedy, and in all the papers there is great talk of the possibility of a Catholic President. But in reality it is almost certain that the election will be won by the Republicans and so the crucial choice will be the Republican Party's decision regarding Nixon and Rockefeller. As for Rockefeller, I hear him spoken about either very negatively or in extremely positive terms. For instance, Max Ascoli,† always a supporter of the most realistic policies, seems to me to have made up his mind to support Rockefeller,

---

* Adlai Stevenson (1900–65), Democrat politician, ran for President in the 1952 and 1956 primaries.
† Max Ascoli (1898–1978), liberal philosopher and sociologist. He left Fascist Italy in 1931 and settled in the USA, where he founded the journal the *Reporter*, a forum for liberal views.

whereas he has no time for Nixon whom he regards as an opportunist ready to support the most contradictory policies depending on which way the wind blows. Others speak to me about Rockefeller as a man lusting for power and devoid of scruples. The reality is that America has nothing new to say in terms of political alignments.

The Latest American Joke

Do you know the difference between the optimist and the pessimist?

The optimist is learning Russian; the pessimist is learning Chinese.

New York, 2 January 1960

Happy New Year to all my friends in Turin!

For the last twenty days I have been without any reply to my letters, indeed I would say without any signs of life except for the minutes of a meeting dated 21 December. I regret this lack of dialogue (basically there was only ever a dialogue with my very early letters) which comes at a time when the hardest work of the winter season ought now to have tailed off. Einaudi Publishing has never succeeded in distance-working, and if you had all sent me criticisms, advice, encouragement, it would have helped me not to feel cut off in the isolation of the individual traveller who is not involved in the production process of a developing company. I have felt this even more in these weeks when the city's Christmas madness has halted my systematic visits to publishers (though I have by now very few left to deal with) and now I am about to leave, around the 12th: Cleveland, Detroit, Chicago then San Francisco, Los Angeles and the South, and for a couple of months my letters will just be reportages of my travels plus, I hope, accounts of books I have read, because I am going to take books with me in the hope of reading them.

On Horseback through the Streets of New York

For the first time in my life I get on a horse. Sunday morning in Central Park. But the stable is rather far towards the west from Central Park and as soon as I am in the saddle I have to go along a lengthy stretch of 89th Street and cross over a couple of Avenues. I ride along high above the roofs of the cars, which are forced to slow down behind the horse's pace. In Central Park the going is good though a bit muddy. I try out a trot and also a bit of a gallop, which is easier. All around, in the marvellously clear air of New York (no city in the world has such clear air and such a beautiful sky), are skyscrapers. Along the lawns in the Park run the inevitable squirrels. My companion, sitting lightly on her horse, shouts technical instructions to me which I don't understand. I have this sensation of dominating New York in a way I have never done before, and I am going to recommend to all visitors to New York that the first thing they should do is a tour on horseback. I met this woman, a writer's wife, at a party yesterday where I was guest of honour (Erich Maria Remarque was also there with his wife, Paulette Goddard, who has aged considerably from the time of *Tempi moderni* but has great eyes and is full of verve, in short she's very nice, whereas with her husband there was an instant feeling of mutual antipathy), anyway this woman, who was young and Jewish but with a real feeling for nature, says a propos of *The Baron in the Trees* that she loves 'to ride', but never 'rides' because her husband never takes her, but that I must certainly know how to 'ride' well. I tell her that I have never been on a horse in my life, so we fix up to meet again the next day and they also lent me a pair of little Mexican riding boots. It is clear that this is 'the right way of approach to America',* because one has to go through all the means of communication in historical sequence and eventually I will arrive at the Cadillac.

---

* Phrase in English in the original.

The Actors' Studio

Often on a Tuesday or Friday morning I go to the Actors' Studio
which is a kind of hovel in the port area, and there are always
many actors, even some famous ones, and directors who sit around,
with Lee Strasberg there in the middle, and each time a group
of actors put on a short play or just a scene, in order to study
some problems, then they explain to their colleagues the problems they encountered in acting it, and the others discuss and
criticize and Strasberg gives his opinion and often delivers an
actual lecture. All this is free, of course: it is a club for actors to
experiment and discuss. Or there are exercises invented by
Strasberg called 'A Private Moment': here an actor without a
script portrays a personal problem, for instance you see someone
in bed who gets up slowly, then is seized by despair, he swears,
tries to get back to sleep, gets up, goes to the window, puts on
a record, then feels less desperate, etc. After this they discuss, etc.
It is all rather funny: this Strasberg (who was one of that group
of playwrights from the '30s when there was also Clifford Odets
and company) is obsessed with the idea of internal sincerity,
which the actor has to 'feel' (which seems a load of rubbish to
me), and the standard question when they perform a scene from
a play is: 'but in that moment were you working on your own
problem or on a stage problem?' because to make your own
psychological problem identify with the problem portrayed in
the play is regarded as the *ne plus ultra*. In short, it is the umpteenth
proof of the weakness of American thought; however, it is a place
where one can breathe a genuine atmosphere, full of passion for
improvement, and it is also the place which symbolizes better than
any other the elements that make up the American spirit in New
York: the Russian component (in this case Stanislavsky), brought
here by the Jews, mixed with the Freudian notion of internal
sincerity, which is rooted in the old Protestant component of
public confession, and all this held together by the fundamental
Anglo-Saxon pedagogical idea that holds that everything can be

taught. At the Actors' Studio two American actors, husband and wife, who saw my little play at Spoleto, the only one I have ever written in my life, asked me to put it on there, so we translated it together and they will perform it in a few weeks, but I will by then be in California. There is also a section of the Actors' Studio for playwrights, but I have never been. There are no books about the Actors' Studio.

Electronic Brains

I have contacted the head office of the biggest producer of calculating machines, IBM. Their public relations are very classy, they received me as though I were the Italian President and put the entire firm at my disposal. When they learned that I was going to Washington, they set up a visit for me to the Space Computing Center, in other words the tracking station which receives all the data and does all the calculations for the Vanguard and various other rockets. I was all pleased with myself, thinking I was going to see things that were almost top secret, whereas this Space Computing Center sits in a shop-window in a street in central Washington and is for show more than anything else; however, it is a functioning centre, though the danger that all the astronauts' data would be lost if a lorry smashed the window in a crash is nullified by the fact that there is another identical centre at Cape Canaveral. However, it was really fascinating: I saw models of rockets and satellites, which in theory should even take off if you turn on certain lights, but the models are always broken. Young mathematicians type on space computer keyboards with hesitant and absent-minded gestures. On the 23rd IBM in New York put at my disposal a Cadillac with a chauffeur and a technical expert from Turin to be my guide at Poughkeepsie, up in Westchester where IBM's huge factory is. This is a factory with 10,000 employees, like a medieval city, and in front of it is a huge carpark for 4,000 cars (these immense carparks full of grey and blue cars, that you see as soon as you leave New York, are one of the things that give you the most authentic feeling of America). I am received by a group of managers who explain to me first the way the whole organization is structured, and one of the first things they tell me is that there is no trade union. Naturally I ask why; 'They don't need them' is their answer. In fact they are all paid better here than elsewhere, the paternalism is quite open, and the colour portrait of Mr Watson* hangs everywhere; I will later learn that on Mr Watson's birthday the employees were invited to the party with a cyclostyled letter explaining that if they did not have a car to go to the party with their wives, a car supplied by the management would come to fetch them at such and such a time; if the wife did not have an evening-dress the management would provide her with one, and a baby-sitter service was also assured for that evening, and at table number such and such places numbered such and such were booked for them, and when Mr Watson came in they all had to stand and sing the following song to the famous tune, etc., and there on the letter were the words of a song in honour of Mr Watson. However, all this is beside the point. I visited the factory, they explained everything about the cores which make up the machines' memory and I also learnt how just through the positive and negative charges in the cores you can represent any number or letter, and all the processes they use to produce those tiny transistors, and then I saw the Ramac, which is the part that carries out the operations even on data input at random, not in any established order. Very beautiful machines with these cascades of threads in beautiful, different colours, producing an effect like a wonderful abstract painting. I had lunch with some managers and researchers, but no alcohol since Mr Watson forbids alcohol in the factory. I visited the labs, wonderful architecture, better than Olivetti, all with moveable walls so they can have rooms of any size they want, and the organization of research is excellent, totally separate from production; all in all, the organization of the

---

* Thomas Watson Jr, president of IBM.

firm is extremely efficient, although when they do a drawing on the blackboard for you to give an outline of the company's structure, they draw lines that continue above Mr Watson and they say: God. Even though I was falling asleep, they explained all this problem about the insulators, you know. I also saw the school they have: wonderful. The staff: two categories, the managerial type who really are quite intimidating, and what we would call the Olivetti type; but of course I was not able to understand the relationship or the dialectic between the two types. It was an amazing sight, all those mathematicians and physicists in their little cells with their green blackboards. The workers were certainly highly qualified, and there was a very smooth rhythm of work; many women, all of them fat and ugly (beautiful women here, too, as in Italian cities, are now only to be found in certain social strata). Many boxes of sweets on every worktop: it's Christmas. Among all these computers were Christmas decorations and banners; many departments organize Christmas parties; loudspeakers broadcast for the workforce of the most advanced technology in the world Christmas carols, a gift from the management of IBM.

Homesick for New York

I am not going to tell you about Washington because it is exactly as one has always imagined Washington from what one has read: artificial, boring, and very elegant, and basically I can even say I liked it, I would not want it to be any other way, but the fact is that I was not even three days in the place and I could not stand it any longer, so homesick was I for New York, and so I raced back here again.

The Cinema

Naturally I never go to the cinema because in the evening I like to see people, but what strikes me is how nobody goes to the cinema, I never find anyone who has been to the cinema or who talks about films. This is of course a feature of Manhattan, and I expect that as I go around America I will see the other side, but certainly this island is a unique case in the world of a society in our time for which cinema does not count at all, very odd for someone who comes from Italy. At most, in our circles, which in New York is not a special category but is *the* city (publishing, journalism, theatre, agents, writers, and all the enormous world of advertising and public relations, plus the world of education and research and the lawyers who are also always concerned with questions over authors' rights, etc.), at most they discuss old silent movies which you can see every day at the Museum of Modern Art, or Ingmar Bergman's films; but for example I have never found anyone who has seen *On the Beach* (which is the only film I went to see, because it interested me as a political symptom even though it is not very good).

Midwest Diary

Chicago, 21 January

I have spent ten days between Cleveland, Detroit and Chicago and in these few days I have had more of a sense of America than in the two months I spent in New York. More sense of America in that I continually found myself saying: yes, this is the real America.

The most typical image of an American town is that of streets flanked by places selling used cars, enormous lots full of white, sky-blue or pale-green cars lined up beneath festoons of little coloured flags, billboards showing not the price but the savings (you can easily get a car for a hundred and even for fifty dollars), and these car-dealers go on sometimes for miles, a bit like a horse-fair.

But Where Is the City?

The truth is that you can go around by car for hours and not find what should be the city centre; in places like Cleveland the city tends to disappear, spreading out across an area that is as large as one of our provinces. There is still a downtown, that is to say a centre, but it is only a centre with offices. The middle classes live in avenues of small two-storey houses that are all the same, even though no two are alike, with a few metres of green lawn in front and a garage for three or four cars depending on the number of adults in the family. You cannot go anywhere without a car, because there is nowhere to go. Every now and again, at a crossroads in these avenues, there is a shopping-centre for doing the shopping. The middle classes never leave this zone, the children grow up without knowing anything except this world populated by small, well-off families like their own, who all have to change their car once a year because if they have last year's model they lose face with their neighbours. The man goes out every morning to work and returns at 5 p.m., puts on his slippers and watches TV.

The poor areas are exactly the same, the little houses are identical, only instead of just one family two or three families live in them, and the building, usually of wood, deteriorates in the space of a few years. What four or five years ago was an elegant suburb is now in the hands of the well-off, black middle classes. The Jews have left their poor ghetto because now in Cleveland they are all more or less rich, and their previous houses have now all become slums for blacks. The churches remain – I mean the buildings – the synagogues in the ex-Jewish areas have now turned into Baptist churches for blacks, but they have retained the candelabra on the windows and the archivolts. The movement of races from one area to another in these big cities is constant: where the Italians once were now you find Hungarians, and so on. The Puerto Ricans have not yet reached the Midwest, they are still concentrated in New York, but here in the last few years there has been a huge amount of Mexican immigration. But the curious feature is that now on the bottom rung of the immigration ladder are the internal migrants, the poor whites from Virginia who come to work up here in the factories, and since they were the last to arrive, they find themselves below the blacks, and their racism and hatred of the anti-segregationist Yankees intensifies.

The Gold Family

In Cleveland I am the guest of the Golds, a typical Midwestern Jewish family. Herbert's father came here from Russia as a boy, became a labourer and greengrocer, and only after the last war did he succeed in becoming the richest hotel owner in Cleveland, but he still lives modestly in his little house, gives a lot of money to Israel which he visits every year, is totally philistine and Americanized, but as in many Jewish families he is proud of having a famous intellectual in the family and totally tolerant of his way of life. His wife is the typical American-Jewish mother, one of this country's great institutions, her Jewish cuisine is excellent, the whole family including the four children exude an extraordinary serenity, the satisfaction of having made it, and she is also Woman of Valour of the state of Israel. Of her children, the eldest is a lawyer and has his office in the hotel (tax consultancy, of course) and the youngest helps his father in the hotel, and besides Herbert there is another son who wants to be a writer, Sidney, who is the real character in the family: he was a manual worker until recently, and also worked at Ford's in Detroit, but he always quits jobs, is half-Communist, wants to be a writer like his brother, and for the time being his father is keeping him (he is thirty-five) because he realizes that to have sons who are writers gives him extra prestige among his fellow citizens. But Sidney is not sharp like Herb, he is naïve and ineffectual and he is set to become the pathetic failure of the area, a poet and a radical.

The Motels

I have lived in several motels (one brand-new one in Cleveland, owned by Gold senior) which are now no longer like wooden cabins, but built with brick, with a huge carpark, surrounded by single-room apartments, often two-storey buildings, each room with a double bed (which by day becomes a divan), TV, radio-alarm, shower, kitchen, fridge, everything organized so that the minimum of service is needed: a paradise for salesmen and lovers, and less expensive than any decent hotel.

The Elections

In intellectuals' houses all the talk is of the election, much more so than in New York. Violently frightened by the face of American Catholicism that I saw in Boston, where the Madonna continues to loom large over the old cradle of Puritanism (Boston is 75 per cent Catholic and now lives under an Italo-Irish dictatorship), I peddle bitter anti-Kennedy propaganda, and generally find fertile terrain among the families of Jewish professors, though on the whole they see Nixon as the danger for them and often they are taken in by the idea that the rise of the Catholic Democrats, who represent nationalities who were poor and working-class until recently, has something democratic about it, and they do not know about the reactionary role performed by Spellman's American-Irish church inside the Catholic world. Then there are some militant Democrats, like the wife of one congressman: he was a Humphrey supporter but was ready to go over to Kennedy if he won the convention; she actually lost her temper completely and chased us out of her house. (Among the middle classes here one meets even intelligent people who feel the need to proclaim constantly that everything is fine, that American culture is first-class – they quote university, theatre and library statistics just like the Soviets – as though they needed to convince themselves before others, yet on the other hand it is here in the provinces, among the same class of people, that you find the most lucid, serious and well-informed critics of American life and society.)

The Prostitutes

After two and a half months in which – incredibly for a European – I have never seen a prostitute on the streets, here in some black districts I rediscover the sight familiar to all Western European cities: prostitutes. There are some in white areas too, but they are usually in certain cafés, and in any case they are very few. The most astonishing thing about New York – which is the result of both Puritanism and freer female morals – is that despite its enormous size you never see a single prostitute. They exist only in provincial towns.

Inter-racial Paternalism

The Karamu is a community centre in Cleveland set up around thirty years ago to promote common cultural activities between whites and 'colored' peoples. Architecturally very beautiful, with theatres, exhibitions by black artists, craft-fairs, museums of African culture, everything in first-class taste, classrooms where every evening I see blacks concentrating on chemistry and biology lessons. I think I'm back in the USSR. I am invited by the theatre's director, a white Jewish man who puts on stage works that involve whites and blacks (amateurs and professionals work for free, he is a professional who prefers to work in the provinces and is paid by this centre), to see the dress rehearsal of a play which opens tomorrow night. We watch the play, but it is a tearjerker, an edifying tale about society along moderate lines on the theme of race (by a black author), an instance of educational parish theatre, or rather exactly like a similar play I saw nine years ago in Leningrad in a similar small theatre run by the Komsomol in a similar pioneers' house, but at least there the hypocrisy was different, not this paternalistic falseness beneath which this institution presents itself to me. I read a brochure about a series of lectures on politics: it is government propaganda. I express my opinion on the play to the director's wife as I accompany her home (she seemed to me to be a very intelligent, liberated and happy woman) but she really believed in good faith that the play was good: she is a prisoner, like many provincial intellectuals, of a solely relative scale of values, engulfed by mediocrity.

My thoughts naturally run to Olivetti,* and here there is the opportunity to check the origin and function of his ideas in a country where they are not a strange growth, but experiences which have emerged empirically in certain areas of 'enlightened capitalism'. You could say in general that Olivetti has more style than his masters, and that on the whole he can make use of the best collaborators that Italy has to offer, whereas here paternalistic cultural initiatives operate on a much more provincial level, since the centralized cultural industry absorbs the ablest into New York and corrupts them in a different way; and here these things reveal their mechanisms more. (Here often with Americans – at least with some of them – I find myself speaking well of Olivetti and presenting him in a totally favourable light; this is one of the few Italian phenomena that Americans can understand and appreciate and it can give them an idea of 'the other Italy' of which they are completely ignorant. I also mention Togliatti,† of course, and speak well of him – you cannot really have a discussion with an American in which you outline first the seriousness and historical legitimacy of certain phenomena, and then their negative aspects – but they don't understand a thing, it's like talking to a brick wall.)

* Adriano Olivetti (1901–60), industrialist and publisher, with socialist leanings. He introduced Taylorism and scientific management into the family firm, but was also active culturally, establishing the Fondazione Olivetti. His Movimento di Comunità, unattached to the main political parties, was popular at the time.
† Palmiro Togliatti (1893–1964), leader of the Italian Communist Party from 1926 until his death. He was highly regarded by the Kremlin, and despite advocating pluralism he sided with Moscow over the Hungarian question in 1956, to the dismay of many left-wing intellectuals, including Calvino, who then left the party.

The Museums

In all these industrial towns of the Midwest there are wonderful museums, with Italian primitives and French impressionists, first-class collections scattered here and there, also a lot of average stuff but never poor quality and every now and again there is a really famous masterpiece (Corallo cover stuff)* which you never expected to find here. I am sorry that I was not able to stop at Toledo, a small steelworks town which is said to have the best museum. Then there are always technical innovations in the way they are set up: in the Cleveland museum there are no custodians in the rooms but in every room there is a camera hanging from the ceiling which swivels round photographing the visitors: by this means a single custodian in his booth can keep an eye on the whole museum. In Detroit's museum you can hire for 25 cents a little cardboard box with a transistor to put against your ear: in each room there is a transmitter with a disc which explains about all the paintings in the room.

Death of a Radical

In Cleveland liberals and Jews are grieving for the death of Spencer Irwin, an old liberal journalist, a newsman on a local paper which although owned by isolationist conservatives allowed him to write what he wanted. I read his last article, on the swastikas in Germany: it is old, fiery democratic rhetoric, provincial-style. Herb went to the funeral: Irwin was a Quaker but the pastors of all the Protestant churches were there along with the rabbi, and each of them said something, and there were also black intellectuals as well as purple-faced alcoholics. Irwin was an ex-alcoholic who had recovered and was one of the heads of Alcoholics Anonymous, a self-help group for alcoholics of all classes.

---

* Calvino is here alluding to the covers of the Einaudi series 'I coralli', which were illustrated with masterpieces of contemporary painting.

The Bar

While waiting for Herb who has gone to the funeral I sit in a very tough-looking bar, a different side of America which I waited in vain to see in New York, with rough guys who look like something out of a film but who are in fact workers from the car factories in Cleveland, women who look like prostitutes but who are probably poor workers as well, jukeboxes (a guy in a beret dances with an old woman, then they leave), bingo machines which are really what we would call pinball (and which exist in New York only in a bar in Times Square), a kind of electronic shooting gallery. In short, our Americanized Italy is more like provincial, working-class America. In the toilet I think I've come across the first piece of obscene graffiti I've seen in America, but it's not: it is a rant against the blacks, though in pessimistic vein (kick out the blacks then who'll be the bosses? The Cucarachas). The bar is frequented by poor whites from the South who emigrated here to work in the factories.

In Detroit I went into dodgy billiard-halls with gamblers at a table playing poker and eyeing up any strangers in case they are police. Small-time, unsuccessful gangster atmosphere like a Nelson Algren book (who I would have liked to be my guide in his home-town of Chicago, but we missed each other because in the days I was there he was not around, so I never got to see Chicago's gangland).

TV Dinners

One also appreciates consumer culture better in the provinces, visiting the big Sears shops which are to be found in every town, and which sell everything, even Lambrettas (which cost more than cars) and motor-boats (in the lakeside towns now is the season when they launch the new motor-boat models for the summer). Sears were famous for their catalogue which allowed even the remotest farmers, in the days when communications were difficult, to shop by mail-order. In the supermarkets the most sensational novelty is the TV dinner: trays which hold a complete dinner, ready to eat, for those who are watching TV and who don't want to interrupt their viewing for even ten minutes to prepare some food. There is a huge variety of TV dinners, each one with a colour photograph of the contents on the wrapper; you just have to take it out of the fridge and eat without needing to take your eyes from the screen.

At the Israeli Temple

Herb Gold gives a lecture on hipsters and beatniks in the temple at Cleveland Heights. It is his father who is really keen on it, because this is his son's debut as a cultural personality in his native town, and it is also an acknowledgment of his own prestige: in the last few years Samuel Gold has become one of the leading lights of his church. The temple is not one of the twelve ortho-dox synagogues of Cleveland Heights, nor one of the temples of the reformed branch (a kind of Jewish Protestantism, with a very simple rite, adopted in order to reconcile Judaism with the American way of life), but it belongs to the 'conservative' cult, which is a halfway house between the two, retaining some of the formal aspects of the rite with an impressive, almost Jesuit open-ness towards other mixes. I accompany the jubilant Gold family to the service and even their most sceptical sons enjoy their parents' satisfaction. I put on the little black cap, like all the faith-ful. There is a wonderful singer, both in terms of his voice and his solemnity of performance. He is accompanied by the organ, an innovation contrary to orthodoxy. The rabbi (no beard, a very open face) reads verses of the psalms and the congregation chant other verses in reply, reading from their little books, and I join in. Among the hymns in the little book there is also 'God Bless America', the famous patriotic anthem. The American flag stands on one side of the altar, as in all American churches, of any persuasion (here on the other side stands the flag of Israel). On the dais there are also young boys with sacred vestments and girls dressed in their best clothes who alternate with the rabbi and the cantor in reading the psalms. Halfway through the service, the rabbi commemorates those in the community who have died this week, including the journalist Spencer Irwin, and then announces Herb's lecture. In order to give it a religious air, the conference had been advertised with the title 'Hipsters, Beatniks and Faith', but Herb does not mention faith, instead he says that the lack of revolutionary political ideals has led to the beatnik ideal of keeping cool, of indifference. Nobody, it seems, objects to this claim that political involvement is a feature of American culture that has been lost today; all that happened, apparently, is that some of the faithful protested to the rabbi at the frequent use of the expressions 'making love' and 'fornication'. Once the lecture is over, the service resumes and Mr Gold is called upon to draw the curtain of the ark.

For the First Time I Drive

an American car, along a stretch of the road to Detroit. The automatic gear-change makes driving very simple, you just have to get used to the fact that you do not have to press the clutch pedal. The strict speed-limits on the motorways make the drivers careful. What is odd, though, is the lack of rules for overtaking, which happens either on the right or the left, as it comes, and nearly always without any signals.

Wonderland

In the motorway service stations, another typical American place, I discover further marvels in the men's room. There is a gadget for relaxing, for those whose legs are tired from driving: you get up on a small platform, put in a nickel, and the machine starts up, making you vibrate for five minutes like someone tormented by St Vitus's dance. Then there is also the automatic shoeshine with its rotating brushes. And in many men's rooms now towels have been replaced by hot-air driers.

American Poverty

has a particular colour which I have now learnt to recognize: it is the burnt red colour of brick buildings or the faded colour of wooden houses which have become slums. In New York poverty seems to belong only to the most recent arrivals, and is something equivalent to a period of waiting; and it would not even seem right that any Puerto Rican should become instantly well-off just because he has landed in New York. In the industrial cities it is clear that the poverty of the urban masses is an essential part of the system, and often it is a poverty which has a European look: black houses which are little more than hovels, old men pushing handcarts (!) full of bits of wood recovered from slums that have been demolished. Of course there is the constant though slow progress of the various social strata as they move up the ladder of well-being, but new groups always take their place at the bottom. And the great vital resource of America, mobility, constant movement, is tending to decrease. The depression of '58 was a huge setback for Detroit and since then Ford have been working in six-month shifts per year, resulting in a permanent state of semi-unemployment; the workers who have been there longest, those with a certain number of years of seniority, have priority over the others in being taken back on; that is, they have their job guaranteed, something new in the general lack of stability in American life, where the proletariat has always provided temporary labour.

The Projects

which means the working-class houses built by the towns or the state to replace the slums, are usually much more depressing than the slums themselves, which if nothing else have a touch of life and cheerful decay about them. Working-class houses, even those built at the time of the New Deal in New York, Cleveland or Detroit, are like prisons built of brick, either high or low buildings but always terrifyingly anonymous, looking out on to deserted squares. Now that the shops along the pavements have disappeared, every village uses its local shopping-centre for supplies. But in Detroit, in an area previously occupied by slums, there now rises the first section of Mies van der Rohe's famous village, the one with the huge vertical and horizontal structures in the midst of greenery. I visit it: there are now showroom flats open for those who want to buy or rent. Up to now it has been all buyers, no one wants to rent. The prices are rather high: to rent a flat costs 220 dollars per month. In short these are dwellings for the upper middle class, professionals and managers; those who lived in the slums that have been demolished have to go and find other slums elsewhere. Among the buyers there are some blacks.

The Classic American Photograph

of the black Baptist church nestling in a shop-window is not a picturesque detail, it is the most common sight as you go around the streets where the blacks live in slums. The Baptist church, the church of the poor blacks, is split by a multitude of internal schisms, every black who has any histrionic-religious skills and the money to rent a shop sets up his own church and starts to rant. Their worship is always based on revival, the immediate emotional and physical presence of divine grace. Some of them become famous millionaires like Father Divine or the other one who died recently.

In the huge, grim but not poor black area of Chicago I see an enormous street advertisement like the ones for Coca-Cola, only the young good-looking boy and girl, well-dressed and well-turned-out, are black rather than white. But as I am going by in a car, I don't have the time to make out what it is advertising. Another day I go by and pay attention: the advertisement ('Have your best comfort') is for a funeral parlour. (Advertisements for funeral agencies are very common in black neighbourhoods.)

Poor Shops

In the land of consumption where everything must be thrown away so you can rush and buy new goods, in the land of standardized production, one learns, surprisingly, that there is a whole under-world market of goods which no one would ever imagine could be bought or sold in America. There are huge stores of second-rate goods, as in the Italian area of Chicago, which are the same as the stores downtown except that the goods are rejects which exude an air of poverty even when they are new. And then there is the whole business of second-hand goods which I thought was a prerogative of New York's Orchard Street, that incredible market street in the poor Jewish quarter, but then you find it exists everywhere; there is a world in America where nothing is thrown away; in Chicago there is an area that is now Mexican, last year it was Italian, and the Mexican shopkeepers have taken over the shops with their own goods and along with Mexican things they continue to sell the old Italian stock. There are also bookshops for the poor where second-hand paperbacks and magazines are sold, as well as a whole range of specialist books, particularly in immigrant languages, Spanish, Greek, Hungarian (not Italian, because Italian immigrants usually don't know Italian as a written language). What emerges as the common cultural denominator of these shops is superstition. In Detroit there is an incense shop, which displays in its window the different kinds of incense required by the various religions, as well as incense for voodoo and witchcraft ceremonies, Catholic religious images, sacred books, conjuring tricks, playing cards, pornographic books. Sidney G. tells me that once the owner, seeing him just browsing, chased him out of the shop: it is likely that in the back-shop they make love philtres or other magic potions for their clientele which is black-Italian-Mexican. In the Mexican quarter in Chicago, there is a shop in which a gipsy reads your palm.

The Bowery

is not unique to New York; every town has a street reserved for drunkards and human debris, where there are very cheap lodgings, really poor shops, restaurants where the alcoholic can, when he has a couple of dollars, obtain a card which entitles him to a certain number of meals for a few cents, so that he knows that he has something to eat for a few days and can therefore drink the rest of his money. Naturally such streets are full of the Salvation Army and other missions, where they can stay warm. I remember a St Thomas Aquinas Reading Room in Detroit, chock-full of down-and-outs pretending to read: a place with a huge window which you can see from the freezing cold street. You have to keep the meeting room locked – as I was informed by a Chicago trade unionist, a member of the U. E.* – otherwise the hoboes come in and sleep on the floor. In America the man who leaves his family and job and ends up an alcoholic and on the streets is a widespread phenomenon, even among those in their forties, a kind of obscure religion of self-annihilation.

Keep it Easy

My host tonight in Detroit was a philosophy professor, now a radio disc-jockey (he introduces the records and makes witty comments in between), he earns a huge amount of money and is very popular. He writes, sings, and even makes records of (mild) protest songs.

The Steel Crisis

is on. The famous strike was caused initially by the industrialists who needed to keep prices high even though stocks were at an all-time high. Probably before the year is out the American economy will have to face, once the elections are over, a serious

---

* United Electrical, Radio and Machine Workers of America.

recession. According to certain left-wing trade-unionists (in Chicago I was moving mostly in those circles) the American economy, caught as it is in a vicious circle of sales on credit and forced consumption, appears to be very fragile, hanging by a thread.

Chicago

is the genuine big American city: productive, violent, tough. Here the social classes face each other like enemy forces, the wealthy people in the strip of skyscrapers along the magnificent lake-shore, and immediately beyond them is the vast inferno of the poor neighbourhoods. You sense that here the blood has drained into the pavements, the blood of the Haymarket martyrs (the German anarchists to whom a very beautiful illustrated book has been devoted, written by the then chief of police), the blood of industrial accidents which helped build Chicago's industries, the blood of the gangsters. In the days when I was there, the famous police corruption case was discovered, which I think even the Italian newspapers mentioned. I would like to stay longer in Chicago which deserves to be understood in all its ugliness and beauty, but even the cold there is nasty, the local woman I have made friends with is trivial and not very chic (so, she's fine for Chicago), and I fly off for California.

San Francisco Diary

5 February 1960

You know what San Francisco is like, all hills, the streets rising up steeply, and a typical old cable-car running along some of the streets; and the scraping sound of the cable beneath street level is the distinctive sign of the city, just as the smoke coming out of the manholes signifies New York. I am living near Chinatown which is the biggest Chinese settlement outside China, now in full celebration mode with rockets being launched for the Chinese New Year which happens around now (the year about to start is the Year of the Mouse). The goods in the Chinese shops are nearly all made in Japan. The Japanese colony in SF is also very numerous, and this city with its mixture of white and yellow peoples looks the way all cities will look in fifty to a hundred years' time. The blacks are outnumbered by the Mexican Indians. The Italians had their quarter in North Beach, near Chinatown, but now they have mostly moved, though the area is still full of Italian restaurants and shops and has become the beatnik quarter. The names and the writing on the shop-fronts are in Italian: as you know, the SFrancisco Italians are Ligurians, Tuscans and northerners, so the old generation knew Italian, unlike the New York Italians who have never known the language nor have they ever learnt English and have been inarticulate for centuries. The ones here also have surnames that are the same as Italian surnames today (whereas the New York Italians' surnames are unknown in Italy, they belong to an Italy that never appeared in our nation's history), and even their faces are similar to ours (while the New York Italians only resemble themselves). In this kind of Chinese-Italian-beatnik Latin Quarter there is a tremendous amount of activity in the streets in the evening, something unusual in America; an espresso-place has even put small tables and chairs on the pavement as though we were in Paris or Rome. I will realize later that this activity only happens on Friday, Saturday and Sunday evenings, and on other evenings everything is closed and deserted.

The Longshoremen's Union

Naturally, the first thing I do is to go and visit Harry Bridges, secretary of the ILWU, the dockers' union which is the only left-wing union with any clout in America, famous for its meeting with Khrushchev. (The ILWU is the West Coast union; as you

know, the longshoremen's union in New York is run by gangsters: remember *On the Waterfront*.) I did not find Bridges very
interesting, but some of his colleagues were. The SFrancisco dockers have become a typical workers' aristocracy thanks to their
union's industrial muscle. They earn about 500 dollars a month,
a totally disproportionate salary for an unskilled workforce. In
their headquarters – modern architecture which is not very beautiful but interesting – the famous recruitment of squads takes
place, required by the ships to load or unload night or day. The
dockers arrive, each of them in a deluxe automobile which they
park on the grass; they come in with their loud-checked over-
alls of every different colour, working-clothes which are new and
clean. Many are black, and many are Scandinavian. When a man
has finished his shift, he tells the union how many hours he has
done, so that the union always has up-to-date lists of the men,
organized round the number of hours worked, and whenever the
employers request workers, the union selects those with fewer
hours worked. The result is that at the end of the year all of them
have done more or less the same number of hours. All this happens
through a system of numbers which appear on luminous boards,
and announcements over the tannoy, a system that resembles the
tote machine at a horse-race or a calculating-machine in the
stock exchange. To be a docker in SFrancisco is the most sought-
after profession, just as in San Remo it is being a croupier at the
casino. This year the union had more than ten thousand requests
to join, but only selected seven hundred men. These statistics give
a clear idea of what working-class prosperity means in America,
even in an area so full of advantages as California where poverty
just does not exist. Choice is of course based also on physical
strength and age: the majority of the longshoremen are giants.
The organization takes enormous pride in the results it has
achieved through its hard-line traditions which are really a lesson
to ponder on for European trade unions. The other evening an
old trade-unionist of progressive views was arguing bitterly with
me over the lack of fight in French and Italian unions, who for

all their political consciousness, which the American working class lacks, nevertheless have never managed through economic strikes to obtain what the American unions manage to extract (and have never managed to defend their political principles, we could add).

A Club

Could San Francisco's secret be that it is a city of aristocracies? An old writer of local history books takes me to lunch at the Bohemian Club. This is the first club along English lines that I have seen in America. Everything, the wood-panelled walls, the gaming-rooms, the paintings from the beginning of the century, the portraits of famous members, the library, are exactly what they would be like in the most conservative clubs in London, which I find deeply moving – as always when I see some glimmer of Anglo-Saxon civilization in this country which is of all countries the farthest that could be imagined from England. And yet as its name suggests, this was eighty years ago the artists' and writers' club, full of heirlooms of Jack London, Ambrose Bierce, Frank Norris, and even Stevenson and Kipling, who both lived in SF, the former for quite some time, the latter just for a few months, and also Mark Twain who was a journalist here when he was still known as Samuel Clemens. Nowadays the members are all around sixty, and they actually have an English look to them: maybe they are some of the few Anglo-Saxon descendants in San Francisco. So is San Francisco really a conglomerate of élites? The San Francisco publishing world does mostly numbered editions, The Book Club of California publishes editions of classics like Tallone in Italy, for instance collections of letters by Californians during the Civil War with reproductions of the manuscript letter, a fascinating new way of presenting history books by including exact reproduction of the documents. SFrancisco is the city where you find the typographers used by the New York publishers. Even the Italians, compared to the other Italian communities in America, have all the characteristics of an élite, although my lunch at Il Cenacolo, the Italians' club, did not suggest a major difference in level from similar locales in New York.

Zellerbach

Near my hotel is the wonderful new skyscraper housing the head-quarters of Zellerbach's paperworks. Z. is from one of the very few Jewish families who lived in SFrancisco before the Gold Rush (1849 is always used as the watershed between California's prehistory and history), Jews who did not mix with the subsequent waves of Central and Eastern Yiddish immigrants (who in any case are few in Calif.) and they constitute an aristocracy on their own.

Ferlinghetti

Ferlinghetti (who, as you know, is called Ferling and who added that ending out of his admiration for Italians, blacks, and other vital and primitive peoples) is the most intelligent of the beatnik poets (the only one with a sense of humour: his poems are a little like Prévert's) and he has not left SF for NY. However, at present he is travelling in Chile so I missed the most authoritative guide to the city's secrets, just as in Chicago I missed out on Algren's guidance. Ferlinghetti has a bookshop, The City Lights, which is the best bookshop among SFrancisco's avant-garde. He sells almost entirely paperbacks, as does Discovery, the other literature bookshop in Columbus Ave. The paperback range, however, covers a very broad price band: besides genuinely popular editions (which are almost always only commercial titles) selling at 35 or 50 cents, there is a whole range (vast numbers of books, reflecting an enormous breadth of interest and intelligence in titles) of soft-cover cultural books costing a dollar and a half or 1.75 or even 2 dollars, and which thus come remarkably close to the price for hardback editions which are around 3 dollars. But the paperback public buy paperbacks even if they are dear and would never buy hardback.

The Provinces

Life is not different from life in NY, just as the social make-up of the city is no different. But at parties here you sense something that is the archetypal provincial atmosphere: gossip here is no longer NY gossip, it already has a provincial inflection. This is particularly true of the small world and artificial paradise of the Berkeley professors, each one of whom lives in his little luxury villa: these all form a row along lengthy streets climbing up the mountain. Actually, more than provincial the atmosphere is colonial: we are on the Pacific.

Truth Is Stranger than Fiction

I chose this hotel, after going round seven or eight others, as it was the most suitable in terms of price, cleanliness and location. No one had recommended it to me. Two days later I discover that Ollier, Claus and Meged, three of my fellow grant-receivers, live there, having all arrived at different times: independently of each other, all four of us chose the same hotel from a thousand small hotels of the same type in this area.

The Monument

I always avoid in these notes any description of the landscapes, monuments or tourist trips in the city. But I have to put this one in. Going through a park near the Golden Gate, suddenly you find yourself facing a huge neoclassical construction, all surrounded with columns, reflected in a lake, a thing of immense proportions; it is in ruins, with plants growing inside it and this huge ruin is all made of papier mâché and rounded off with great care. It produces a surreal, nightmarish effect, not even Borges could have dreamt up anything like this. It is the Palace of Fine Arts, built for the PanAmerican exhibition in 1915. Tourist brochures, oblivious to its grotesqueness, point it out as one of the finest pieces of neoclassical architecture in America and maybe this is even true. There is in it above all a dream of what culture was in the eyes of 1915 millionaire America, and the building in its present state is well-placed to illustrate someone or other's definition of America having passed from barbarism to decadence with nothing in between. Now that the building is falling to pieces, the San Franciscans, who are really keen on it, have decided to rebuild it in stone, with all the metopes sculpted in marble. The State of California is putting in five million dollars, the municipality another five million, the Chamber of Commerce another five million and the final five million will be collected from the public.

Sausalito

The sea in the bay and nearby is cold even in summer, and despite its latitude and vegetation (eucalyptus and redwoods) the beautiful marine and woodland areas near SF have nothing Mediterranean about them, because the colours, given the permanently cloudy and rainy sky and the fog which comes in daily, are not even like those of the most gloomy days in Liguria's Santa Margherita, they are more like the colours of a Scandinavian fjord. Or of a lake: Sausalito, which of the various tourist villages and yacht marinas is the one that has taken on an intellectual hue, full of boutiques, and inhabited by writers, painters and homosexuals, is just like Ascona.

The Professor

Like nearly every young writer, Mark Harris (we read but rejected his comic novel *Wake Up, Stupid* months ago) teaches creative writing in a college, the State College of SFrancisco. What he is specifically expert at is baseball: he has three novels on baseball. When he speaks about American literature, of the difficulty of writing literature in a society which is so prosperous and where the problems still have to be discovered, he says some not unintelligent things. But he is totally devoid of any information about European literatures, of any inkling of what has happened and is happening across the Atlantic. Not that he is totally without interest: he listens in astonishment to even the most obvious information you give him. He does not know that there was a civil war in Spain. (He will certainly have read Hemingway, but in the way that we read about wars between maharajahs in the South Seas.) The philosophy professor in the same college, whom I did not meet but Meged did, knows about only one philosopher: Wittgenstein. Of Hegel's philosophy he knows only that it is metaphysical and that it is not worth his while bothering about it, while of Heidegger and Sartre he says that they are essayists not philosophers.

Babbitt

Mario Spagna (pronounced Spagg-na, and known as Spag), whose family originally hail from Castelfranco d'Ivrea (but he does not know any Italian, just a few words in Piedmontese dialect), and who takes me in his car to see the surrounding country, was introduced to me by his neighbour Mark Harris as your typical, average American. At the age of fifty he took early retirement from his job with Standard Oil in order to cultivate his inner spirit. He writes mainly letters to senators and congressmen. He reads the papers, cutting out the items which concern in particular the local parliamentarians and giving them his advice and approval. He has also written an article which was published: 'Facing the Mirror', urging young people to look at themselves in the mirror not out of vanity but to examine their conscience. He has spent several years working out a project for a Temple of Peace and Beauty to be built on the slopes of Mount Timalpais and which should become the seat of World Government of the United Nations.

Do It Yourself

I never emphasize in my notes the fact that all of American life, and all their highly active social life, runs without any service personnel, and that American houses, almost always constructed with great efficiency and enthusiasm, have been painted (the walls, that is), and have had stairs put in, and all the various bits of carpentry, etc., carried out by the owners themselves, because of the non-existence or prohibitive cost of labour for such jobs. Tony O.'s beautiful, elegant house (he's a professor at Berkeley) was entirely built by himself, both the masonry and the wood, from the foundations to the roof, but he is not the only one to have done so. For many of the well-off, middle-class intellectuals, making yourself a home means literally making it with your own hands.

Europe

The writer N. M. M.* is the third of three famous English sisters, who were very beautiful in their day. One was Hitler's lover, another is the wife of Sir Oswald Mosley, the leader of the English Fascists. This one, who is a Communist, was the wife of Neville Chamberlain's son, who died fighting with the republicans in Spain: after that she came to America where she is very active in all the democratic, anti-racial committees.

Public relations

The brochure that Mr C., public relations man, has given me about his agency, I only manage to read now, on the bus taking me to his vineyard in Moon Valley (of Jack London memory) where he has invited me to spend Sunday. God, what kind of a host have I ended up with? Here he is photographed with Cardinal Spellman, 'his good friend', being congratulated by the cardinal

---

* Calvino is confused here. This is not Nancy but her sister Jessica Mitford, who eloped with Esmond Romilly, a nephew of Winston Churchill.

for the mission carried out for the State Department to save Brazil from Communism (thanks to Mr C.'s public relations initiative 'within a year the tide had turned against the Communists'). Elsewhere the brochure defines public relations (which C.'s staff carry out on behalf of various corporations and occasionally for the State Department): 'One branch of public relations may deal with creating news and getting it published. Another branch does quite the opposite, to prevent or reduce the impact of unfavorable news.' We are in the heart of Americanness here: there is a naïvety in the way it presents itself so openly which is paralleled only by certain kinds of naïve Soviet propaganda. I foresee an afternoon of uncomfortable political discussions. But no: in his private life Mr C. is a sensitive, reasonable and discreet person, both in his beautiful house built entirely by himself and full of wonderful Mexican ornaments, and in his vineyard which is maintained without a labour force (there are very few skilled vinedressers in the area: as is well known, there are no more peasants in America, except in the South; one of his neighbours who has a considerable wine-making firm as a side-line had to get someone over from France to prune the vines), while his vines are nibbled at by deer beneath a fine rain. In one of his books, on Mexico, which he gives me to read, alongside the usual anti-Communist discourse typical of the American press, there are also critical analyses of the Mexican Church which are serious and full of common sense. And the conversation on European and American political issues stays on a level of reasonable liberalism. He too is worried by the Catholic advance ('And your friend Cardinal Spellman?' 'Well, he's a good guy, but the other priests …'). But he does not dwell on Communism (apart from the inevitable question on the situation of Italian Communism that all Americans ask): public relations also features sensitivity and tact among its characteristics. The cuisine that he and his wife (an architect) prepare directly over the fire is the best that I have tasted in my whole trip.

A Beatnik Party

I am invited to a beatnik party. There have been police raids lately to stamp out the marijuana traffic, and someone is always on guard at the door in case the police arrive. (There have also been beatnik rallies in the streets to protest against the 'Fascist systems' and to advocate the decriminalization of drugs.) Here, in the house of someone I don't even know, the only drink is wine, poor-quality wine at that, there are no chairs, nowhere to dance, there are blacks who play the drums, but there is no room, there are several good-looking girls but the nicest ones are usually lesbians, and in any case you don't really get to know anyone, there is no discussion, and the inevitable drug-addict, who at similar parties in New York is a decent, clean person, here is squalid and filthy and goes around offering heroin or Benzedrine. In short, the 'bourgeois' parties are better, at least there are better drinks (I forgot to say that among the crowd at this party there was also Graham Greene, who now lives in SFrancisco, but I did not even manage to see him).*

Kenneth Rexroth

is certainly the most notable person I have met in America: I do not know his poetry (he has written about twenty books of verse and several works of criticism plus many translations from Japanese classics and other poets) but as a person he made a tremendous impression on me. An old anarcho-syndicalist, he acted for many years as a trade-union organizer. He is everyone's enemy, and every now and then bursts out into brief bouts of scornful laughter. His favourite targets are the ex-Communists and ex-Trotskyites of *Partisan Review*, Trilling and company. He is a handsome old man with a white moustache, he was also a boxer

---

* Again Calvino's information is incorrect: Greene was not living in California at the time, but was visiting San Francisco on a round-the-world tour with Michael Meyer.

in his youth, and he receives me dressed in an old soldier's jerkin and a cowboy shirt. He is optimistic about the future: even though there are no political or ideological movements here, technical progress, etc. will bring in something new. In any case even if Hitler had won, if all the anti-Fascists had been killed and all the books burnt, etc., history would have started again from scratch, but everything would have turned out the same, only a question of time. But what are the new groupings, forces, tendencies which might allow us to catch a glimpse of tomorrow's America? This is the question I ask everyone, always without any great results, and I also ask him it. He says that in the universities where he goes to read his poetry he is encountering a new generation, still rather amorphous, but full of interest and revolutionary urges. The beatniks are a superficial phenomenon, the rent-a-mob rebels of Madison Avenue. But the real young generation is to be found in the universities. There is also the black movement in the South, and Luther King is the great black leader who is now in Ghana (there is now an interesting relationship between the black movement here and the new African states): these are more or less things which I had heard people in NY say, and I've not yet managed to meet this famous new university generation, at least not in any illuminating way. Rexroth also talks to me (respectfully) about the groups of Catholic anarchists, Dorothy Day's movement which I had heard about in New York, where she is active, publishing a magazine rather like *Témoignage Chrétien*. Also a part of this group is our own author J. F. Powers and the poet Brother Antoninus, who seems to me to be a bit like our Father Turoldo. Rexroth is writing a lengthy autobiography, which he says can be translated in Europe because he has done all the things that Europeans expect an American to have done. Now he works as a literary critic on SFrancisco radio (SF has its own independent radio station, which is very good, autonomous and offers excellent international news coverage. It is the sole source of information here, because the SF newspapers are of very low quality and the *New York Times* arrives here three days late. I have lived through and am still living through these days of the French crisis cut off from any source of information except the skeletal coverage in the local papers, which are all obsessed with the Finch crime).

The Chinese New Year

I was looking forward to the New Year parade (last night, 5 February), thinking it would be a great people's festival with the famous dragons, but I was disappointed. There was a military parade of marines, local politicians went by in de luxe limousines, then leaders of the Chinese community who had the same gangsterish, Fascist look as the heads of the Italian community, young boys all in line like the GIL in Mussolini's Youth Movement and similar organizations, the anti-Communist committee, and a huge number of young 'Misses' all very Americanized. At the end there was a dragon, very long and beautiful, but there was absolutely no sense of popular spontaneity, rather an 'imperialist' or if you prefer 'American-Fascist' atmosphere which is the first time I've come across it on my trip. (But other sources tell me of a very different spirit in Chinatown: in the Chinese cinema, which shows only films in Chinese, produced in Formosa or Hong Kong, they apparently showed films made in Communist China for two consecutive months, before the Americans realized.)

In Short

I expected so much from SF, I had heard so much about it, now that I have spent a fortnight here (also because I was waiting to arrange with my colleagues to leave by car with some of them), now that I am leaving, well, I cannot say deep down that I really know much more about it than I did before, that I have got to know it properly, and basically maybe I am not terribly interested. Life is monotonous here, I did not meet any exceptional people (apart from Rexroth), I had no success with women (not that the city is greedy with its treasures, it's just the way it turned out, perhaps I am now entering a downward spiral). From the moment I left New York I have heard nothing but criticism of New York, rather in the same way as we criticize Rome (though of course it is totally different), yet this is all justified; however, New York is perhaps the only place in America where you feel at the centre and not at the margins, in the provinces, so for that reason I prefer its horror to this privileged beauty, its enslavement to the freedoms which remain local and privileged and very particularized, and which do not represent a genuine antithesis.

California Diary

Los Angeles, 20 February

Memories of a Motorist

I leave SFrancisco on 7 February with Ollier Pinget Claus and wife in a Ford that we hired and which we will leave in LA. We take turns at driving. It's not difficult, just a bit laborious because it doesn't hold the road perfectly. The traffic system of parallel lines instead of overtaking on the left is better and far less dangerous than in Italy. Of course where the road narrows, with just two lanes for traffic in either direction, overtaking happens practically just like in Italy. But the problem is always that of staying between the lines, and if you change lane you must be sure no one is coming up behind you. The speed limits are very strict and have to be obeyed because there are constantly police cars and motor-cycles with radar control. In built-up areas it is 25 or 35 miles an hour, while the overall limit in the State of California is 65 miles per hour. Our car is not an automatic (only the more expensive ones are), which means that out on the open road it is fine, but in LA with all the traffic that there is and the constant traffic lights you realize that not having to change gear is a tremendous relief. The problem of parking is very serious in LA as well. The minute we arrive we leave the car for just a few minutes in a no-parking area and when we come back we cannot find it: the police have already had it towed away by a little lorry with a crane and we are forced to spend half a day getting it back from a garage which is used for this purpose. All the systems to help traffic flow work with miraculous speed: one night in SFrancisco coming back with a friend from a party a little bit merry, the car ended up stranded, off the road; it was raining, we ran to a public telephone to call the emergency services, and we had not even got back to the car but the lorry was already there pulling the car out.

It Is Not True What Everyone Always Says

that the only way to see America is to go across it by car. Apart from the fact that it is impossible given its enormous size, it is also deadly boring. A few outings on the motorway are enough to give an idea of what small-town and even village America is like on average, with the endless suburbs along the highways, a sight of desperate squalor, with all those low buildings, petrol stations or other shops which look like them, and the colours of the writing on the shop signs, and you realize that 95 per cent of America is a country of ugliness, oppressiveness and sameness, in short of relentless monotony. Then you go across even deserted areas for hours and hours, like those we crossed amid the forests and coasts of California, certainly among the most beautiful places in the world, but even there you feel a certain lack of interest, perhaps because of that absence of human dimensions. But the most boring thing about travelling by car is spending the evening in one of those tiny anonymous towns where there is absolutely nothing to do except to have it confirmed that the ennui of a small American town is exactly how it has always been described, or even worse. America keeps its promises: there is the bar with its wall adorned with hunting-trophies of deer and reindeer; in the public bar there are farmers with cowboy hats playing cards, a fat prostitute seducing a salesman, a drunk trying to start a fight. This squalor is not just to be found in the small anonymous towns but also, in a slightly more alluring form, in famous holiday centres like Monterey and Carmel; and there too in this dead season it is very difficult to find a restaurant that will serve dinner.

In These Earthly Paradises

where American writers live, I would not live if you paid me. There is nothing else to do but get drunk. A young lad called Dennis Murphy or something similar, who has written a bestseller, *The Sergeant*, which has now been translated and published in Mondadori's Medusa series – he has just received a copy of it which he shows me, convinced that Mondadori is a small publisher – arrives in the morning with his wrists slashed. During the night he got drunk and put his fists through the windows of his villa. As for Henry Miller who lives here at Big Sur, we already know that he is not receiving any visitors because he is writing. The old writer (now over seventy) has recently remarried, and his new wife is nineteen years old, so all the rest of his energies are devoted to writing in order to finish the books that he still wants to write before he dies.

Hotels for the Elderly

My friends avoid motels convinced (completely wrongly) that they cost more so we end up in filthy, flea-ridden small hotels. A permanent feature of hotels are the old folk who live in them and spend their days and evenings in the lounge watching television. California is the great refuge for old people who have ended up on their own all over the United States: they come to spend their years in its mild climate living off their savings in a small hotel. But also in New York the majority of hotel guests are the elderly, particularly old women.

The Pacific

is a sea which is completely different, with these sheer coastlines formed not of rock but of earth, and these harbours with their high, wooden palisades. The marine vegetation is also totally different: the waves cast up on to the beach seaweed that has a wooden texture but is as pliant as a whip, three or four metres long, with a little bearded head. You can fight whipping duels with this incredibly long and robust seaweed. Just below the surface of the water and on the shore there is neither sand nor rocks, but rather a porous, breathing mass of marine organisms. The seabed is alive, made up of molluscs which are open like eyes, dilating and contracting with the beat of each wave. And even in the days of full sunlight there hovers over the ocean a shadow of mist and vapour.

Los Angeles

From the moment I arrived in America, everyone told me that Los Angeles was horrible, that I would really like SFrancisco but would hate LA, so I had convinced myself that I would definitely like it. And indeed I arrive and am immediately enthusiastic: yes, this is the American city, the impossible city, it's so enormous, and since I only enjoy being in huge cities it is just right for me. It is as long as if the area between Milan and Turin were just one single city stretching north as far as Como and south as far as Vercelli. But the beauty of it is that in between, between one district and the next (they're actually called cities and often they are nothing but endless stretches of villas, big and small), there are huge, totally deserted mountains which you have to cross to go from one part of the city to another, populated by deer and mountain lions or pumas, and on the sea there are peninsulas and beaches that are among the most beautiful in the world. Furthermore it is a really brash city, dull, with no pretence at having monuments or quaint features – not like SFrancisco which is the only American city to

have a 'personality' in the European sense: there is no problem loving
SFrancisco, everyone can do it – but LA, this really is the American
landscape, and here at last the extremely high and widespread quality of life in California does not appear to be an island of privilege,
but, linked as it is to a big industrial city of these dimensions, seems
to be something structural. But after a few days in Los Angeles I
realize that life here is impossible, more impossible than in any other
place in America, and for the temporary visitor (who, on the other
hand, can usually enjoy a city better than its residents) it is actually
a source of despair. The huge distances mean that a social life is practically impossible, except for the residents of Beverly Hills who can
socialize among themselves, as can those of Santa Monica or of
Pasadena and so on; in other words, one falls back into a provincial
existence, even though a gilded one. Otherwise you have to face car
journeys of forty minutes, an hour, an hour and a half, and I always
have to rely on someone to give me a lift, or I drive my friends'
cars but I get tired and bored; and there is no public transport except
the odd bus, and the taxis are very rare and very expensive. To this
lack of form there corresponds a lack of soul in the city: you do
not even find that vulgar soul like you get in Chicago and which
I hoped to find again here; in truth it is not really a city, but an
agglomeration of people who earn, who have excellent conditions
for working well but no links with others. In any case Piovene* has
described Los Angeles very well, so I will not dwell on it, but refer
you to his chapter on it, which is excellent.

The Suburbs

When you see how these professors – both the good ones and
the mediocrities – live in this paradise on earth, and also see the
extraordinary money the university devotes to research, you say
to yourself that the price of all this must be the death of the soul,

---

* Guido Piovene (1907–74), novelist and journalist. He wrote Catholic novels in
the Bernanos tradition as well as a travelogue, *De America* (1953).

and certainly here even the most robust souls, I believe, would soon start to perish. A city made of a thousand suburbs, Los Angeles is also the suburb of the world, in everything, even in cinema: in reality it is not so much that cinema is 'done' here as that 'people come to do cinema here'. I who always am obsessed with living in the centre in every city, here too I go to stay in a hotel down-town, but here downtown is only a centre full of offices, nobody lives there, and my friends from the Department of Italian at UCLA persuade me to go and stay in a motel at Westwood, where I will be nearer them. I feel so at home in motels that I could spend my whole life there; and this is a Mormon motel, oppo-site an absurdly enormous Mormon temple, closed to everyone except the elders of the sect, next to a neat area inhabited by Japanese (who work cutting the lawns in front of the houses in nearby neighbourhoods) and Mexicans. However, I lose contact with other parts of the city, and to a certain extent I lose the desire to look up the many people whose addresses I have been given and for whom I have been given letters of introduction (even telephoning is complicated: each district has its own phone-book, you cannot find the other phone-books here, most tele-phone calls are made via the operator as though they were long-distance calls), and so for the first time since I came to America, instead of doggedly trying to multiply my contacts with the locals, I allow myself to be carried along in the routine of life enjoyed by the Italian professors who live in their own little world.

On Cinema, so I Have Nothing to Tell You

When I left New York Arthur Miller was here, but he has now gone, his secretary's letter informs me, so I have missed the oppor-tunity to meet the most famous woman in America (however, I hope to find them again in New York), and from my contacts in the cinema world I extract only boring official visits to the Walt Disney and Fox studios, with the usual Western villages which have been meticulously reconstructed. These months in

Hollywood (I use the word Hollywood in the European sense: as you know, Hollywood is now a district of restaurants, theatres and night-clubs, a kind of Broadway, but it has nothing more to do with cinema production; the studios are elsewhere, in the country) are a dead season since in April in California everyone makes their tax return, and the tax officials come to check the number of film-rolls that have been shot and base their taxes on that. So the film-makers try to shoot as little as possible in these months, and send the rolls they have used to Arizona. When the tax inspection is over, they have them sent back: this is a trick that everyone knows about, but as far as the law is concerned they are in the clear. So at 20th Century Fox there was only one film being shot, some science-fiction thing. The only interesting detail I noticed was this guy, among the technicians, dressed as a cowboy, with game-bags full of little stones and a sling in place of a pistol. He is the person whose duty it is to frighten the ducks (the scene was set on a tropical river) by firing stones when the director needs a flight of ducks in a certain direction.

In short, I'm telling you all this to say that I'm sorry but I was not invited to any party full of famous divas, directors and producers. Here is not like New York, here people plan important parties two months in advance, given the general dispersal. And in any case, since the Chaplins are no longer here, life is not the same, etc.

Tree-houses

I'm bathing in the swimming pool in Chiquita's house, an acrobatic dancer, in Malibu. Her husband always plays a bodyguard in films. She has had herself built a wonderful house in a tree which sways in the wind. As a theorist of this kind of existence, I visit it and have myself photographed. I later discover that it is not the acrobat's idea: the psychoanalyst I visit the next day also has one in his villa; tree-houses are very common in California.

I Am not Going to Mexico

from here, as I had planned, along with the other writers on the grant. I discover that my visa is valid only 'for one admission', so if I leave I cannot come back in again. The others, though, all have visas 'for unlimited admissions' and off they go. I could only go there when I leave the United States, before coming back to Italy, if my thirst for new emotions has not been satisfied.

The Best and Biggest Ranch in California

I have been able to visit is the Newhall family's ranch. Huge orange and walnut groves. Again without any human presence, as always in American agriculture, everything is done by machine, even the walnut harvest. The picking of oranges, on the other hand, is entrusted to a union of specialized Mexican labourers. I also saw cowboys: they were passing between the palisades, behind which the cows are kept, in huge spaces, bored and chewing their synthetic feed which is brought to them by conduits and appropriately graded by a nearby windmill. They will never see a prairie in their life, neither the cowboys nor the cows.

Accidents of a Pedestrian

'Here anyone going on foot will be arrested immediately' was what we jokingly said on arrival in Los Angeles, where there are no pedestrians. In fact, one day I try to go by foot for a stretch through Culver City, and after a few blocks a policeman on a motorbike comes alongside and stops me. I had crossed a street – one that was narrow and deserted, what's more – while the light was at red. In order to avoid the fine – 'the ticket' – I explain that I am a foreigner, etc., that I am an absent-minded professor, etc., but he has no sense of humour, makes a lot of fuss and asks a lot of questions because I do not have my passport with me (in America I have noticed – even before this – that documents are totally pointless); he does not give me a ticket, but he keeps me there for a quarter of an hour. A pedestrian is always a suspicious character. However, he is protected by the law: whenever one crosses the street at any point, all the cars halt, as they do in Italy but only at the zebra crossing. Since they are few in number, like the redskins, they are trying to preserve them.

In Short,

you do not really want me to tell you about the villas of the film stars along Sunset Boulevard, about the prints on the cement at the Chinese Theatre, about the inevitable visit to Disneyland and Marineland (which actually is something amazing: circus games not just with seals and dolphins, but with the most enormous whales!). This instalment of the diary has turned out a bit flat, since here I ended up being a bit of a tourist, partly because once I had become free of the company of my colleagues, on arriving here (I hate being in a group; only if I am alone and constantly changing company do I feel I'm travelling) I was constantly undecided whether to leave the next day or stay longer, forever allowing myself to become seduced by amorous adventures which the city doles out in generous quantities but which never succeeded in transmitting their excitement to the following days, and if I am not in a state of continual tension I do not enjoy my travelling, and so I am also unsure about the next stages of my trip, caught between the desire to see EVERYTHING and the desire to return as soon as possible to New York where I always have 'a good time'.

Meantime I will now cross Nevada Arizona New Mexico, using airplanes, Greyhound buses and the train. Between the end of the month and the beginning of March I will be at:

C/o IIE
1300 Main Street
Houston 2, Texas

Otherwise I have always a reliable NY address:

C/o F. J. Horch Ass.
325 East 57th St
New York 22, NY

Diary from the South-west

I arrive in Las Vegas by plane, late on Friday evening. In this city full of hotels and motels there is not a single vacancy to be found. This holiday weekend (Monday 22 February is Washington's birthday) has ensured that everything was booked up more than a month in advance and not only by people from Los Angeles but all over the country, because a stay in the gambling capital is *de rigueur* for every American, like a trip to Mecca. You all know what Las Vegas is like, in the middle of the most squalid desert in Nevada, an old gold-diggers' village, and even now it is not very large, consisting virtually of just two streets, the old Main Street with all the most famous gambling houses, and the new lengthy Strip, a road in the desert that is all neon signs, even more so than Broadway, with marvellous motels, casinos, and theatres which show the most famous nude women performers in the whole world, the *Folies Bergère*, Lido, etc., as well as the most famous Broadway singers and actors, except that on Broadway there are never more than five or six major revues on at any one time, whereas here there are around twenty theatres and you can even see three shows a night since they go on until four in the morning. As for gambling, it continues round the clock, twenty-four hours out of twenty-four, practically everywhere, because every public space is a casino and all you find here are public spaces, and where there are no roulette or baccarat tables there are rows and rows of those famous one-armed bandits from the time of the pioneers, so you see crowds of frantic people frantically playing these machines, like workers in a factory

(Piovene's image, which conveys the idea perfectly). As you know, Nevada is the only State where gambling is permitted, prostitution is legalized, divorce possible after six weeks' residence, marriage possible at any time as long as you swear you are not already married. I arrive, climb into a taxi with a man from Washington, a navy employee and fanatic of these shows, and the taxi driver very scrupulously takes us round all the motels but everywhere there is the luminous sign saying No Vacancies, so he ends up renting us a room in his own house, a modest little house, which I share with the Washington employee, and I am happy at this rare opportunity to be able to see every now and again at close quarters the life of the average American. He is a serious well-behaved man, gambles very little and cautiously, is very careful not to go with women who in any case would cost a fortune, but his main ambition is to see as many shows as possible, he has come this far by plane for that very reason, he spends three practically sleepless nights in order to catch three shows a night, and you know how boring shows like the *Folies Bergère* are, and he sends the programme from every theatre (here you can send it like a postcard paid for by the theatre) to his friends and colleagues in the office to show them what fine things he has seen. The taxi man is also a good guy, with a good respectable little family, his wife is a Sunday school teacher, and in the taxi the first thing he does is to explain to us the benefits of legalized prostitution: 'I believe in legalized prostitution.' I have to say that Las Vegas has not been a disappointment: it is all just as you have read about so many times, with wedding chapels in the middle of the gambling-dens and the farce theatres with their advertisements for the quickest marriages (this is even more brazen than I had imagined: these little churches are really fair booths built like candy boxes with little statues of Cupid in front; they have names like The Stars' Wedding Chapel and their billboards have Hollywood-style close-ups of happy couples kissing), but what is genuine here is a huge authentic sense of vitality, crowds of people with loads of money constantly on the move. I have to say I like Las Vegas; I seriously like the place. Not at all like the gambling cities in Europe, actually the complete opposite thanks to its plebeian, Western feel, and very different from places like Pigalle. Here you sense tremendous physical well-being, this is a productive, brash society enjoying itself as a community, between one plane and the next, and here you can genuinely sense that the pioneers, gold-diggers, etc. have shaped this absurd city-cum-gambling-den in the desert. I am aware I am saying things that are incredibly banal, but I am travelling through a banal country and I cannot find a better way to cope than living and thinking about this in a banal way. (I won't tell you how all the local colour – Western, pioneer, goldrush, and beyond that Indian and Mexican – is the object of tourist exploitation and rhetoric, and is chopped up into tiny souvenirs in quaint little shops, all enough to make you feel sated with it for the rest of your life.)

Contrary to What

I said in the previous instalment, there is no other way to tour America than the car. Trying to cross it on Greyhound buses, as I did through Nevada, Arizona and New Mexico, means missing all the most famous tourist attractions, unless you stop in each place and try to organize local expeditions with guided tours or similar arrangements which would make you waste a lot of days to no end, since all the things 'to see' are never on the highways. But the fact is that the 'monuments' (nearly always here we are dealing with natural monuments: canyons, petrified forests, etc.) are never such awe-inspiring sights, and I have noticed that nature in America does not arouse powerful emotions in me: it is just a question of checking things you have seen in the cinema; so I ignore without regret Death Valley (which can be nothing other than a desert more deserted than anything I have seen in these last few days) and the Grand Canyon (which must only be a canyon that is more of a canyon than the others) and in a single stage of the journey I enjoy all the gradations of the Arizona desert and the romantic squalor of the Western villages and enter New Mexico.

Depressed Area

The bus crosses New Mexico and it is already dark and in the first village we stop at, at the usual bar where we have a snack, everything is already changed: the intangible colour of poverty (which I had completely forgotten about in California) here encloses everything, the people are nearly all Indians in Indian dress, poor women with children waiting for the bus, the drunk, the beggar, and the familiar, indefinable feel of underdeveloped countries. New Mexico, that tremendous reserve of escapist, Lawrencian exoticism for intellectuals and artists from the United States (though most of them prefer the more robust and genuine Mexico itself, which is by now an obligatory destination for all the holidays intellectuals take, and a rich source of decorative furnishings which means that New York intellectuals' houses are all more or less small-scale Mexican museums; and Mexico has become for the USA something that fulfils the role Greece has for Europe), is in reality – in terms of the presence of its culture – not up too much (the pre-Hispanic remains are very few and not very big; and with neo-Spanish remains you never know where what is genuine ends and the fakes begin – I was not in the Hollywood studios for nothing! Albuquerque is not up to much, Santa Fe is very beautiful, though when you examine it closely it is above all well-presented) but it conveys the idea of what life is like in an underdeveloped area – in fact it is difficult to imagine anything more underdeveloped than this – that is tacked on to the least underdeveloped country in the world.

25 February

Today I went to Taos and liked it enormously: as a mountain area it is marvellous, and also as a place of refuge for intellectuals it is not a fake, the Indian pueblo is very genuine, the intellectuals here are nice and not just commercial, the literary appeal – D. H. Lawrence – is tangible since all his friends are still alive, there are wonderful collections of Indian and neo-Hispanic ware (the neo-Hispanic stuff is from the famous flagellant sect who are still alive out here) and there are two ski resorts just a few miles away: in short, a place where I would not mind staying at all. Tonight in Santa Fe I was invited to the house of a famous Franco-American furniture designer and architect who was born in Florence and whose house is full of simply wonderful stuff, genuinely from the Mexican people, completely unexpected: I've never seen anything like it before. Today there is an evening of great celebration in Santa Fe because at the theatre is the only show of the year: the Ballet Russe from Monte Carlo! I am not going because I passed up – in one of my rare moments of economic wisdom – the only chance to have a ticket that someone wanted to sell; none the less, I participate in the excited atmosphere of the little community of voluntary exiles: I really enjoy being in countries at unusual moments, when people are excited and happy. So, I was talking about underdevelopment: certainly this is a wasteland, farming consists of a few vegetables and fruit for local consumption, hardly any factories, yet the Indians enjoy the benefits they are allowed thanks to the New Deal and the Americans' guilty conscience, and have unemployment subsidies, total tax exemption, lands, forests and fishing reserves (they live in a kind of primitive Communism and the authorities' efforts to teach them the advantages of private initiative are pointless), hospitals with free health-care, schools and priority in all possible types of employment (plus of course the exploitation of the fact that they are this State's great tourist attraction). Don't get me wrong, the poverty is still terrible, but when you consider the geographical conditions, which are much worse than any part of southern Italy, well the people of Basilicata could only dream of being able to live like them. A wise people, the Indians are perhaps the only poor people to live in a depressed area and not be prolific, and yet their population, which was heading for extinction, has in recent years been slightly on the increase.

The Pueblos

I go into the pueblo of San Domingo near Albuquerque and find myself in a familiar landscape: the poor suburb slums of Rome, identical. The low, squat little Indian houses are the double of those in Rome's Pietralata or Tiburtino districts, except that here they are built in adobe (the mud bricks that the Indians learnt to bake from the Spanish and which form the essential building material for all New Mexican architecture) but they are then covered in whitewash so they all look the same. And the people all have the same look about them as they shelter from the cold in their blankets, the children playing in the mud (but staying clean) and coming up (amazingly!) to ask for charity (or rather to sell the usual coloured pebbles). (However, in this pueblo there is a church with amazing Indian paintings. As you know, the Indians in this formerly Spanish area practise both Catholicism and pagan rites: one really should stay here till a Sunday to see these famous fiestas but I haven't really come to America to study primitive folklore.) At Taos where the biggest pueblo is, some of these flat houses are piled one on top of the other, and this gives the village an Algerian look (but of an earthen colour, not white) and the fact that in these cold, snowy days the Indians go around muffled up to their noses in multicoloured blankets contributes to this Islamic look. In any case, it is all just like Alberobello: even the interiors of the houses are just like inside a *trullo*. The Indians have cars, but because of the wishes of the elders they do not have electricity or any other source of heat or light in the pueblos except the fireplaces inside the little houses and the cooking-stoves in the street. Consequently they have neither radio nor TV. (It is clear that the Indian communities have no future and in the whole country there is a debate about what will happen to them, between those who favour conservation of the community at all costs and the supporters of assimilation. The fact is that the Indians rarely emigrate from their inhospitable lands and they are the ones who are most reluctant to assimilate; but now the children are studying at high school and are beginning to become Americanized. However, this is the only place in the United States where a dialectical element in the colonized people lives on – though it is hard to say to what extent. As my friend Ollier – an ex-colonial civil servant in Morocco – rightly observed, America is in everything a colonial country where what has been eliminated is the colonized people, the main characteristic, contradiction, vitality and significance of all colonies.)

Local Tradition

has been conserved admirably by the Anglo-Saxon Americans (but only in the last thirty years or so, I believe) and these museums, like the one of Navajo ritual paintings, for instance, are kept with the usual care and access to finance typical of the US in all things cultural, and the same goes for all the Hispanic antiquities and for the way that the old Hispanic-Mexican architecture is being continued by today's architects. The people of Spanish origin, however, are not at all interested in the conservation of monuments to their own culture. Protestant architects construct beautiful churches in adobe and in the Hispanic-Mexican style and in them install surviving masterpieces of popular religious wooden sculpture; the Catholic priests fling in the usual tacky rubbish of current religious iconography.

Lawrenciana

Naturally, being in the Taos area, I went to see Angelino Ravagli, the husband of Frieda Lawrence, who died three years ago, and the man who is thought to have inspired the character of the gamekeeper in *Lady Chatterley's Lover*. I speak to him in Ligurian dialect because (although he is from the Romagna by birth) he

101

is really from Spotorno and he met the Lawrences when he rented them his villa there and then followed them across the world, all the way to Taos (to a ranch in the mountains which was given to D. H. by a female admirer who is still alive here and which Frieda decided to pay for with the manuscript of *Sons and Lovers*, but the ranch has now been left by Frieda in her will to the University of New Mexico which sends young writers there every summer to write), and then when D. H. died he married Frieda. Ravagli is the executor of Frieda's will and co-owner of the rights for D. H.'s books (the few that are not in the public domain) along with Frieda's children and her first husband, the German. He really regrets the money he could have made with *Lady Chatterley* in America but now cannot: however, perhaps he might be able to make this money if the literary agent, etc.; a question that I do not need to explain to you. (However, in fact nobody abroad really understands the question of the Lawrence literary rights.) Now he has sold this house where they came to stay after D. H.'s death and he does not know what to do with himself in Taos on his own and will go back to Italy where he has a wife to whom, according to Italian law, he is still married, and several children all in the professions, one a graduate in agriculture in Turin whose address he gives me. Angie is of course a very simple man but he is not plebeian, as the Lawrences certainly believed, but rather petit-bourgeois (he was a captain of the bersaglieri; is interested in Malagodi's political programme;* in his bedroom he has a picture of Eisenhower painted by himself because he has now started painting); however, he is of course very much a warm human being, as they say, and very friendly, what with all the chaos of this weird existence, and here in Taos he is very popular: many people have come to live here to be near the Lawrences, like for example a curious poet, Spud Johnson,

* Giovanni Malagodi (1904–91), politician. He was Secretary of the Italian Liberal Party 1954–72 and then its President, before becoming President of the Senate in 1987.

who has taken over the Taos newspaper which is intriguingly called *El Crepusculo*. At Christmas Aldous Huxley came here with his wife and Julian and they spent Christmas with Angie; Aldous, through his Turinese sister-in-law, has bought a flat at Torre del Mare near Spotorno.

Atomic Matters

In some vague way this is an accursed land, so it is natural that it was in this desert that they secretly invented the atomic bomb and continue to manufacture it, thus bringing to life the Indian legend that is unique to this area that here a power capable of destroying the earth was unleashed. Then it turned out that it was precisely here that they discovered uranium, but this was later and now uranium is starting to become the only hope of wealth for the area. Naturally I was only able to view the laboratory sites from the outside (and there are also research laboratories on human resistance to space flights and on the effects of radiation on animal and vegetable organisms), and in these few days I have not been able to approach any scientists, something that I regret but also perhaps it's better that way because from the few and far between glimpses I have had I have formed the idea that scientists are the only group which can lead to something new in America, because many of them possess alongside what is predictably the most advanced technical expertise a highly sophisticated knowledge of the humanities, and above all they are the only intellectuals with any power, and with any say; this idea of mine, I was saying, I fear very much could be undermined by further meetings with them. Scientists' links with arts people are not regular; I have asked about this all around, and they say yes, perhaps there are a few like I describe. However, here atomic questions remain shrouded in a veil as in Indian legends; a local guy in all seriousness shows me a woodland area where spies would meet to exchange atomic secrets but then the FBI discovered them.

The People Around Here

Going around without a car has the advantage that it forces me wherever I go to mobilize the whole village around my person, but certainly by now after several months of this it is always the same thing. Here I am sent from one old lady to another who runs an Indian antiques shop or a bookshop or other cultural enterprise. But deep down now that I know the terrifying dullness of American life I understand more the people who come to live here, just as I understand more the way they love Italy, which previously got on my nerves.

Texas

How do you go about acquiring an image of Texas? That's what I have continued to ask myself in all these months, convinced that this State which is so peculiar in terms of its spirit and economic life was in reality difficult to capture in a very short stay, such as the one I intended to devote to it, and staying in a big city I would just see a big city like so many others and not 'the real Texas', whereas staying in a little country town I would miss so many aspects. Consequently, having made up my mind to stay in Houston, which is the biggest city of the once-biggest State in the Union, I was not expecting to receive any strong impressions of local colour. Instead, I arrive when the Fatstock Show is on, the live-stock display, and when it's on the biggest rodeos of the year in the whole of America take place here. So I arrive and the city is full of cowboys from all over Texas, and from all the livestock-rearing States, but they are all dressed as cowboys, even those who are not cowboys, old men, women, kids, the whole Texan spirit is flaunted here in a way that makes this place ostentatiously, visibly different from the rest of the States. And on the famous desire for independence in Texas, there is no need to conduct a special inquest; many cars have written on them: 'Built in Texas by Texans', and in the city's flagstands the Texan flags clearly outnumber the Federal ones. What comes over is an impression of a country in uniform, these middle-class families marching in formation all wearing stetsons and fringed jackets, proudly displaying their practicality and anti-intellectualism which has developed into their mythology, fanaticism, and alarming belligerence. Luckily it is a mythology that is constantly tied to work, to production, to business, to this enormous amount of livestock, whose display I witness surrounded by a troupe of a hundred or so Pakistani students who have come here to study agriculture. And so there is a hope that, even though Texas feels itself ready to make war on Russia, immediately if need be, as some of them claim, nevertheless deep down the isolationism of the agricultural mentality will have the upper hand (as you know, Texas managed to go to war with Germany a year before Pearl Harbor, sending a volunteer corps with the Canadian air force).

The Rodeo

The rodeo, which is held in an indoor stadium as big as the Vél d'Hiv, is also a mixture of practicality and mythology. The majority of the exploits in which the cowboys engage are operations they perform in their daily work: mounting a horse with or without a saddle, lassoing a calf or bull in a certain number of minutes; but in between one competition and another you get interludes of totally fake Western mythology: the singing cowboys from TV, who are greeted with wild enthusiasm. However the cowboys' technique is excellent: chasing a calf on horseback, lassoing it with a rope, flinging yourself on to it to turn it over on to its back, managing to tie its legs with the help of the horse which has to keep the lasso taut.

We Are Now in the South

Despite the Texan spirit, the man who drives me on a tour round the city (there is nothing to see: the usual city full of houses and little green lawns, sprawling and shapeless; the black areas that already have the air of poverty of the South) puts his seat-belt on when he drives, because the statistics show that in the majority of accidents, etc. He is a good man, a financial agent, who works for the Democrats: he is the only one who does so here, he is one of the few liberals and he fights for the blacks' right to vote. But I will talk to you about this when I am in Louisiana or the Deep South. Tonight I am leaving for New Orleans, which is now at the height of Mardi Gras.

Diary from the South

Montgomery, Alabama, 6 March

New Orleans

Despite warnings from everyone, I arrive in New Orleans without any hotel reservation, on Monday the 29th, right in the middle of the Mardi Gras celebrations (Mardi Gras in America – or rather in New Orleans: the only place where it is celebrated – is an elastic term meaning our '*Carneval*', whereas a 'carnival' usually refers to a funfair.) I arrive early in the morning, all the hotels are of course full to the brim, and I start roaming around the Vieux Carré, which is exactly as it looks in photographs, all the houses with little balconies and colonnades in wrought iron. I am used to encountering anything 'antique' in America only in minimal proportions but swollen and falsified by rhetoric and propaganda; here, though, I must say that New Orleans is really all New Orleans, decadent, decaying, smelly, but alive. It is a controversial question whether the New Orleans style is more French or Spanish: the present look of the old town is the one given it by the Spanish who governed it for sixty years, before it returned to the French for a few months in 1803 and was then sold by Talleyrand to Jefferson. Now Franco has presented the town with majolica plaques with the street names from the time

of Spanish domination, so that the much-vaunted French spirit
of the town (many families still retain a cult of Napoleon, as is
also shown by the furniture) is countered at every street corner.
To cut a long story short, I find a ghastly room which costs me
a fortune in a dusty apartment hotel in the middle of Royal
Street, and – from the spotless, disinfected world of the motels I
have become used to – I am plunged into a Tennessee Williams
atmosphere where everything disintegrates into pieces through
old age and filth; in a dark closet between my bedroom and the
porch a ninety-year-old woman is kept enclosed all day. The
Garden District, where the French families went to live in the
nineteenth century, is totally different (whereas the Vieux Carré
became the black quarter until about ten years ago when it was
rediscovered as the great tourist attraction of the South and it
became an area of antique shops, hotels and night-spots) and it
is all big villas, many of them fine examples of plantation houses
with columns and everything. New Orleans closed in on itself
in its French aristocratic pride and remained one of the most
impoverished and backward cities in the States, and the consequences of the Civil War did the rest; now it is recovering a
certain prosperity as an oil city and as a harbour for South
American fruit and minerals. The harbour is an Italian quarter,
the heart of one of the most ancient Italian settlements in the
United States, with families originally from Sicily and the Lipari
Islands who have never spoken Italian in previous generations
and often have no idea even of their origin. But I am here to
see the famous Mardi Gras; and indeed this is in itself a *Carneval*
town, with its eighteenth-century décor, like Venice. Even nature
here wears a *Carneval* mask: oaks and sycamores in the huge parks
have their branches covered in Spanish moss, a parasite with flow-
ing tendrils and festoons. Mardi Gras lasts a week and paralyses
the whole town and consists of a series of parades of floats which
are not anything special compared to the *Carneval* floats in
Viareggio or Nice – because in any case the floats and grotesque
masks actually come from Viareggio: from last year's Viareggio

Carneval: special firms there sell them on and export them here. And even the black element, which I expected to be one of the main attractions, is not very prominent. To be sure there are blacks mixed up in the enormous crowds, and black musicians on the floats, and some of them improvise dances in the streets, but they are a very small percentage and the only specifically black element are the bearers of the enormous torches in the night-time parades, who often move in a way that emphasises this ritual's primitive symbolism. The fact is that the blacks have their own Mardi Gras, in their own neighbourhoods, and nobody is willing to take me there because of the danger that a large number of drunk blacks represents; however, from what I hear, there are often white tourists who organize expeditions to the black areas to see the black *Carneval* (but without getting out of their cars, of course): the route they take is always along streets that no one ever knows in advance. Well, on my first evening, particularly as luck had it that I found myself without a companion, I got bored and ended up going from one burlesque joint to another, drinking awful whiskey and trying to start discussions with the girl dancers about unionization, but they were only interested in making me buy them drinks, the usual racket, and so on. However, the next day, which is Mardi Gras itself, when the whole city plus half a million visitors go mad for twenty-four hours, I see that this is something really big and unique, even by European standards, because the protagonists here are the people themselves, displaying great imagination in their masks and sheer vitality. In short, an impressive mass spectacle: it has imagination, joy, sensuality, vulgarity and atmosphere, all in the right proportions, and all done in such a way as to redeem the decadent atmosphere of the place with waves of popular feeling. In a word, eighteenth-century Venice could not have been very different, as I tried to explain in an interview for local television. It is intensely cold, but most of the people are almost totally naked; unfortunately, the beautiful girls are outnumbered by homosexuals in female dress: New Orleans is a big centre for transvestite clubs, and homosexuals converge there from all over America, and *Carneval* is the ideal opportunity for displaying their particular ingeniousness in cross-dressing. People drink hurricanes, tall glasses of rum and fruit juice, and beer out of cans, which are then abandoned on the side of the pavement as harbingers of the desolation of Ash Wednesday, along with the pearl necklaces which are thrown during the parades, each with a little tag (strange are the routes of leisure products): 'Made in Czechoslovakia'. In short, this New Orleans is just that decaying place that we all knew about, and you can live here only if you know how to make the decadence functional, namely all the antique-dealers, furniture dealers, etc. I forgot to say that the majority of the stories told by the guides about happenings in New Orleans' historic houses were invented by Faulkner; because when he was young, Faulkner lived here for a few years working as a guide taking tourists around the place; and the stories he told were all invented by him but they were all so successful that all the other guides also started to tell them and now they are part of Louisiana's history. I was also invited into the villas of the upper class; in fact the most luxurious and aristocratic house that I have been in in this country was certainly here (built a few years ago but all in plantation style and all its accessories authentic), visiting a woman for whom I had a letter of introduction; not having a clue who I was, she invited five or six corporation presidents, who made me listen to the most reactionary discourses that I have heard in the whole journey: enough to make you despair, because the American ruling class understands nothing but power-politics, is a thousand miles away from starting to think that the rest of the world has problems to solve, that Russia offers the way to some solutions and they don't. The usual pronouncements for and against Nixon were made in these terms; and a man from Investments and Securities supported Nixon because at this point in time you need 'a tough, ruthless guy'. In any case, the Southerners talk too much, just the way we imagine they do; when I left, with me in the limousine to the airport there were some men coming back, I think, from a local Democratic Party convention; and what do you think they were talking about? They were against the Yankees and the Easterns [*sic*] who are stirring up the blacks, because where they live there are very few blacks, but we'd like to see them here where the blacks outnumber us forty to one etc. etc., all the things that you usually hear white Southerners say. Even slightly more sophisticated and adventurous people always talk about this as well, only they do it ironically, expressing blandly anti-segregationist views. Those who are anti-segregationist either eke out the miserable, frightened and isolated existence of the American progressive (I will need to devote a whole instalment to them, to their condition as exiles), or if they are rich or privileged, they close themselves in isolation and don't see anyone and are careful not to express their opinion, like the philosopher (a friend of Abbagnano) James Fiebleman, who has written twenty-two books, particularly on aesthetics, and has a wonderful modern house full of statues: 4 Epsteins, 1 Manzù, 1 Marini. In short, this is a place that would make you shoot yourself; the only thing to do is act like the Italian professor at the local university, a young man called Cecchetti, about whom I have no idea whether he's any good as a literary critic, and who in his opinions is very conservative ('I would not send my children to school with black kids, but not for racial reasons, you know, only for social reasons: the blacks all belong to the lower classes'), but he is someone who does the only intelligent thing to be done to justify the fact of living in America: he plays the stock exchange. Spending the mornings at the local branch of Merrill Lynch, Fenner, Pierce and Smith, following on the ticker-tape the dealings on the New York stock exchange, the fluctuations on the electronic noticeboard, studying the right moment for buying and selling, with the tele-printer in the room displaying the latest news on which to base your dealings, studying the ups and downs of all the major American firms, reading the *Wall Street Journal* the minute it arrives, that is the only way to live the life of a big capitalistic country in a way that is not passive, it is in fact the real democratic aspiration of

America, because even if it does not give you any chance of influencing events, other than speculation on the financial markets, nevertheless it keeps you plugged into the mechanism in its most advanced and active area, and requires constant attention – in this country of frighteningly local and provincial interests – to the whole system. I would not hesitate to declare that in this country where the man who follows and determines party policies is in the vast majority of cases the spokesman for very specific and nearly always reactionary interests, where even the unionized worker refuses to think anything outside strict economic increases for his category, the crowd – the enormous crowd – of owners of small quantities of shares, of small speculators in this highly sensitive stock exchange system represents the blueprint for the most modern citizenry.

Montgomery, Alabama, 6 March

This is a day that I will never forget as long as I live. I have seen what racism is, mass racism, accepted as one of a society's fundamental rules. I was present at one of the first episodes of mass struggle by the Southern blacks: and it ended in defeat. I don't know if you are aware that after decades of total immobility black protests began right here, in the worst segregationist State in the country: some were even successful, under the leadership of Martin Luther King, a Baptist minister, advocate of non-violent protest. That is why I came here to Montgomery, the day before yesterday, but I did not expect to find myself right in the middle of these crucial days of struggle.

The scene today is Alabama's Capitol (which was the first Confederate Capitol, in the early months of the secession, before the capital moved to Richmond), a white building like the Washington Capitol, on a wide, climbing street, Dexter Street. The black students (from the black university) had declared that they would go to the Capitol steps for a peaceful protest demonstration against the expulsion of nine of them from the university, who last week had tried to sit down in the whites' coffee shop in Court Hall, the State court building. At half-past one there was a meeting of the students at the Baptist church right beside the Capitol (the church where King had been minister, but now he is based in Atlanta directing the whole movement – though in these days he is back here – and his church has another local leader). But the Capitol was already ringed by policemen with truncheons and Highway Police in their cowboy hats, turquoise jerkins and khaki trousers. The pavements were swarming with whites, mostly poor whites who are the worst racists, ready to use their fists, young hooligans working in teams (their organization, which is only barely clandestine, is the Ku Klux Klan), but also comfortable middle-class people, families with children, all there to watch and shout slogans and obscenities against the blacks locked inside the church, plus of course dozens of amateur photographers taking shots of such unusual Sunday events. The crowd's attitude varied between derision, as though they were watching monkeys asking for civil rights (genuine derision, from people who never thought the blacks could get such ideas in their heads), to hatred, cries of provocation, crow-like sounds made by the young thugs. Here and there, along the pavement, there are also a few small groups of blacks, standing aside, men and women, dressed in their best clothes, watching silently and still, in an attitude of composure. The waiting becomes more and more unbearable, the blacks must by now have finished their service and must be ready to come out; the Capitol steps are blocked by the police, all the pavements are blocked by the crowd of whites who are now angry and shouting 'Come out, niggers!' The blacks start to appear on the steps of their church and begin singing a hymn; the whites begin to make a racket, howling and insulting them. The fire-fighters arrive with their hoses and position themselves all around; the police begin to give orders to clear the streets, in other words to warn the whites that if they stay it is at their own risk and peril, whereas the small groups of blacks are dispersed roughly. There is a sound of horse-hooves and the scene is invaded by cowboys wearing the CD (Civil Defense) armband, a local militia of volunteers to keep public order, armed with sticks and guns; the police and militia are there to avoid incidents and see that the blacks clear off, but in reality the whites remain in charge of the street, the blacks stay in their church singing hymns, the police manage to send away only the most peaceful whites, the white thugs become more and more menacing and I who am keen to stay and see how things turn out (naturally, I am on my own; the few pro-black whites cannot allow themselves to be seen in these situations, well-known as they are) find myself surrounded by tougher and tougher looking characters, but also by youths who are there as though to see something funny, and just to make a noise. (I will later learn – though I did not see him – that there is also a white Methodist minister – the only white man in Montgomery with the courage to make a stand for the blacks – and as a result his house and his church have already been bombed twice by the KKK – who was there in front of the church and had organized his white congregation into providing a service to take the blacks safely from the church door to the cars; but, I repeat, I did not see him; the images in my head are of an all-out racial war, with no halfway houses.) Then begins the most painful part to watch: the blacks come out of the church a few at a time, some head down a sidestreet that I cannot see, but which I think the police have cleared of whites, but others go down Dexter Avenue in small groups along the pavements where the white thugs have gathered, walking away silently with their heads held high amid choruses of threatening and obscene sneers, insults and gestures. At every insult or witticism made by a white, the other whites, men and women, burst out laughing, sometimes with almost hysterical insistence, but sometimes also just like that, affably, and these people, as far as I am concerned, are the most awful, this all-out racism combined with affability. The most admirable ones are the black girls: they come down the road in twos or threes, and those thugs spit on the ground before their feet, standing in the middle of the pavement and forcing the girls to zigzag past them, shouting abuse at them and making as though to trip them up, and the black girls continue to chat among themselves, never do they move in such a way as to suggest that they want to avoid them, never do they alter their route when they see them blocking their path, as though they were used to these scenes right from birth.

Those who are not used to these things are the whites, because the blacks had never dared do such things, and of course they don't know what to say except that there has been infiltration by Communists. The first battle was the one about buses, last year. The boycotting of the buses following an incident (the arrest of a black girl who had wanted to sit on a seat reserved for whites) was the first mass protest by the blacks and it was successful. Then they tried to mount a legal action to have the whites' park open to blacks, but the town council ordered all parks to be closed, and so the city was for the whole summer, and still is today, without a public park, a swimming-pool, etc. These protests were organized by this young black political activist, Luther King (who like all the others is officially a Baptist Church minister), who has no particular social or political programme except equal rights for blacks. Actually there is no doubt that once they gain equality the blacks will be even more conservative than the rest, as has happened with other minorities once they emerge from poverty, the Irish and the Italians; but for the meantime, this spirit of struggle is something unique in America today and it is important that there is also a mobilization of black students, who usually think that they have made it and try only not to cause trouble. With this courtroom coffee-shop row, last week the whole city went into a state of tension like in a civil war, the KKK put bombs in several houses (I visited some of the people who had been bombed) and a few days ago they clubbed a black woman over the head with a baseball bat and the judge did not find the KKK person accused guilty despite witnesses, photographs, etc. The thing that is difficult for a European to understand is how these things can happen in a nation which is 75 per cent non-segregationist, and how they can take place without the involvement of the rest of the country. But the autonomy of the individual States is such that here they are even more outside Washington's jurisdiction or New York public opinion, than if they were, say, in the Middle East. And there is no possibility (or perhaps they lack the ability?) for the black movement here to find allies, neither for King nor for the more left-wing activists, who maintain (correctly) that the crucial point is that of being allowed to vote. King now has allies in the colonial peoples' movement, but they can only provide moral support; he was recently in Ghana, Egypt, and India; he was also invited to Russia, but refused because otherwise, etc. So the minute I arrived in Montgomery, into the hottest part of this situation, I learnt that King was in town and I got them to take me to him. He is a very stout and capable person, physically resembling Bourghiba a bit, with a little moustache: the fact that he is a pastor has nothing to do with his physical appearance (his second-in-command and successor, Abernathy, a young rather fat man who also has a small moustache, looks like a jazz-player), these are politicians whose only weapon is the pulpit and even their non-violence does not really have a mystical aura about it: it is the only form of struggle possible and they use it with the controlled political skill which the extreme harshness of their conditions has taught them. These black leaders – I've approached several of them in the last few days, of different tendencies – are lucid, decisive people, totally devoid of black self-pity, not terribly kind (though of course I was an unknown foreigner who had turned up to nose around in days which were very eventful for them). The race question is a damnable thing: for a century a huge country like the South has not spoken or thought about anything else, just this problem, whether they are progressives or reactionaries. So I arrive escorted by blacks in the sacristy of Abernathy's church and King is there along with another black minister who is also a leader, and I am present at a council-of-war meeting where they decide on this Sunday's course of action which I have just described to you; then we go to another church where the students have gathered, in order to give them this instruction, and then I stay for this dramatic, moving meeting, I the sole white among three thousand black students, perhaps the first white to do so in the whole history of the South. Naturally I have come here also with introductions to extremely racist, ultra-reactionary high-society ladies, and I have to divide my days with acrobatic skill so that they do not suspect what a deadly enemy they are harbouring in their midst (above all whites are forbidden by law from entering blacks' houses or getting into a car with them). From the Baptist church I move on to the city's theatre where respectable people have gathered for the gala première of the Chicago Ballet, to which I have been invited by the local paper's gossip columnist, a good friend of the Dominican dictator, Trujillo. Today, however, after the Capitol, I have ten minutes of peace to calm down after all the emotion, then a high-society lady comes to collect me and shows me, as we drive along, their factory of gherkins in vinegar, and hints vaguely at the day's 'troubles' caused by that agitator Luther King. This famous Southern aristocracy gives me the impression of being uniquely stupid in its continual harking back to the glories of the Confederacy; this Confederate patriotism which survives intact after a century, as though they were talking of things from their youth, in the tone of someone who is confident you share their emotions, is something which is more unbearable than ridiculous.

8.3.60

Meanwhile, Monday 7 March I crossed Alabama and Georgia by bus, through the poverty-stricken countryside, the blacks' wooden shacks, the squalid little towns. The sad conclusion is that the American economy has not got the slightest capacity to solve the problems of the underdeveloped areas; everything that was done was carried out at the time of the New Deal; after that, absolutely nothing, and the economic collapse of the South hits you in the eyes, and I am not surprised that they still talk about the Civil War as though it were yesterday; nothing has been done in a hundred years to repair the ruin of the South caused by the War of Secession.

Consequently, my impressions of the South would be very dark if I had not discovered

Savannah

I stopped at Savannah, Georgia, to sleep and have a look at it, attracted only by its beautiful name and by some historical, literary or musical memory, but no one said I should go there, no one in any State of the United States. AND IT IS THE MOST BEAUTIFUL CITY IN THE UNITED STATES. Absolutely, there is nothing to compare with it. I don't know yet what Charleston, South Carolina, is like, where I will be going tomorrow and which is more famous. This is a town where nobody ever comes (despite having a top-class tourist infrastructure and knowing how to present its attractions – relating to both history and town planning – with a sophistication unknown elsewhere; but this is perhaps the secret of its charm, that internal American tourism, which is always so phoney, has not touched it). It is a town which has remained practically unchanged, just as it was in the prosperous days of the South at the start of the nineteenth century, in the heyday of cotton; and it is one of the only American cities to have been built with unique urban planning, of extreme rational regularity and variety and harmony: at every second intersection there is a small tree-lined square, all identical, but always different, because of the pleasantness of the buildings which range from the colonial period to that of the Civil War. I stayed there spending the whole day going round from street to street, enjoying the forgotten pleasure of feeling a city, a city which is the expression of a civilization, and it is only in this way by seeing Savannah that you can understand what type of civilization the South was.

Of course it is a city of the utmost and lethal ennui, but ennui with a style, full of rationality, Protestantism, England. A boring, fussy city with detailed instructions in hotel bedrooms on the route to follow in case of an air-raid alarm; the most famous personality born here is the founder of the Girl Scouts; in a house where I went (because I was naturally curious to get to know the inhabitants) they served me tea, I mean tea, no whiskey, nothing alcoholic, just tea, the first time this has happened to me in this country. Here too, as elsewhere in the South, old ladies do nothing but talk of their ancestors, though here you understand what being a Southern gentleman or gentlewoman is really about, whereas in Montgomery they are frighteningly uncouth despite being rich – relatively rich for the South – while here everything exudes an air of genteel poverty (the city lives really off its port, which is the first harbour that I've seen which has a flavour of old America) and the attitude towards the blacks is one of sentimental paternalism. But tomorrow I will tell you all about

9.3.60

Charleston

Full of wonderful so-called *ante bellum* houses (pre- the War of Secession) and some even date from the eighteenth century, but filthy and falling apart. And as a city nothing to compare with Savannah.

And now?
     I could go to North Carolina where I have been
     invited to the University at Chapel Hill.
Or turn back towards the west, to
Colorado, where I have several invites.
     And from there fly to Wyoming, where I have been
     invited to a ranch.

118

And from there fly to the far north-west, to Seattle
in Washington State. Having omitted the
north-west is a mistake I cannot forgive myself.
   And come back, stopping in Chicago, where I
   stayed only a few days and the city certainly
   has much more to be discovered.
But I would certainly also like to go back
to the two big cities in California.
   I would like to continue to go zigzagging
   round the whole continent, as I have been doing
   now for the last two months.
Instead,
   I am going back to New York to spend the two months that
   still separate me from my return to Europe, because New York,
   rootless city, is the only one where I could think I have put
   down some roots, and in the end two months of travel are not
   enough, and New York is the only place I could pretend to
   reside.
Two months which in the event will be
shortened by a series of invitations,
each one of three or four days and for
which I have already made precise note of the commitments
and dates:

> in a college of millionaire girls
> in Bennington, Vermont
> at Yale University
> again at Harvard University
> once more in Washington.

So now I am tortured by the thought that my
days in New York will fly away in a twinkling,
and the only thing I regret is
not being able to stay long enough in this city
about which for two months I have heard nothing but criticism

and I share all the criticisms that people make about it however

[Unpublished. Calvino tells the story of his journey to the United States in letters sent to the Einaudi publishing house.]

The Cloven Communist

I meet Italo Calvino in San Remo. This is a kind of very brief summer ritual: it never lasts more than ten minutes and those minutes correspond exactly to the sum of our silences. But this time the rule, which has been in force now for many years, is no longer valid: there are too many reasons for making an exception. First of all the publication of a large volume by Einaudi, Our Ancestors, *which contains not in any strict order* The Cloven Viscount, The Baron in the Trees *and* The Non-Existent Knight; *also the author's journey to America. I do not know where to begin, but I am quite clear in my own mind about my intention to get Calvino to talk for our readers, and I suddenly find that, making a rapid mental sketch of this Ligurian writer, I come up against the image of Cesare Pavese. This is in a certain sense an obligatory point of reference, a way of anchoring Calvino to his roots or rather of bringing together his natural development (everything that relates to the Liguria in which he grew up) and his intellectual formation, and perhaps something else as well. On this occasion there is an important date, one that offers the pretext for reflecting on quite a long period in our history. This is the tenth anniversary of the death of Pavese and it takes place exactly on the 27th of this month. I go back to the pain and surprise of those days, make a quick calculation of everything that has happened since, of what we have become both individually and as a family and it is in this very context that I find the first question to put to Calvino. The rest will come later: his work, his trip to America, his political ideas. For the time being, starting from the memory of Pavese means genuinely anchoring ourselves to our own history.*

Ten years on from his death, what is your opinion of Pavese's works? What has time brought out and what has it, on the other hand, left aside? Finally, if you feel you are in his debt, in what sense do you think we should speak of such a debt?

A few weeks ago some friends from Rome came to Turin to make a documentary about Pavese's city. I took them around, showing them the places where we went together: the River Po, the bars, the hills. Certainly in these ten years many things have changed, more than I expected. Already there is a 'Pavese era', with its own very distinct face – that twenty-year period 1930–50 which only now appears to us with a single physiognomy, spanning the war, unified in the look of the streets, in the design of objects, in the way women looked, in the way people behaved, and also in the psychological climate and the world of ideas. This is already enough to relegate Pavese to the past, but also to reaffirm his worth in a dimension that we previously did not pay enough attention to: he was the author of a fresco of his time which is without equal and which was articulated throughout his nine brief novels, as though it were a tightly packed and complete *comédie humaine*. How many things are there that, precisely because they are distant and almost incomprehensible today, turn out to be charged with fascinating poetic force! Where on earth can you find these days young people faced with long days and endless nights, who don't know what to do or where to go, bored because of their own virginity and the void around them, not because they are sated and have a void inside them as they do today? And yet how authentic and credible it is, how we suffer this torment when we read Pavese! And this problem of solitude, what was it? Yet everything is so clear, painful and distant, just as Leopardi is clear, painful and distant.

Pavese's nine novels have a stylistic and thematic unity which is extremely compact, yet each of them is so different from the next. I used to think *La casa in collina [The House on the Hill]* and *Tra donne sole [Amongst Women Only]* the best of them, each in its different way, but I reread recently *Il diavolo sulle colline [The*

Devil in the Hills] which, I remember, was the novel of his that
I understood least, when Pavese gave me the manuscript to read.
Now I see that it is a story that has many layers it can be read
on, perhaps the richest of his novels, containing a highly complex
and lively philosophical debate (though with maybe a bit too
much discussion) and containing as if in concentrated form all
the essence of Pavese the thinker (the Pavese of the diary and
the essays), all fused into a narrative which is exciting, first-class,
brim-full of things.

Of course no one in Italian literature followed the Pavese route.
Neither in terms of language, nor in that way he had of extract-
ing a poetic tension from a realistic, objective story, and not even
in his despair, which initially seemed the element that was most
likely to catch on. (Even internal suffering is something seasonal;
who today wants to suffer?) Pavese has gone back to being 'the
most isolated voice in Italian poetry', as the blurb read on an old
edition of his *Lavorare stanca [Hard Labour]*, a blurb dictated, I
think, by himself.

Even I myself, who am meant to be his disciple, in what sense
do I deserve that label? What links me to Pavese is our common
taste for a style that is both poetic and moral, a kind of tough-
ness, and a love of many of the same authors: all things that I
inherited from him, from the five years of almost daily contact I
had with him; and that is no small amount. But in my own work,
in the last ten years, I have moved away from the climate that
prevailed when Pavese was the first reader and arbiter of everything I wrote. And who knows what he would say now! Some
critics get it completely wrong, saying that my fantasy tales derive
from Pavese's ideas on 'myth'. What has that got to do with them?
Actually in his final essays Pavese maintained that one cannot
endow with a poetic ('mythic', he would have said) force images
from other epochs than our own, in other words he condemned
a type of literature which coincidentally I was to undertake less
than a year after he died. The truth is that our ways of working
were always different; I do not start from considerations of poetic

method: I career down dangerous roads, hoping always to survive through 'natural' strength. Pavese did not; as far as he was concerned, there was no such thing as a poet's 'nature'; everything was rigorous self-construction based on will power, he never took a step unless he was certain of what he was doing, in literature; if only he had been the same in his life!

Seeing that you have touched on the subject, can you tell us why for some time you have preferred in your writing to work on the reflected images of reality, on the ideas that sustain it, and have moved away from the direct and immediate music of things.
I tried to answer this question in the preface to the volume *Our Ancestors* which gathers together my three lyric-epic-comic novels, *The Cloven Viscount, The Baron in the Trees, The Non-Existent Knight.* Now that cycle is complete, finished, it's there for whoever wants to study it or enjoy it; it's not up to me any more. For me the only thing that counts is what I am going to do next, and for the moment I do not know what that will be. But as I told you earlier, I never start out from an idea of poetic method, I never say: 'I will now do a realistic-objective story, or a psychological or fantasy one.' What counts is what we are, and the way we deepen our relationship with the world and with others, a relationship that can be one of both love for all that exists and of desire for its transformation. Then you put the point of the pen on the white page, work out a certain angle so that it produces the black signs which make sense, and wait to see what comes out of all this. (It is also true that you often end by tearing everything up.)

I have heard that you are preparing a book about your impressions of your journey through the United States. Do you think that travelling helps a writer these days? In your case, what positive and negative experiences did you draw from your trip to America?
When I set out for the United Sates, and also throughout my travels there, I swore that I would never write a book on America

(there are already so many!). Now, however, I have changed my mind. Travel books are a useful, modest and yet self-contained way of writing literature. These are books that have a practical use, even though, or precisely because, countries change from year to year and in fixing them as you have seen them you record their changing essence; and in such books you can express something that goes beyond the description of places one has seen, a relationship between yourself and reality, a process of knowledge.

These are things I have come to believe only recently; up until yesterday I believed that travelling could only have an indirect influence on the substance of what I write. Here what was relevant was that I had had Pavese as my mentor, the great enemy of travelling. He used to say more or less that poetry comes from a germ that you carry in you for years, perhaps for ever; what influence can having spent a day or week here or there have on this incredibly slow maturation process? Certainly, travelling is a life experience, which can mature or change something in us like any other experience, this was what I thought, and a journey can help us write better because it has helped us understand something more of life; someone visits India, for instance, and on returning home will write better, say, his memories of his first day at school. In any case, I have always enjoyed travelling, leaving aside its effect on literature. And it was also in this spirit that I made my recent American trip: because I was interested in the United States, in what it is really like, not to undertake, I don't know, some 'literary pilgrimage' or because I wanted 'to be inspired by it'.

However, in the United States, I was seized, as never before, by a desire to know and possess fully a polymorphous and complex reality, something Other. What happened was something like falling in love. Lovers, as everyone knows, spend a lot of time arguing; and even now that I have returned, every so often I find myself arguing inside myself with America; but in any case I continue to live inside that experience, I fling myself avidly and jealously on everything I hear or read about that country which

I claim to be the only one to understand. Seeing that in this case I was seized by 'the music of things', as you said earlier, Carlo, I really ought to hurry and try to put it down on paper.

Negative aspects of travel? Everyone will say that it distracts you from that horizon of set objects that constitute your own poetic world, it disperses that absorbed concentration which is a condition (one of the conditions) conducive to literary creation. But in the end, even if it is a dispersal, what does it matter? In human terms, it is better to travel than to stay at home. First of all live, and then philosophize and write. Writers above all should live with an attitude towards the world which effects a greater acquisition of truth. That small something which will reflect this on the page, anything, will be the literature of our time, nothing else.

What then does the return home represent, what value do your memories have as someone from Liguria?
Ligurians divide into two categories: those attached to their own place like limpets stuck to a rock, whom you could never move; and those who regard the world as their home and wherever they are they find themselves at home. But even the latter category, and I belong to them, as perhaps you do, too, come back home regularly, and stay attached to their land as much as the former. My own area, the Western Riviera, has become unrecognizable in the last fifteen years, but perhaps precisely because of that fact rediscovering behind all this cement the traces of a Liguria of my memory is an operation of patriotic *pietas* that betrays even more my love and trepidation for the place. It is just like scraping away today's dominant commercialized mentality to find the old ethical substratum our families used to have, and that in your case, Carlo, must be one of a Catholicism with Jansenist overtones, whereas for me it is a secular tradition, deriving from Mazzinian and free-thinking Masonic roots, all geared towards an ethics of 'achievement'. What binds me to my home area, above all to the land we had above San Remo, is the memory of my

father, which seems to grow deeper and deeper, one of the strangest personalities and existences, yet also one of the most characteristic of the generation that grew up after the Risorgimento, and the last Ligurian to be typical of a Liguria that no longer exists (typical even in the fact of his having spent a third of his life on the other side of the Atlantic).

However, I realize that these are sentimental factors whereas rationally I have always sought to look at things from the point of view of the most advanced standpoint of the world of productivity, the sectors of society which are most decisive for the history of humanity, whether these be in industrial Europe, America or in Russia. When I was younger this contradiction preoccupied me considerably: if I knew that the world that counted was the one that I have just described, why in creative terms did I have to remain bound to the Riviera which survives on a subsistence economy, caught between the false prosperity of tourism and an agriculture which is largely that of a depressed area? And yet, when I wrote stories set in the Riviera, the images came to me very clearly, precisely, whereas when I wrote about the industrial world everything turned out less focused, greyish. The fact is that we write well about what we have left behind, since it represents something finished (though later you discover it is not over at all).

You always have to start out from what you are. Sociological criticism could perform this concrete service instead of moving around in generic terms as it does: define the true essence of every writer from his own point of view, uncover his real social background which perhaps is in total contrast with appearances. In my case they could perhaps discover that deep down they will find the rural smallholder, an individualist, a hard worker, mean, hostile to the State and to the taxman, who, reacting against an agricultural economy which brings no returns, and to the remorse he feels for having left the country in the hands of tenants, proposes universal solutions to his crisis: Communism or the industrial world or the rootless life of globe-trotting intellectuals, or maybe just rediscovering on the page the harmony with nature that has been lost in the real world.

If you had to write a brief account of your political experiences, which points would you want to emphasize? Which friendships helped you become what you are? Did ideas or real people count more?
A few months ago, I was just back from America, there was that series of lectures in Turin on Fascism and anti-Fascism: for each one the Teatro Alfieri was packed, and in the middle of that crowd I recognized the faces of that little big world which makes up anti-Fascism, the people of the Resistance, back together again no matter what road they had taken in the meantime, and in addition very many young people. Well, that was wonderful: we are still here, and we still count; in fact shortly afterwards we had some proof of that.

Men always count more than ideas. For me ideas have always had eyes, nose, mouth, arms and legs. Political history for me is above all a history of human presences. Just when you least expect, you realize that Italy is full of wonderful people.

My generation was a fine generation, even if it has not done everything it could have. Certainly, for us, politics retained for years perhaps an exaggerated importance, whereas life is made up of so many things. But this passion for civic society provided our cultural development with some sinew: if we got interested in many different things it was for that reason. Even if I look around, in Europe, in America, at our contemporaries and those who are younger than us, I have to say that we were sharper. Among the young people who have grown up in Italy after us, the best of them know more than we did, but they are all more theoretical, their ideological passion derives from books; our first passion was action; and this does not mean being more superficial: quite the reverse.

As you can see, I am trying to give an overall outline, to delineate a continuity between the time when I was part of a political organization and now when I am more a 'free-booter'.

Because what counts is whatever is continuous, the positive element that is recognizable in every reality. My political ideas now? Perhaps I don't have much of a sense of current questions, but I regard myself as an ideal citizen of a world based on an understanding between America and Russia. Of course, that means hoping that many things will change on both sides, it means counting on the new men who are certainly emerging on both sides. And China? If America and Russia can together solve the undeveloped world's problems, the most painful routes will be avoided. There has been so much pain already. And Italy? And Europe? I don't know, if we can think in terms that are not parochial but on a world scale (that is the least we can ask in this interplanetary era) we can be not passive pawns of the future but its real shapers.

[Interview with IC by Carlo Bo, *L'Europeo*, XVI, 35, 28 August 1960.]

Political Autobiography of a Young Man

I. A Childhood under Fascism

1) I was sixteen in 1939, so in replying to the question about the ideas I grew up with before the war, I have to beware of generic approximations, I have to try to reconstruct a network of images and emotions rather than ideas.

The danger for those writing autobiographical memoirs in a political key is that excessive weight is given to politics compared to the weight it really has in childhood and adolescence. I could begin by saying that the first memory of my life is that of a socialist being beaten up by Fascist lynch-squads, something which I think few among those born in 1923 can manage to remember; and indeed it is a memory which must probably refer to the last time Fascist squads used coshes, in 1926, after an attempt on Mussolini. The person attacked was Professor Gaspare Amoretti, an old Latin teacher (father of a Communist from the *Ordine Nuovo* group who later fell in Japan on a mission for the Third International), who at that time was living in the annexe of our villa at San Remo. I remember clearly that we were at dinner when the old professor came in with his face beaten up and bleeding, his bowtie all torn, asking for help.

But to make everything that you will see and hear in your life stem from your first childhood memory is a literary temptation.

One's perspectives in childhood and adolescence are different; disparate impressions and judgments are placed alongside each other without any logic; even for those who grow up in an environment which is open to opinion and information a line of judgment is formed only with the passage of time.

As a child listening to the adults' discussions in our house, I always felt that it was taken for granted that in Italy everything was going wrong. And during adolescence I and my companions at school were almost all hostile to Fascism. But it is not at all inevitable that just because of this my road towards anti-Fascism was already marked out. At that time I was very far from seeing the situation in political terms, as a struggle of one ideology against another, and from working out perspectives towards a solution for the future. Seeing that politics is an object of contempt and obloquy in the eyes of the best people, the most spontaneous attitude for a young person is to think that it is an area that is irredeemably corrupt, and that one has to look for other values in life. The distance between judging Fascism negatively and having a political commitment to anti-Fascism was so great it could not be conceived of today.

However, now I have to beware of another error or habit typical of those who write autobiographical memoirs: that of tending to configure your own experience as the 'typical' experience of a particular generation and ambience, emphasizing the more common aspects and ignoring the more particular and personal ones. Unlike what I have done at other times, I would now like to turn the spotlight on those aspects which most depart from the 'typical' Italian experience, because I am convinced that one can gain more truth from the exception than from the rule.

I grew up in a little town which was rather different from the rest of Italy when I was a child: San Remo, which was at that time still populated by elderly English people, Russian grand dukes, eccentric and cosmopolitan types. And my own family was rather unusual both for San Remo and for the Italy of that time: my parents were no longer young, both scientists, lovers of nature, freethinkers, very different in personality from one another, and both opposed to the political climate of the country. My father, who was from San Remo, from a family that supported Mazzini and republican, anticlerical and masonic ideas, had been in his youth an anarchist, a follower of Kropotkin and then a Socialist Reformist; he had lived in Latin America for many years and had not been through the experience of the First World War; my mother, who was from Sardinia, from a secular family, had grown up in the religion of civic duty and science, had been a socialist in favour of intervention in the war in 1915 but with a tenacious faith in pacifism. When they came back to Italy after years overseas they found Fascism establishing its power and an Italy that was totally different and difficult to understand. My father tried in vain to put his skills and honesty at the service of the country, and to consider Fascism along the same lines as the Mexican revolutions he had lived through and with the accommodating, practical spirit of the old Ligurian reformist that he was; my mother, whose brother was one of the university professors who had signed Croce's manifesto,* was intransigent in her anti-Fascism. Both were cosmopolitan by vocation and experience and both had grown up under the general urge towards renovation of pre-war socialism, and their sympathies were not so much with liberal democracy as with all the progressive movements that were out of the ordinary: Kemal Atatürk, Gandhi, the Russian Bolsheviks. Fascism fitted into this picture as one route among many, but a wrong route, led by ignorant and dishonest people. The critique of Fascism in my family, apart from attacking its violence, incompetence, greed, suppression of freedom of speech and aggression in foreign policy, was directed above all at its two cardinal sins: the alliance with the monarchy and the reconciliation with the Vatican.

---

* In 1925 the Fascist Education Minister, Giovanni Gentile, issued a pro-Fascist manifesto signed by 250 intellectuals, including Pirandello; the Idealist philosopher Benedetto Croce responded with an anti-Fascist manifesto, signed among others by the poet Montale.

Young children are instinctively conformist, so realizing that I belonged to a family that was unusual created a state of psychological tension with the prevailing environment. The thing which most distinguished my parents' anti-conformism was their intransigence on the question of religion. At school they asked that I be excused from religious instruction and not ever have to attend Mass or other religious services. While I was at a Waldensian primary school or attending an English college as an external pupil, this fact did not cause me any problems: Protestant, Catholic, Jewish and Russian Orthodox pupils were all mixed up together in varying proportions. At that time San Remo was a city with churches and priests of all denominations, as well as strange sects that were then fashionable such as Rudolf Steiner's anthroposophists, and I considered my family's attitude as one of the many gradations of religious opinion I saw represented around me. However, when I went to the state high school, being exempt from religious classes in this climate of general conformism (Fascism was already in its second decade of power) exposed me to a situation of isolation and forced me at times to shut myself off in a kind of silent passive resistance towards my teachers and fellow-pupils. Sometimes the religious lesson was in between two other classes and I would wait in the corridor, causing misunderstandings with teachers and janitors passing by who thought I had been sent out as a punishment. What happened with new pupils was that they always thought I was Protestant because of my surname; I would deny this but was unable to reply to the next question: 'So what are you then?' The expression 'freethinker', said by a schoolboy, would make people laugh; 'atheist' was too strong a word for that age; so I refused to answer.

My mother delayed my enrolment in the Fascist scouts, the *Balilla*, as long as possible, firstly because she did not want me to learn how to handle weapons, but also because the meetings that were then held on Sunday mornings (before the Fascist Saturday was instituted) consisted mostly of a Mass in the scouts' chapel. When

I had to be enrolled as part of my school duties, she asked that I be excused from the Mass; this was impossible for disciplinary reasons, but my mother saw to it that the chaplain and the commander were aware that I was not a Catholic and that I should not be asked to perform any external acts of devotion in church.

In short, I often found myself in situations different from the others, looked on as though I were some strange animal. I do not think this harmed me: one gets used to persisting in one's habits, to finding oneself isolated for good reasons, to putting up with the discomfort that this causes, to finding the right way to hold on to positions which are not shared by the majority. But above all I grew up tolerant of others' opinions, particularly in the field of religion, remembering how irksome it was to hear myself mocked because I did not follow the majority's beliefs. And at the same time I have remained totally devoid of that taste for anti-clericalism which is so common in those who are educated surrounded by priests.

I have insisted on setting down these memories because I see that now many non-believing friends let their children have a religious education 'so as not to give them complexes', 'so that they don't feel different from the others'. I believe that this behaviour displays a lack of courage which is totally damaging pedagogically. Why should a young child not begin to understand that you can face a small amount of discomfort in order to stay faithful to an idea? And in any case who said that young people should not have complexes? Complexes arise through a natural attrition with the reality that surrounds us, and when you have complexes you try to overcome them. Life is in fact nothing but this triumphing over one's own complexes, without which the formation of a character and personality does not happen.

Of course I must not make things out to be more exciting than they were. My childhood experiences had nothing dramatic about them, I lived in a comfortable, serene world, I had an image of the world that was varied and rich in contrasting nuances, but no awareness of all-out conflicts. I had no notion of poverty; the only social problem I ever heard mentioned was that of the Ligurian smallholders, on whose behalf my father campaigned, those owners of minuscule pieces of land, tormented by taxes, by the price of chemical products, and the lack of roads. There were of course the poverty-stricken masses from other regions of Italy who were beginning to emigrate to the Riviera: the wage-earners who worked on our land and filed into my father's study to be paid every Saturday for the week's work were from the Abruzzi or the Veneto. But these were people from distant lands, and I could not imagine what poverty really meant. I did not find it easy to relate to working people; the familiarity and friendliness that my parents showed towards the poor always made me feel ill at ease.

The ideas regarding the political struggle already taking place in the world did not reach me, only its external images, which simply lay beside one another as in a mosaic. The most read papers in San Remo were from Nice, not Genoa or Milan. During the Spanish Civil War *L'Eclaireur* supported Franco; *Le Petit Niçois* was for the Republicans, and at a certain point it was banned. In our house we read *Il Lavoro*, a Genoa paper, as long as it remained – as it did well into the Fascist period – the only paper whose editor was an old socialist, Giuseppe Canepa. Canepa was an old friend of my father's, who I remember sometimes coming to lunch at our house. But this must have been around 1933, since my parents enjoyed enormously its anti-Hitler column signed by 'Stella Nera', who was Giovanni Ansaldo.* Once a Zeppelin passed overhead, full of Nazi brownshirts, and the boy next to me, Emanuel Rospicicz, who was a Polish Jew, said: 'If only it would crash and kill them all.' I was in the fourth year of primary school, at the Waldensian School: it must have been 1933. In my house

---

* Giovanni Ansaldo (1895–1969), journalist. Originally a Fascist, he went on to become the editor of the main Naples daily, *Il Mattino*.

there were always comings and goings of young people from all over – Turks, Dutch, Indians – who had grants to attend the institute that my father directed; once a heated argument arose between two Germans, a Nazi and a Jew. My mother's best friend, from Switzerland, often went to France and attended the international peace and anti-Fascist demonstrations at the Salle Pleyel: she did not tell us, but (we later found out) she secretly tested their passwords on us. At the time of the Popular Front in France, at afternoon snack-time our mother would make us stand to attention facing east and say: '*Pour le pain, pour la paix, pour la liberté.*'

At the same time, of course, I attended the assemblies and parades of the Fascist armed scouts, the *Balilla Moschettieri*, and later of the *Avanguardisti*. The pleasure in missing these, of being suspended from school for not attending an assembly or not putting on your uniform on call-up days, became more intense around the time of going to high school, though even then more than anything else this was simply a bravado display of student disobedience. But what it was like living through this period of Fascist demonstrations I have already tried to represent in three stories which are set in the summer of 1940; there is no point in going back over that here.

In short, until the Second World War broke out, the world seemed to me to have a range of different gradations of morality and behaviour, not opposites but placed alongside each other. At one extreme was the stern anti-Fascist or even pre-Fascist rigour which was incarnated by my mother with her moralistic, secular, scientific, humanitarian, pacifist, animal-loving austerity (my father was another response on his own: a solitary walker, he lived more in the woods with his dogs than among other humans: hunting in season, and looking for mushrooms or snails in the other months). After that one gradually moved through various levels of indulgence towards human weakness, approximation and corruption which became more and more marked and cloying as one went through the Catholic, military, conformist and bourgeois vanity fairs, until you reached the opposite extreme of total vulgarity, ignorance and bluster which was Fascism in its smug sense of triumph, devoid of scruples and sure of itself.

This kind of picture actually did not impose on us categorical decisions, though it might seem like that today; a boy then saw open to him various options, including that of rejecting his parents' world as a nineteenth-century sarcophagus out of touch with reality, and of choosing Fascism which seemed much more solid and vital; in fact my (younger) brother, from the age of thirteen to sixteen, called himself a Fascist just to rebel against our family (but as soon as the German occupation began the rebellion stopped and the family was united in support of the partisan struggle). I at that same age – the time of the Spanish Civil War, which seemed a clear sign of the defeat of the values my parents believed in – accepted their world of values as a tradition and defence against Fascist vulgarity, but I was heading down the road of pessimism, an ironic and detached commentator, someone who wanted to keep himself aloof: any progress was an illusion, things could not be worse in the world.

2) The summer in which I began to enjoy my youth, society, girls, books, was 1938: it ended with Chamberlain and Hitler and Mussolini in Munich. The Riviera's *belle époque* was over. There was a year of tension, then the war on the Maginot Line, then the collapse of France, Italy joining in the war, and the dark years of death and disasters. I do not think that my memories can be very different from those of the average contemporary of mine: neither as regards our anxiety for the events of the war, nor as regards our reading and our discussions of that time.

I would like to flag here an environmental change which took place around me and was not without consequences. With the war, San Remo stopped being the cosmopolitan crossroads that it had been for half a century (stopped for ever: in the post-war period it became part of the suburb of Milan–Turin) and what came back to the fore were its characteristics as an old Ligurian provincial town. Imperceptibly this was also a change of horizons. It came naturally to me to immerse myself in this provincial atmosphere, which for me and my contemporaries, who almost all belonged to the old middle-class families of the town, the children of upright anti-Fascist or at least non-Fascist professionals, acted as a defence against the world around us, a world by now dominated by corruption and madness. As for my own family, what counted now for me was not so much their exotic experiences as my father's old heritage of dialect, rooted as it was in places and property. This was a kind of local ethics, which orientated our choices and friendships and was made up of diffidence and scornful superiority for everything that was beyond the range of our crude and ironic dialect, our brusque common sense.

In 1941 I had to enrol in university. I chose the Agriculture Faculty, concealing my literary ambitions even from my best friends, almost concealing them from myself. A few months spent in Turin, reluctantly attending the university, gave me the mistaken notion that city people thought about nothing besides supporting either Torino or Juventus or supporting one of the two radio orchestras, and this confirmed my enclosure in my provincial shell.

So we grew up jealously guarding a cult of individuality which we thought was exclusive to ourselves, despising the youth of the big cities whom we considered a spineless lot; we were 'hard guys' from the provinces, hunters, snooker-players, show-offs, proud of our lack of intellectual sophistication, contemptuous of any patriotic or military rhetoric, coarse in our speech, regulars in the brothels, dismissive of any romantic sentiment and desperately devoid of women. Now I realize that what I was constructing was a shell in which I intended to live immune from every contagion in a world which my pessimism led me to imagine would be dominated forever by Fascism and Nazism. It was a form of refuge in an obstinate and reductive morality, but which ran the risk of exacting a high price: refusal to participate in the course of history, in the debate on general ideas, areas which I had given up on as lost for ever, in enemy hands. So we accepted, more through lack of experience than lack of courage, external forms of Fascist discipline which were imposed on us, just so as not to get into trouble, whereas I never became involved – again because of this kind of contemptuous refusal to participate – in the political discussions which I nevertheless knew were happening in the Fascist University Youth (GUF) movement, even in the nearby provincial capital. (And this was wrong, because through that kind of environment I would have entered into contact earlier with the young militants of the anti-Fascist organizations and I would not have come to the Resistance unprepared.)

But this enclosed attitude (which nowadays we could define as 'political indifference', by analogy with the attitude that prevailed after the war in those on the opposite side) did not last long, as it soon came into conflict with everything that was in the air. And in any case this phase of provincial isolationism was never total. For instance, one of the school friends I was closest to was a boy from the South who had come from Rome, Eugenio Scalfari.* By now Eugenio was at the University of Rome and would come back to San Remo in the holidays: it could be said that my 'political' life began with my discussions with Scalfari who at first belonged to the fringe groups of the Fascist University Youth, but then was expelled from the GUF, and became involved with groups that had very confused ideologies at the time. Once he wrote to me asking me to join a party that was being formed: the name they proposed was 'the aristocratic-social party'. So, gradually, through the letters and the summer discussions with Eugenio I found myself following the reawakening of clandes-

---

* Eugenio Scalfari (1924–), journalist and writer, founder of the popular weekly magazine *L'Espresso* and the major daily paper *La Repubblica*.

tine anti-Fascism and developing a sense of direction in my reading: 'Read Huizinga, Montale, Vittorini, Pisacane'; the new publications that came out in those years marked so many stages in the disordered literary-ethical education we had.

We also talked a lot about science, cosmology, the fundamentals of knowledge: Eddington, Planck, Heisenberg, Einstein. Our provincial town was in those days full of unusual cases of individual cultural advances: a young man from San Remo, who was a fanatic for English and American culture, managed in the middle of the war to acquire an at that time legendary knowledge in epistemology, psychoanalysis and jazz and we listened to him as though he were some sort of oracle. One summer day, Eugenio Scalfari and I created an entire philosophical system: the philosophy of the *élan vital*. The next day we discovered that it had already been invented by Bergson.

At that time I was writing short tales or apologues with a vaguely political (anarchoid-pessimistic) message. I would send them to Scalfari in Rome who managed to have one of them published in the GUF's broadsheet: it seems it caused a few problems but nobody knew who I was. At that time my political ideas and my writings were oriented towards an anarchism that was not bolstered by any ideological underpinning. In the summer of 1943, after the fall of Mussolini on the 25th of July, we found a common platform with Scalfari and other friends, calling ourselves 'liberals' (a major influence here was the reading of De Ruggiero's *Storia del liberalismo*), which was something as vague as my anarchism. Sitting around in a circle on a huge flat stone in the middle of a stream near our land we met to found the MUL (University Liberal Movement). Politics was still a game, but not for long. They were days of frenzy, subsequently known as the '45 days'. The Communists came back from exile; we plied them with questions, requests, discussions, objections.

Then came [the armistice of] the 8th of September. Eugenio went back to Rome. After a few months I joined the undercover Communist organization.

3) On the 25th of July I had been disillusioned and offended that a historical tragedy such as Fascism should finish with an act of routine administration like a motion of the Grand Council. I was dreaming of the revolution, the rebirth of Italy in the struggle. After the 8th of September this dream became reality: and I had to learn how difficult it is to live out and live up to one's dreams. My choice of Communism was not at all dependent on ideological motivations. I felt the necessity to start with a clean sheet, so I had defined myself as an anarchist. As for the Soviet Union, I had the full array of the usual objections and diffidence, but I was also influenced by the fact that my parents had always been unswervingly pro-Soviet. But above all I felt that at that juncture what counted was action, and the Communists were the most active and organized force. When I learnt that the main partisan leader in our area, the young doctor Felice Cascione, who was a Communist, had fallen fighting against the Germans at Monte Alto in February 1944, I asked a Communist friend if I could join the party.

I was immediately put in touch with comrades who were workers, and had the job of organizing students in the Youth Front, and one of the things I wrote was cyclostyled and sent round secretly. (It was one of those semi-humorous apologues, like many I had written and would continue to write, and it concerned the anarchist-type objections which conditioned my support for Communism: whether the army, police, bureaucracy would survive into a future world; unfortunately I have not kept a copy, but I always hope I'll find an old comrade who has.)

We were in the most peripheral fringe of the chequer-board of the Italian Resistance, devoid of natural resources, of Allied help, of authoritative political leadership; but this was one of the most fierce and ruthless trouble-spots for the whole twenty months, and it was one of the areas that had the highest casualty rate. It has always been difficult for me to recount in first person my memories of the partisan war. I could do it in several narrative keys, all of them equally truthful: from the re-evocation of the various emotions in play, the risks, anxieties, decisions, deaths, to an emphasis on the heroic–comic narration of the uncertainties, mistakes, blunders, misadventures which befell a young middle-class lad, who was politically unprepared, with no real experience of life, and who had lived at home with his family until then.

I cannot omit to record here (especially as this person has already appeared in these notes) the role my mother played in my experience of those months: she was an example of tenacity and courage in a Resistance which she saw as being one with natural justice and family virtues, exhorting her two sons to join the armed struggle, and behaving with dignity and firmness before the SS and the Fascist militia, and in her long detention as a hostage, not least when the blackshirts three times pretended to shoot my father in front of her eyes. The historical events which mothers take part in acquire the greatness and invincibility of natural phenomena.

But here I am meant only to trace the history of my political ideas at the time of the Resistance. And I would distinguish two attitudes which were both present in me and in the reality surrounding me: one was the Resistance as a highly legal act against Fascist subversion and violence; the other was the Resistance as a revolutionary and subversive act, as something passionately identified with the rebellion of the eternally oppressed and outlawed. I was alternately sensitive to one or other of these attitudes, depending on the events in which I found myself involved and on the harshness of the struggle, and on the people whom I found myself close to: the friends of my usual middle-class anti-Fascist environment, or a completely new stratum of society, which was more sub-proletariat than working-class, which was my major discovery about humanity, because up until then I had always thought of anti-Fascism as a tendency among cultured élites, not amongst the poor masses.

Communism too was these two attitudes together: depending on the psychological situation I was in, the unified legalistic party line, and Togliatti's speeches which I happened to read in cyclostyled sheets, sometimes seemed the only word of calm wisdom amid the general extremism, at others they seemed something incomprehensible and remote, beyond the reality of blood and fury in which we were immersed.

After the Liberation, the first Marxist theoretical text I read was Lenin's *State and Revolution*, and the prospect of the 'withering away of the State' was enough to absorb my originally anarchist, anti-State and anti-centralizing aspirations into the ideology of Communism. This is where the prehistory of my ideas ends, and the conscious history begins, at the same time as my participation in post-war political life, which for me took place mostly within the workers' movement in Turin, and in tandem with my participation in the world of literature. In order to say something new about my subsequent experience (which was articulated above all in the works I published and in my public activity on behalf of the party) I should have to go down deeper, beyond the limits of time and space at my disposal. There will be plenty of opportunity to continue the account or to start it again from scratch. One sees one's past more and more clearly as time goes by.

4) In defining my youthful ideas I used the terms anarchism and Communism. The first stands for the need for the truth about life to be developed in all its richness, over and above the deadening effect imposed on it by institutions. The second represents the need for the world's richness not to be wasted but organized and made to bear fruit according to reason in the interests of all men living and to come.

The first term also means being ready to break the values that have become consolidated up until now, and that bear the mark of injustice, and to start again from scratch. The second also means being ready to run risks involved in the use of force and authority in order to reach a more rational stage in the shortest time possible.

These two terms or orders of needs and risks have been to varying degrees co-present in my way of considering political ideas and actions, in the years when I was part of the Communist party, just as they were before that and as they have remained since. Placing an emphasis on one or other of the two elements, or one or other of the two definitions I have given of each, has been the way in which I followed the historic experiences of these years.

Today my main concern is to see that the positive definition of the two terms, the one I gave first, can come true by paying the lowest possible of the costs I outlined in the second. The problems that are now troubling the world seem to me to be contained in this crux.

II. The Generation that Lived through Difficult Times

1) and 2) For those who were sixteen at the outbreak of the war and twenty at the armistice of 8 September 1943, the reply to the first two questions in the survey cannot involve a genuine exposition of ideas but rather a series of memories of childhood and adolescence, selected according to the way they impinged upon what was only a potential political awareness. This was what I tried to do in the replies published in *Il Paradosso*, 5:23–24, but the more I think about it the less satisfied I am with that lyrical–moralistic account of my 'prehistory'. Political development proper begins when will, choice, reasoning and action come into play: that is to say, it is already a part of adult life. Consequently, in republishing this survey in book form, I think it is more useful to develop my replies to questions 3 and 4, which in the journal I had merely sketched out; and for questions 1 and 2 just to summarize what I had written then.

Before the war, I can speak not so much of a set of ideas as a conditioning – by my family, geography, the society we moved in and also my own psychology – which led me spontaneously to share anti-Fascist, anti-Nazi, anti-Franco, anti-war and anti-racist opinions. This conditioning and these opinions would not have been enough on their own to make me commit myself to the political struggle. Between a negative judgment of Fascism and active anti-Fascist commitment there was a distance then which perhaps today we are unable to appreciate. When you see that politics is an object of obloquy and ridicule in the eyes of the best people around you, the most spontaneous attitude for a young person is to conclude that it is a field that is irredeemably corrupt, something you must avoid, and that you must look for other values in life.

It was then that another form of conditioning entered into play: historical conditioning. The war quickly became the daily backdrop to our lives, the only object of our thoughts. We found ourselves immersed in politics, or rather in history, even without any choice of will. What did the outcome of that all-out conflict that bathed Europe in blood mean for the future of the world and for the future of each one of us? And how ought each one of us to behave in those events that were so far beyond the scale of our will power? What is the role of the individual in history? And does history have any sense? And does the concept of 'progress' still have any meaning?

These were the questions that we could not but ask ourselves: and that was how I developed the attitude I have never lost, of casting every problem as an historical problem, or at least to winkle out of each problem the historical kernel. If the term 'generation' has a meaning, ours could be characterized by this special sensitivity to history as a personal experience; and this applies particularly to Italy, and also more or less to all the countries where there was a rupture caused by the war and the Resistance.

Our experience of history was different from that of preceding generations, and it was in implicit or explicit polemic with them; and reasons for polemics were not hard to find: if there was ever a young generation able to put their parents in the dock, that was us, and this is always a fortunate position. However, it was not a total rupture: we had to find among our parents' ideas those that we could hold on to in order to begin again from scratch, those which they had not been able to or were not in time to turn into action. Consequently ours was not a nihilistic or iconoclastic generation or a generation of 'angry young men': on the contrary, we were precociously endowed with that sense of historical continuity which turns the real revolutionary into the only kind of 'conservative' possible, namely he who, in the general catastrophe of human affairs when they are left to biological impulses, knows how to choose what needs to be saved and defended and developed and made to bear fruit.

Alongside the problem of our participation in historical events, I would like to mention another one that was fundamental in our experience: the problem of the means which history – and therefore we ourselves – must use.

For many of us, right from boyhood, rejecting the Fascist mentality meant above all repudiating weapons and violence; so the involvement in the armed partisan struggle meant above all overcoming powerful psychological blocks within us. I had grown up with a mentality which could more easily have led me to become a conscientious objector than a partisan; and yet all of a sudden I found myself in the middle of the most bloody fighting. However – as was said by the man who first defined this position of commitment for us, and who was first to pay for it with his life – 'this most recent generation has no time to develop inner dramas: it has found a perfectly constructed external drama'. The tragedy of our country and the ferocity of our enemies increased as the settling of scores approached; the logic of the Resistance was the very logic of our urge towards life.

One could have fallen, as a reaction, into extremism, because it seemed to us that there could never be satisfactory revenge for so many outrages; or, in order to discipline this emotional impulse, fall into a cold politicized legalism.

But from all these components fused together into one single burning vitality, what emerged was the partisan spirit, that is to say that ability to overcome dangers and difficulties on impulse, a mixture of warlike pride and self-irony as regards that very warlike pride, a sense of being the real incarnation of legal authority and self-irony regarding the situation in which we found ourselves incarnating it, a manner that was sometimes boastful and truculent but always animated by generosity, an anxiety to make every noble cause our own. At a distance of so many years, I have to say that this spirit, which allowed the partisans to perform the marvellous deeds they did, remains even today a human attitude that is without peer, for moving in the hostile reality of the world.

3) At the Liberation I naturally found myself channelled into active politics, following on from the excitement of the Resistance. Having 'been a partisan' seemed to me as it did to many other young people an irrevocable event in our lives, not a temporary condition like 'military service'. From that point on we saw our civilian life as a continuation of the partisan struggle by other means; the military defeat of Fascism was only the premise; the Italy for which we had fought still existed only in theory; we had to turn it into a reality on so many levels. Whatever activity we wanted to undertake in social and economic life, it seemed natural to us that it should be integrated with participation in political life, that it should derive its meaning from that.

After the Liberation I confirmed my membership of the Communist party, which I had joined during the Resistance primarily to participate in the fight against the Germans and Fascists in the most active and organized units, and the ones that had the most convincing political line.

Communism represented what were (and basically will remain) the two poles of political attraction between which I have oscillated. On one side our rejection of the society which had produced Fascism had led us to dream of a revolution which would start with a clean slate, and build on its own the basic instruments of government, and, triumphing over the inevitable trail of mistakes and excesses that accompanies every revolution, would manage to form a society which was the antithesis of bourgeois society (it was the image of the October Revolution that we had in our heads, that is to say much more a starting point than an end point). On the other hand, we aspired to a civilization that was the most modern and progressive and complex from a political, social, economic, cultural point of view, with a ruling class that was highly qualified, in other words with culture inserted at every level of leadership in politics and productivity. (But maybe we formed this image later than 1945 and now I am backdating it arbitrarily? No, it was already alive then, and was inspired not only by a certain Western progressive climate – Roosevelt's New Deal, the British Fabian Society – but also by aspects of the Soviet world.)

But for those of us who were members then, Communism was not only a cluster of political aspirations: it was also the fusion of these with our cultural and literary aspirations. I remember when, in my provincial city, the first copies of *l'Unità* arrived after the Liberation. I opened the Milan edition: its deputy editor was Elio Vittorini. I opened the Turin edition: Cesare Pavese was writing on the cultural page. As luck would have it, these were my two favourite Italian writers, about whom I knew nothing up until then except two of their books and some of their translations. And now I discovered that they were in the field that I too had chosen: I thought this was how it had to be. And similarly the discovery that the painter Guttuso was a Communist! And Picasso too! That ideal of a culture that was integral to political struggle appeared to us in those days as part of natural reality. (But in fact it was not like that: we were to bang our head against the brick wall of the relationship between politics and culture for fifteen years, and the problem is still not solved.)

I settled in Turin, which represented for me – and indeed it really was at that time – the city where the workers' movement and the movement of ideas helped form a climate which seemed to combine the best of a tradition and a prospect for the future. Turin meant both the old workers' high command of *Ordine Nuovo* and the anti-Fascist intellectuals who had kept alive a moral and civic line in Italian culture: around both groupings were the young people who had emerged from the Resistance, full of interests and energy. My development followed both paths simultaneously: on the one side I became linked to the Einaudi publishing house, around which there gravitated people of widely differing ideological tendencies and temperaments but always committed to an interest in historical problems, and where there was much debate and everyone kept their eyes open on everything that was being thought about and written about in the world; at the same time I participated in party activity – also collaborating on, and for a certain period editing, *l'Unità* – thus getting the chance to know the majority of the 'old gang', those who had been close to Gramsci. (I will always remember the serene clarity, rigour and gentleness of Camilla Ravera, who was for us the model of an intellectual with a humane form of political culture which we would have liked to revive and re-establish in the midst of our reality which was full of contradictions and harshness; and particularly the figures of workers' leaders, like Battista Santhià, whose rebellious temperament had accepted discipline and patience.)

But I would not like to give a sugary picture of the early years of my political formation, as though the discovery of the tragic aspects of Stalinism only happened later for us. I became a Communist just when the arguments were raging about the Stalin–Trotsky split, the elimination of internal opposition by Stalin, the mystery of the famous 'confessions' at the Moscow trials, and the Soviet–German pact. These were all events that preceded my involvement in political life, but still burning questions and the subject of constant polemics between ourselves and our friends/enemies in the non-Communist left. I accepted these facts, in part convincing myself that 'they were necessary', in part putting them aside while I waited to be able to explain them better to myself, and in part I was confident that they were temporary aspects of Communism, not justifiable ideologically and consequently destined to be re-debated in the more or less near future (a perspective which turned out to be – at least vaguely – accurate).

So it was not that I was ill-informed on the facts, but I did not really have very clear ideas on what these many facts meant. My 'class' of 1945–46 young lefties was inspired above all by a desire for action; the one after us – say about five or ten years after us – is driven above all by a desire for knowledge: they know everything about the sacred texts and collections of old newspapers but they do not love active political life as we loved it.

At that time we were not terrified by contradictions, on the contrary: every different aspect and form of language of that highly complex organism that was the Italian Communist party was a different pole of attraction working also on each one of us; where the call of the 'new party', of the 'working-class government' ended, one continued to hear the extremist voice of the Italian people's old love of faction, and the cold watchwords of international strategy smothered the capacity for compromise of *ad hoc* tactics. In that period we had not yet distinguished a clear dialectic of different currents; not that our militancy in the party was ever docile or conformist: we always had particular questions we wanted to see debated, and these were always full of general implications as well, but we were capable of finding ourselves one minute in favour of the workers and ideological rigour, the next minute being more tactical and courting liberalism, depending on the circumstances.

That was how it came about that I found myself admiring alternately one or other of the two major Communist leader-figures in Turin: Mario Montagnana and Celeste Negarville. Both of working-class origin, with a very difficult but glorious past in each case during the twenty years of clandestine operation, prisons and exile, Montagnana and Negarville were so different in psychology and mentality as to incarnate two conflicting souls within Communism. My more strictly party education took place under the shadow at times of one, at times of the other, and I was fond of both men, though in different ways, and I also felt myself in sharp conflict now with one, now with the other. I feel I have stayed close to the memory of both men, and it is for that reason that I want to remember them both together.

Mario Montagnana was the incarnation of the revolutionary rigour typical of the old working-class area of Borgo San Paolo, and had stayed faithful – often in open polemic with the official party line – to a workers' intransigence which was entirely underpinned by a morality of almost puritanical inflexibility. He was my editor when I worked on the Turin edition of *l'Unità*. He had gone into journalism from the factory floor, as a young man, when Gramsci was editor; and he always had in mind the paper made by workers for workers, with news about the shop-floor and the different departments, news that reflected workers' opinion on every event. He admitted through clenched teeth that many things had changed in the factory world and the life of the people from the time of his early militancy, and he always tried to place every situation and problem against the ideal image of that proletarian culture of those times, making no concessions to the class enemy, a fierce fighter in the sacrifices and the struggles whether minimal or serious, rigid about party discipline, an ascetic more from a sense of dignity and pride than from necessity.

Our relations were strained as though between a father and son, perhaps precisely because, as between father and son, there was an affection and respect which he had in me and I held for him, and this turned into an antagonism: in him because he saw I was different from what he had hoped, and in me for always disappointing him. He was an old-fashioned man; but in educating us in a revolutionary discipline that he had maintained despite everything, he injected a moral warmth, a genuine passion for human worth, which rescued his obsession with rigour from any calculated coldness.

Celeste Negarville was about ten years his junior (he was forty at the Liberation) but already represented a different epoch. The revolutionary proletariat had made him enjoy the pleasure of the larger political game, and he used this experience with all the composure of the most expert and skilled member of the ruling classes. It was said that in Rome at the Liberation this ex-worker, a hero of conspiracies and prison terms now turned government minister, had impressed everyone with his unsuspected personality, that of a real gentleman, with his intelligence, elegance and love of life, and at the same time his bond with the masses which was what gave him his strength. When I began to follow his career, which was on his return to Turin, the exciting time was over, and there was now no hope of being able to develop Italian democracy on the basis of the unity of the anti-Fascist forces. In the harsh, noisy world of a big working-class city as the Cold War intensified, this Machiavellian prince, open-minded and a bit of a fixer, clever and even contemptuous in the way he used people, never touched by egalitarian or populist worries, was often criticized by the younger members: we found him cynical, exploitative, with no interest in specific problems, and distant from the passion for truth and justice of the rank and file. Gradually we realized that his political vision was larger, more intelligent and modern, and we understood him better in human terms: his refinement shone out through the layer of bitterness and scepticism that settled over him as time passed, through the inertia of his return to an easy-going plebeian obtuseness, through the dissatisfaction of a man who refuses to accept that he is growing old. Not yet aware of the struggle between the various tendencies within the party, we based all our judgments on individuals on moralistic and psychological criteria, as the rank and file usually does: of course we did not understand very much about what was going on, but we were inclined to try to understand the reality of men and the world they lived in by going outside fixed ideas, and this effort in our attentions and judgments was not without fruit.

With Stalin's death, Negarville rediscovered his verve, revealing a passion for sincerity which must have always lurked within him; a conscience which had always remained clean and critical in the face of all the involutions of international Communism. In the debates of those years, he was among the most ready to carry forward the process of renewal which had been started by the 20th Congress; and we now saw to what extent what we had complained of as his cynicism had in reality been the defence of a moral sensitivity and of an objectivity in personal judgment that he had always keenly felt, though without ever disobeying the rules of the game in internal Communist policy, which is one of staying silent and waiting when the power relations are not favourable to your own line.

Montagnana, on the other hand, in the years when we felt a process of renewal developing in the party, was always one of the fiercest opponents of new ideas, whether in the political or trade-union arena. I never had the chance to see him now except at meetings or official events, and he seemed to me a man going against the movement of the times and people's consciences. In the debates of 1956 he defended the methods and the men of Stalinism with a ruthlessness that bordered on the cynical, but I recognized deep down his extreme moralism which led him to identify with all the harshness, even the tragic and painful harshness which his generation of Communist militants had accepted and made their own, paying for them in person, with their own skin or with their consciences.

And I found that the old 'cynicism' of Negarville had been more alive – both in its moral conscience and its awareness of history – than Montagnana's almost 'religious' attitude: Montagnana too had certainly suffered for everything that he could not accept or justify, but he had sacrificed all his reservations for a fanatical support of theory that had become a prop for the inhumanity of political systems.

Today the figures of these two Communists, now dead, come together in my memory and my judgment with all their good and bad points: at a time when every truth had to be paid for with many lies, both had tried to keep alive their own truth which was as contradictory and abused as the history of those years was.

I realize that having set out to tell the story of those who were young at the Liberation, I have ended up talking about the old. But the process of defining our generation – and perhaps this is true not just for our generation – also meant attempting to understand fully the experience of those who preceded us.

4) For some years now I have stopped being a member of the Communist party, and I have not joined any other party. I see politics along more general lines, and I feel less involved and responsible for it. Is this a good thing or a bad thing? I now understand so many questions I did not understand previously, by looking at them from a less immediate perspective; but on the other hand I know that we can only understand fully what we do in practice by assiduous, daily application. The Soviet Union and the United States are as much at the centre of my interests and worries as before, because the images I have for our future come from these two sides. I get less worked up about the things that are wrong in the USSR, not least because there are fewer of them; I get more worked up when America does something wrong, not least because it continues to do so on all sides. From Europe I continue to expect not political solutions but ideological developments, and these continue not to materialize. All in all, many things have changed in the general political situation, but the basic 'scale of values' I believe in has not changed very much.

I would like to point out here at least two things which I have believed in throughout my career and continue to believe in. One is the passion for a global culture, and the rejection of the lack of contact caused through excessive specialization: I want to keep alive an image of culture as a unified whole, which is composed of every aspect of what we know and do, and in which the various discourses of every area of research and production become part of that general discourse which is the history of humanity, which we must manage to seize and develop ultimately in a human direction. (And literature should of course be in the middle of these different languages and keep alive the communication between them.)

My other passion is for a political struggle and a culture (and literature) which will be the education of a new ruling class (or new class *tout court*, if class means only that which has class-consciousness, as in Marx). I have always worked and continue to work with this in mind: seeing the new ruling class taking shape, and contributing to give it a shape and profile.

[The first part of this essay appeared in the journal *Il Paradosso*, 5:23–24 (September–December, 1960). The second part was published in the collective volume *La generazione degli anni difficili* [*The Generation that Lived through Difficult Times*] (Bari: Laterza, 1962).

In 1960 *Il Paradosso*, a Milan journal dealing with youth culture, conducted a survey involving people from politics and literature who had grown up under Fascism to give younger people an account of the experience of those who had gone before them. The enquiry, entitled '*La generazione degli anni difficili*' was divided into four themes which correspond to the four sections of the text:

1) The ideas you grew up with until the advent of war.

2) What effects did the war have on your development? Did it represent a collapse, or modification, or confirmation of your ideas?

3) When, or why did you decide to commit yourself to political activity, and what contingent considerations affected your choice?

4) If possible, state the scale of values in which you believed then, and the history of that scale of values down to the present.

The answers were later collected in the volume with the same title, published by Laterza in 1962 and edited by the enquiry's promoters (Ettore Albertoni, Ezio Antonini and Renato Palmieri). For that publication in book form I preferred to recast totally my response, or rather to begin my autobiographical account from the point where I had interrupted it in the journal article. I publish here the two texts in succession. As for the convictions expressed in the second piece, they – like every other work in this collection – are only the testimony of what I believed at that particular time and not necessarily afterwards. (Author's note.)

The general title ('Political Autobiography of a Young Man') and the title of the first piece ('A Childhood under Fascism') are Calvino's.]

A Letter in Two Versions

1

Dear Mr Ricci,

Here is my CV. I was born in 1923 under a sky
in which the radiant Sun and melancholy Saturn were housed
in the harmonious Libra. I spent the first twenty-five years of my
life in what was in those days a still-verdant San Remo, which
contained cosmopolitan eccentrics amid the surly isolation of its
rural, practical folk; I was marked for life by both these aspects
of the place. Then I moved to industrious and rational Turin,
where the risk of going mad is no less than elsewhere (as Nietzsche
found out). I arrived at a time when the streets opened out
deserted and endless, so few were the cars; to shorten my journeys on foot I would cross the rectilinear streets on long obliques
from one angle to the other – a procedure that today is not just
impossible but unthinkable – and in this way I would advance
marking out invisible hypotenuses between grey right-angled
sides. I got to know only barely other famous metropolises, on
the Atlantic and Pacific, falling in love with all of them at first
sight: I deluded myself into believing that I had understood and
possessed some of them, while others remained for ever ungraspable and foreign to me. For many years I suffered from a
geographical neurosis: I was unable to stay three consecutive days

157

in one city or place. In the end I chose definitive wife and dwelling in Paris, a city which is surrounded by forests and hornbeams and birches, where I walk with my daughter Abigail, and which in turn surrounds the Bibliothèque Nationale, where I go to consult rare books, using my Reader's Ticket no. 2516. In this way, prepared for the Worst, and becoming more and more dissatisfied as regards the Best, I am already anticipating the incomparable joys of growing old. That's all.

> Yours sincerely,
> Calvino

[From the book *Tarocchi (Tarot Cards)* (Parma: F. M. Ricci, 1969). At the end of this volume in the '*I segni dell'uomo*' series there is a biographical note by the author of the text, in the form of a facsimile of an autograph letter to the publisher, Ricci.]

2

Dear Mr Ricci,

Here is my CV. I was born in 1923 under a sky in which the radiant Sun and melancholy Saturn were housed in the harmonious Libra. I spent the first twenty-five years of my life in what was in those days a still-verdant San Remo, where two worlds clashed, one cosmopolitan and eccentric, the other rural and enclosed; I was marked for life by both these aspects of the place. Then I moved to industrious and rational Turin, where the risk of going mad is no less than elsewhere. I arrived at a time when the streets opened out deserted and endless to the pedestrian that I was; to shorten my journeys which consisted of a series of right angles, I would mark out invisible hypotenuses while crossing the grey streets; a way of proceeding that today is not just impossible but unthinkable. Chance led me to cross other famous cities, on the sea and on rivers, on ocean and channel, on lake and on fjord, falling in love with all of them at first sight: some I believed I had understood and possessed, while others remained for ever ungraspable and foreign to me. For many years I suffered from a geographical neurosis: I was unable to stay three consecutive days in one city. Having said that, I could not but marry a foreigner; a foreigner everywhere, who had naturally ended up in the only city which was never foreign to anyone. That is why, dear FMR, we often meet at Orly airport.

As for my books, I regret not having published each one under a different *nom de plume*: that way I would feel freer to start again from scratch each time, just as I always try to do anyway.

Yours,
    Calvino

[From the book *Tarots* (Parma: F. M. Ricci, 1974). Written in French, unpublished in Italian. When Franco Maria Ricci asked me for an autograph copy in French of my earlier biographical letter, I decided to rewrite the text completely. (Author's note.)]

Objective Biographical Notice

Italo Calvino's father was an agronomist from San Remo who had lived for many years in Mexico and in other tropical countries; he had married a junior lecturer in botany from Pavia University, who was from a Sardinian family and who had followed him on his travels: their first-born son was born on 15 October 1923 in a suburb of Havana, just before the parents' definitive return to Italy.

Italo Calvino spent the first twenty-five years of his life almost without a break in San Remo, at Villa Meridiana, which at that time was the headquarters of the Experimental Floriculture Centre, and in the family's ancestral land at San Giovanni Battista, where his father cultivated grapefruit and avocados. His parents, who were freethinkers, did not give their son any religious education. Italo Calvino attended regular schooling in San Remo: his nursery school was the St George School, his primary school the Waldensian School, and secondary schooling was at the G. D. Cassini Royal High School. After obtaining his school-leaving certificate, he enrolled in the Agriculture Faculty of Turin University (where his father was the professor in charge of tropical agriculture) but he never got beyond his first exams.

During the twenty months of German occupation, Italo Calvino went through experiences common to the young people of his age who had avoided the call-up to the Fascist Social Republic of Italy: he undertook conspiratorial and partisan activity, fought for several months in the 'Garibaldi' Brigades in the violent war-theatre of the Maritime Alps, along with his sixteen-year-old brother. His father and mother were taken hostage by the Germans and held for several months.

In the period immediately after the Liberation, Calvino was politically active on behalf of the Communist party (of which he had been a member in the Resistance) in the Imperia area and among the students in Turin. In this same period he began to write short stories inspired by the life of guerrilla warfare he had led, and he made his first cultural contacts with Milan (Elio Vittorini's *Il Politecnico*) and Turin (the Einaudi publishing house).

The first short story he wrote was read by Cesare Pavese who passed it on to the journal that Carlo Muscetta ran in Rome (*Aretusa*, December 1945). In the meantime Vittorini had published another of his stories in *Il Politecnico* (on which Calvino also collaborated with articles on social problems in Liguria). Giansiro Ferrata invited him to send other stories to the Milan edition of *l'Unità*. In those days daily papers consisted of a single sheet, but a couple of times a week they began to come out with four pages instead of two: Calvino also worked on the third page, the cultural page, of the Genoa edition of *l'Unità* (winning a short-story prize jointly with Marcello Venturi) and of the Turin edition (where for some time Alfonso Gatto was one of the editors).

In the meantime the student changed faculty, transferring to the Arts Faculty, at the University of Turin, and enrolling directly in the third year of the literature course, with the special permission granted to war returnees. He lived in an unheated attic: he wrote stories and as soon as he finished one he would take it to be read by Natalia Ginzburg and Cesare Pavese who were getting the Einaudi publishing offices back on their feet. In order not to have him always hanging around, Pavese encouraged him to write a novel; he received the same advice from Giansiro Ferrata in Milan who was on the jury of a competition for an unpublished novel launched by the publisher Mondadori to provide the first sample of new post-war writers. The novel that Calvino finished just in time for the deadline of 31 December 1946 (*The Path to the Spiders' Nests*) would not impress Ferrata or Vittorini nor would it make it into the final shortlist (which consisted of Milena Milani, Oreste del Buono, Luigi Santucci). Calvino let Pavese read it, who recommended it, though with some reservations, to Giulio Einaudi. Einaudi was enthusiastic about it and launched its publication, even going so far as putting up posters. It sold 6,000 copies: quite a success for those days.

In the same month that his first novel was published, November 1947, Calvino scraped a degree in Arts with a thesis on English literature (Joseph Conrad). But it could be said that his development took place entirely outside university lecture theatres, in those years between the Liberation and 1950, debating, discovering new friends and mentors, accepting unsteady and occasional jobs, in that climate of poverty and feverish undertakings that was typical of the time. He had begun working at Einaudi in the publicity and press office, a job he would continue to hold as his permanent employment in years to come.

The atmosphere at the Turin publishing house, with its preponderance of historians and philosophers over critics and writers, and its constant debates between the supporters of different political and ideological tendencies, was fundamental in the intellectual formation of the young Calvino: gradually he found himself assimilating the experience of a generation slightly older than himself, of men who had already been moving in the world of literature and political debate for ten or fifteen years now, who had been militants in the anti-Fascist movement in the Action Party or the Christian Left movement or the Communist party. A major influence (not least because of his opposition to Calvino's non-religious outlook) was the friendship, moral influence and vital volubility of the Catholic philosopher Felice Balbo, who at that time was a full member of the Communist party.

After almost a year as editor of the cultural page of the Turin edition of *l'Unità* (from 1948 to 1949) Calvino realized that he did not have what it takes to become a good journalist or a professional politician. He continued working with *l'Unità* off and on for several years, with literary pieces and above all with trade-union surveys, articles on industrial and agrarian strikes and factory occupations. This link with the practical side of political and union organization (which also involved close friendships with comrades of his own generation) occupied him more than the ideological or cultural debates, and helped him overcome the crisis caused by the condemnation and expulsion from the party of friends and intellectual groupings to whom he had been close (Vittorini and *Il Politecnico* in 1947; Felice Balbo and *Cultura e realtà* in 1950).

What he was still not sure about was his literary vocation: after the publication of his first novel, Italo Calvino tried for years to write others in the same vein of picaresque social realism, but they were all mercilessly torn to pieces and rejected by his mentors and advisers. Fed up with those laborious failures, he abandoned himself to what came more spontaneously to him: he was basically a teller of stories, and he wrote *The Cloven Viscount* in a spurt of creativity. He thought he should publish it in a journal and not as a book so as not to give too much importance to what was simply a bagatelle, but Vittorini insisted on turning it into a short book for his '*Gettoni*' series. It received an unexpected unanimity of approval from the critics; it even inspired a fine article by Emilio Cecchi, which in those days meant the consecrating (or co-opting) of the writer into 'official' Italian literature. In Communist circles it stirred up a small polemic over the question of 'realism' but, balancing that, it also received authoritative approval.

From that success Calvino's 'fantasy' output took off (though this was a term already current among critics right from the time of his first novel) and at the same time a number of works portraying contemporary experiences in an ironic Stendhalian key. To define these alternating works Vittorini coined the formula 'realism with a fantasy thrust' and 'fantasy with a realistic thrust', a formula that became fashionable. Calvino tried also in theoretical terms to articulate the different elements of his thought and poetics: he gave the most structured outline of his programme in a lecture he delivered in Florence in 1955 ('*Il midollo del leone*' ('The Lion's Marrow'), *Paragone*, 6:66).

In this way Italo Calvino carved out his place in 1950s Italian literature, in an atmosphere that was now very different from that at the end of the 1940s, the period to which he continued to feel tied in terms of ideas. The literary capital of Italy in the 1950s was Rome, and Calvino, though remaining explicitly 'Turinese', now spent much of his time in Rome, enjoying that fun-loving city and a great many friends and associates, among whom the serene figure of Carlo Levi dominated.

It was in those years that Giulio Einaudi commissioned from his 'fabulous' author the volume of *Italian Folktales*, which Calvino selected and translated from the dialects of the nineteenth-century collections made by folklorists, both published and unpublished. This also had an academic component (in terms of the research, the introduction and the notes) which briefly aroused in Calvino a dormant vocation to be an academic.

Meantime the period of the great political debates approached which would shake the apparently monolithic world of Communism. In 1954–5, in a climate of truce amid the struggles between the various groupings of Italian Communist intellectuals, Calvino collaborated regularly on the Roman weekly journal *Il Contemporaneo*, run by Salinari* and Trombadori.† At the same time his discussions with the Milanese Hegelian Marxists were very important for him: discussions with Cesare Cases and especially with Renato Solmi, and behind them Franco Fortini, who had been and would continue to be an implacable opposing voice

---

* Carlo Salinari (1919–78), Marxist literary critic, expert on Manzoni and Boccaccio, and champion of realist literature.
† Antonello Trombadori (1917–93), Marxist art critic, journalist and politician. He co-edited with Salinari the left-wing journal *Il Contemporaneo* in the 1950s and 60s.

for Calvino. Having got involved in the battles inside the Communist party in 1956, Calvino (who was also collaborating on the Roman journal *Città Aperta*) resigned from the party in 1957. For some time (1958–59) he took part in the debates about forming a new socialist left and worked on Antonio Giolitti's* journal *Passato e Presente* and the weekly *Italia Domani*.

In 1959 Vittorini began the publication of a series of journal issues containing literary texts and critical pieces (*Il Menabò*) that reacted against the prevailing literary climate, and insisted that Calvino's name appear alongside his own as co-editor. Calvino published in *Il Menabò* a number of essays in which he sought to sum up the international literary situation: '*Il mare dell'oggettività*' ('The Sea of Objects') (*Il Menabò*, 2 (1959)), '*La sfida al labirinto*' ('The Challenge to the Labyrinth') (*Il Menabò*, 5 (1962)), and also an attempt at outlining a general ideological map entitled '*L'antitesi operaia*' ('The Working Class as Dialectical Antithesis') (*Il Menabò*, 7 (1964)). The criticisms his friends made on this last text persuaded him to abandon definitively the field of theoretical speculation.

In 1959–60 Calvino spent six months in the United States of America. In the ten years that followed, his journeys outside Italy became more frequent. In 1964 he married: his wife is Argentinian, of Russian origin, a translator from English who lives in Paris. In 1965 his daughter was born.

In recent times documents to establish Calvino's biography have become increasingly rare: his public appearances have grown fewer, his presence is less felt, he no longer works on newspapers, he no longer gets on young people's nerves by siding with them or against them. Very little is known about his travels since he is one of the few Italian writers who does not write travel books or

---

* Antonio Giolitti (1915–), Communist MP in the 1950s, he was in the reformist wing of the party during and after the events of Hungary in 1956, after which he joined the Socialist party. Giolitti's expulsion from the PCI was one of the reasons that led Calvino to resign as well.

reportages. His detachment from the official world of literature was sealed in 1968 when he refused a substantial literary prize.

The author of *The Baron in the Trees* seems more determined than ever to keep his distance from the world. Has he reached a condition of indifferent detachment? If you know him, you would think that it is more the heightened awareness of how complicated the world is that forces him to stifle within himself outbreaks of hope as much as those of anguish.

[Written in 1970 for a volume in the Einaudi series '*Gli Struzzi*', *Gli amori difficili (Difficult Loves)*, following the series' requirements for biographical notes. (Author's note.)]

Hermit in Paris

For some years now I have had a house in Paris, where I spend part of the year, but hitherto this city has never appeared in the things I write. Maybe to write about Paris I ought to leave, to distance myself from it, if it is true that all writing starts out from a lack or an absence. Or else be more inside it, but for that I would need to have lived there from when I was young, if it is true that it is the first years of our existence, not the places of our maturity, that shape the world of our imagination. Or rather: a place has to become an inner landscape for the imagination to start to inhabit that place, to turn it into its theatre. Now Paris has already been the inner landscape of such a huge part of world literature, of so many books that we have all read, and that have counted in our lives. Before being a city of the real world, Paris for me, as for millions of other people in every country, has been a city that I have imagined through books, a city that you appropriate when you read. You start in childhood, with *The Three Musketeers*, then *Les Misérables*; at the same time, or immediately afterwards, Paris becomes the city of History, of the French Revolution; later, as your youthful reading progresses, it becomes the city of Baudelaire, of that wonderful poetry of over a hundred years ago now, the city of painting, of the great novel cycles, Balzac, Zola, Proust …

When I used to go to Paris as a tourist, it was still that Paris that I visited, it was an already known image that I recognized, an image to which I could add nothing. Now the accidents of life have taken me to Paris with a house and family there; if you like, I am still a tourist, because my activity, my work interests are still in Italy, but of course my way of existing in the city is different, made up of the hundreds of small practical problems of family life. Perhaps, if it identified with my personal vicissitudes, my own daily existence, and lost that aura which is the cultural and literary reflection of its image, Paris could become again an inner city, and I could write about it. It would no longer be the city about which everything has already been said, but just the city in which I happen to live, a city without a name.

Occasionally I decide spontaneously to set totally imaginary stories in New York, a city in which I have lived for only a few months in my life: who knows why, perhaps because New York is the simplest city, at least for me, the epitome of a city, a kind of prototype of a city, as far as its topography, its visual appearance, its society is concerned. Whereas Paris has huge depth, so much behind it, so many meanings. Perhaps it intimidates a little: I mean the image of Paris, not the city itself; on the contrary, it is the city where as soon as you set foot in it you immediately find it familiar.

When I think about it, I have never happened to set any of my narratives in Rome, and yet I have lived more in Rome than in New York, perhaps even more than in Paris. Rome is another city which I cannot speak about, another city about which too much has been written. However, nothing of what has been written about Rome can be compared with what has been written about Paris: the only thing they have in common is this: both Rome and Paris are cities about which it is difficult to say anything that has not already been said; and even their new aspects, every change they undergo, immediately finds a chorus of commentators ready to note it.

But perhaps I do not have the talent to establish personal relations with places, I always stay half in the clouds, with just one foot in the city. My desk is a bit like an island: it could just as well be in some other country as here. And besides, cities are turning into one single city, a single endless city where the differences which once characterized each of them are disappearing. This idea, which runs through my book *Invisible Cities*, came to me from the way that many of us now live: we continually move from one airport to another, to enjoy a life that is almost identical no matter what city you find yourself in. I often say, and I have said it so often that I have now become a bit bored with it, that in Paris I have my country home, in the sense that as a writer I can conduct part of my activity in solitude, it does not matter where, in a house isolated in the midst of the countryside, or on an island, and this country house of mine is right in the middle of Paris. In this way, while the part of my life that is connected with my work takes place entirely in Italy, I come here when I can or have to be on my own, something that is easier for me to do in Paris.

Italy, or at least Turin and Milan, is an hour from here; I live in an area from where it is easy to get to the motorway and then to Orly airport. You could say that at the rush hour when the city streets are blocked by traffic, I can get to Italy more quickly than, say, to the Champs Elysées. I could almost commute; we are now close to a time when it will be possible to live in Europe as though it were one single city.

At the same time, we are close to the time when no city will be able to be used as a city: you waste more time on short trips than on long journeys. When I am in Paris, you could say that I never leave this study; from long-standing habit, every morning I go as far as St Germain-des-Prés to buy the Italian papers, using the Métro. So I am not really much of a flâneur, the man who strolls through the Paris streets, that traditional figure immortalized by Baudelaire. That's it: international journeys as much as short journeys in the city are no longer an exploration of a series of different places: they are simply movements from one point to another between which there is an empty interval, a discontinuity, a parenthesis above the clouds if it is an air trip, and a parenthesis beneath the earth if it is a city journey.

I have always been at ease using the Métro, from the time I first arrived in Paris as a young man and discovered that this means of transport, so simple to use, put the whole city at my disposal. And perhaps there is something of my fascination with the underground world in this relationship of mine with the Métro: the novels of Jules Verne I like most are *The Black Indies* and *Journey to the Centre of the Earth*. Or it is the anonymity that attracts me: these crowds in which I can observe everyone one by one and at the same time disappear totally myself.

Yesterday on the Métro there was a man with bare feet: not a gipsy or a hippie, a man with glasses like me and so many others, reading the paper, looking a bit like an academic, the usual absent-minded professor type who had forgotten to put on his socks and shoes. And it was a rainy day, and he was walking about barefoot, and nobody was looking at him, no one seemed interested. The dream of being invisible ... When I find myself in an environment where I can enjoy the illusion of being invisible, I am really happy.

The exact opposite of how I feel when I have to talk on the television, and I feel the camera pointing at me, nailing me to my visibility, to my face. I believe that writers lose a lot when they are seen in the flesh. In the old days the really popular writers were totally anonymous, just a name on the book cover, and this gave them an extraordinary mystique. Gaston Leroux, Maurice Leblanc (just to mention a couple who have spread the myth of Paris among thousands of people) were very popular writers about whom no one knew anything; there have been even more popular authors whose first name was not even known, just an initial. I believe that this is the ideal condition for a writer, close to anonymity: that is when his maximum authority develops, when the writer does not have a face, a presence, but the world he portrays takes up the whole picture. Like Shakespeare, of whom no portrait remains that can help us understand what he was like, nor any information to explain anything genuinely about him.

Today, by contrast, the more the author's figure invades the field, the more the world he portrays empties; then the author himself fades, and one is left with a void on all sides.

There is an invisible, anonymous point which is the one from which the author writes, and that is why it is difficult for me to define the relationship between the place where I write and the city surrounding that space. I can write really well in hotel rooms, in that kind of abstract, anonymous space which hotel rooms are, where I find myself facing the blank page, with no alternative, no escape. Or perhaps this is an idealized condition which worked most of all when I was younger, and the world was there just outside the door, packed with signs, accompanying me everywhere: it was so physical that all I had to do was detach myself from it just a short step to write about it. Now something must have changed, I write well only in a space which is mine, with books to hand, as though I always needed to consult something or other. Maybe it is not so much for the books themselves, but for a kind of interior space they form, as though I identified myself with my ideal library.

And yet, I never manage to keep a library of mine together: I always have some books here, others there: when I need to consult a book in Paris, it is always a book I have in Italy, and when I have to consult a book in Italy it is always a book in my Paris house. This need to consult books when writing is a habit I have developed over the last ten years or so; previously it was not like that: everything I wrote had to come from memory, and formed part of lived experience. Even all my cultural references had to be something I carried within me, was part of me, otherwise it did not conform to the rules, it was not something I could put on to the page. But now it is exactly the opposite: even the world has become something I consult every so often, in fact the leap from this bookshelf to the world outside is not as great as it seems.

I could say then that Paris ... well, here's what Paris is: it is a giant reference work, a city which you can consult like an encyclopaedia: whatever page you open gives you a complete list of information that is richer than that offered by any other city. Take the shops, which is the most open, communicative discourse a city uses to express itself: we all read a city, a street, a stretch of pavement, by following the row of shops. There are shops which are chapters of a treatise, shops which are entries in an encyclopaedia, shops which are pages of a newspaper. In Paris there are cheese shops where hundreds of cheeses, all of them different, are displayed, each labelled with its own name, cheeses covered in ash, cheeses covered in walnuts: a kind of museum or Louvre of cheese. They are aspects of a civilization which has allowed the survival of differentiated forms on a scale big enough to make their production economically profitable, while still maintaining their *raison d'être* in presupposing a choice, a system to which they belong, a language of cheeses. But above all this is a triumph of the spirit of classification and nomenclature. So if tomorrow I start writing about cheeses, I can go out and consult Paris like an enormous cheese encyclopaedia. Or consult certain grocers where you recognize still what nineteenth-century exoticism was, a mercantile exoticism that was part of early colonialism, the spirit that inspired the Universal Exposition.

Paris has the kind of shops where one feels that this is the city which gave shape to that particular way of regarding culture which is the museum, and the museum in turn has given its form to the most varied activities in daily life, so that the galleries in the Louvre and the shop-windows form a continuum. Let's say that everything in the street is ready to go into the museum, or that the museum is ready to absorb the street. It is no accident that my favourite museum is the one dedicated to the life and history of Paris, the Musée Carnavalet.

This idea of the city as encyclopaedic discourse, as the collective memory, is part of a whole tradition: think of the Gothic cathedrals in which every architectural and ornamental detail, every space and element, referred to notions that were part of a global wisdom, was a sign that found echoes in other contexts. In the same way we can 'read' the city like a reference work, just as we read Notre-Dame (even though we read it through Viollet-Le-Duc's restorations), capital by capital, pluvial after pluvial. And at the same time we can read the city as the collective unconscious: the collective unconscious is a huge catalogue, an enormous bestiary; we can interpret Paris as a book of dreams, an album of our unconscious, a catalogue of horrors. So on my walks as a father, accompanying my little girl, Paris opens up to my consultations with the bestiaries of the Jardin des Plantes, the serpent and reptile sections where iguanas and chameleons stay happily together: they are fauna of prehistoric epochs, and at the same time they are the dragons' cave which our civilization drags along behind it.

The monsters and ghosts of the unconscious which are visible outside us are an old speciality of this city which not by chance was the capital of surrealism. Because Paris, even before Breton, contained everything that then became the raw materials of the surrealist vision; and surrealism later left its mark, its traces, recognizable throughout the city, if nothing else in a particular way of appreciating the power of images, as in the surrealist bookshops, or certain small cinemas, like Le Styx, for instance, which specializes in horror films.

The cinema too, in Paris, is a museum, or encyclopaedia to consult, not just for the quantity of films in the Cinémathèque, but for the whole network of cinemas in the Latin Quarter: those tiny, foul-smelling cinema halls, where you can see the latest film by a new Brazilian or Polish director, or old movies from the silent age or the Second World War. With a bit of careful study and a bit of luck every spectator can reconstruct the history of cinema piece by piece: I, for instance, have a weakness for 1930s films, because they were the years when cinema was for me the whole world, and in this area I can find some real treats, let's say, in the sense of a search for lost time, seeing films from my childhood, or catching films I had missed when

I was young, which I thought I had missed for ever, whereas in Paris you can always hope to find what you had thought lost, your own past or someone else's. So yet another way to see this city: like a huge lost-property office, a little bit like the moon in *Orlando Furioso* which gathers up everything that has been lost in the world.

So now we are entering into the limitless Paris adored by collectors, this city which invites you to make collections of everything, because it accumulates and classifies and redistributes, where you can search as in an archaeological excavation. The collector's experience can still be an existential adventure, a search for the self through objects, an exploration of the world which is at the same time a realization of the self. But I cannot claim to have the collector's instinct, or rather that instinct reawakens only with impalpable things like the images of old films, a collection of memories, of black-and-white shadows.

I have to draw the conclusion that Paris for me is the city of my maturity: in the sense that I no longer see it in the spirit of a discovery of the world, which is the adventure that belongs to youth. In my relations with the world I have moved from exploration to consultation, that is to say that the world is a collection of data which is there, independent of me, data which I can compare, combine, transmit, maybe even occasionally enjoy, but always slightly from the outside. Beneath my house there is an old suburban railway line, the Paris-Ceinture, almost unused now, but twice a day a little train still goes by and then I remember Laforgue's lines, which say

> *Je n'aurai jamais d'aventures;*
> *Qu'il est petit, dans la Nature,*
> *Le chemin d'fer Paris-Ceinture!*
> (I shall never have any adventures;
> How small in the middle of Nature
> Is the Paris-Ceinture suburban line!)

[This text was derived from an interview with Valerio Riva for Swiss Italian TV in 1974. It was published in the same year in a limited edition, in Lugano by Edizioni Pantarei with four drawings by Giuseppe Ajmone. (Author's note.)]

Where I Was on 25ᵗʰ April 1945

There had been a fire in a wood: I remember the long line of partisans coming down between burnt pine-trees, the hot ash under the soles of our feet, the trunks still white-hot in the night.

It was a march that was different from the others in our life of constant movement in those woods. We had finally received the order to come down from the hills to attack our own town, San Remo; we knew the Germans were retreating from the Riviera; but we did not know which strongholds they still held. These were days when everything was shifting and our leaders were certainly kept informed on an hourly basis; but here I am trying to stick just to my memories as an ordinary partisan in the Garibaldi Brigades following my detachment and limping because of an abscess on my foot (from the moment the frost had hardened and crumpled the leather of my boots, my feet had constantly been plagued by sores). It seemed certain that this time Germany was done for, but we had had too many illusions in those years and too often we had been disappointed: so we preferred not to make any forecasts.

The front nearest us – on the French border – showed no sign of moving: for eight months, namely from the moment of France's liberation, we had heard the rumble of cannons on the Western front; for eight months freedom was just a few kilometres away, but meanwhile the life of the partisans in the Maritime Alps had become harder and harder because, as a back route to the front line, our area was of crucial importance for the Germans who had to keep the roads clear at all costs; that was why they never gave us any peace, nor we them; and that was why our area was one of the zones that suffered the highest percentage of casualties.

Even in those weeks when spring was in the air (it was, though, a very cold April) and we felt that victory was imminent, that feeling of uncertainty that had shaped our lives for so many months still persisted. Even in the final days of the war the Germans had reappeared by surprise and we had suffered mortalities. Just a few days prior to this, while on patrol, I had nearly fallen into their hands.

The last camp our group made was, if I remember correctly, between Montalto and Badalucco: the fact that we had already descended into the area of olive groves was in itself a sign that this was a new season, after the winter up in the chestnut-tree zone which meant constant hunger. By this stage we were not able to reason in any other way except in terms of whether something was good or bad for our survival as partisans, as though this existence was still to last who knows how long. The valleys were once again covered in leaves and bushes, meaning a better chance of staying under cover during enemy fire, like that clump of hazel trees which had saved our lives, mine and my brother's, twenty days earlier, after action on the Ceriana road. As long as our lives hung by a thread, it was pointless conjuring up even the notion that a new life was about to dawn, one without machine-gun fire, reprisal raids, the fear of being caught and tortured. And even afterwards, when peace had come, rediscovering the habit of functioning in a different way would take time.

It seems to me that that night we slept for only a couple of hours, lying on the ground for the last time. I thought that the next day there would be a battle for possession of the Via Aurelia, my thoughts were those you have the night before a battle, rather than about the imminent Liberation. It was only the next day, seeing that our descent continued without any interruption, that we realized that the coast was already liberated and that we were marching directly on San Remo (in fact after some rearguard clashes with the town's partisan groups, the Germans and Fascists had retreated towards Genoa).

However, even that morning, the Allies' ships had appeared off the San Remo coast and started the daily naval bombardment of the town. The town's National Liberation Committee had assumed power under the bombardment and as its first act of government had ordered that 'Liberated Zone' be painted in huge white letters on the walls of Corso Imperatrice so that the warships could see it. When we got near Poggio, we began to encounter the people of the town standing on the sides of the road: they had come out to see and cheer the partisans marching along. I remember that the first people I saw were two elderly men with their hats on, coming along and chatting about their own business as though it were any old holiday; but there was one detail about them that would have been inconceivable up to the day before: they had red carnations in their lapels. In the following days I was to see thousands of people with red carnations in their lapels, but they were the first.

I can certainly say that for me that was the first image of freedom in civilian life, of freedom without any risk to life any more, which appeared to us just like that, nonchalantly, as though it were the most natural thing in the world.

As we gradually got closer to the town, the crowds of people grew, as did the rosettes, the flowers, the girls, but coming nearer to my home brought back the thought of my parents who had been held hostage by the SS, and I did not know whether they were alive or dead, just as they did not know if their sons were alive or dead.

I see that these memories of Liberation Day are more concerned with 'before' than 'after'. But that is the way they have remained in my memory, because we were all caught up in what we had lived through, while the future as yet did not have a face, and we would never have imagined a future which would make these memories gradually fade as has happened in these thirty years.

[*Domenica del Corriere*, April 1975. Supplement issued to commemorate the thirtieth anniversary of the Liberation, containing twenty-eight pieces on 'That day, 25 April 1945 ...' (Author's note.)]

Dialect

1) 2) and 3) Dialect culture retains its full force as long as it is defined as a municipal culture, something strictly local, guaranteeing the identity of a town, a country area, a valley, and differentiating these with respect to other neighbouring towns, country areas, valleys. When a dialect starts to become regional, in other words a kind of inter-dialect, it has already entered the purely defensive phase, in other words its decadence. Regional dialects like 'Piedmontese', 'Lombard', and 'Veneto' are relatively recent and bastardized creations, and today they need to be seen in the context of the major mass emigrations, seen as related to the dramatic situation which both for the immigrants and for the indigenous peoples is represented by this enforced clash of cultures, which are no longer the previous local cultures nor are they yet a new culture which transcends them.

The situation of dialects was different in the Italy which lasted up until a quarter of a century ago, where municipal identity had very strong characteristics and was self-sufficient. In the days when I was a student, in other words already in a society which spoke the standard language fluently, dialect was still what marked us out, what distinguished those of us from San Remo from our contemporaries from Ventimiglia or Porto Maurizio, and gave rise to frequent jibes among us; not to mention the even stronger contrast between the dialects of mountain villages, like Baiardo and Triora, which reflected a completely different sociological situation, and so these dialects lent themselves easily to being caricatured by those of us living in the coastal towns. In this world (which to tell the truth was very narrow) dialect was a way of defining ourselves as speaking subjects, of giving a shape to the *genius loci*, in short of existing. It is not at all my intention to mythicize nostalgically that very narrow cultural horizon, merely to state that in those days there existed an expressive vitality, in other words the sense of particularity and precision, which disappears when dialect becomes generic and lazy, as it does in the 'Pasolinian' age of dialect: Pasolini sees dialect solely as a residue of popular vitality.

Lexical richness (as well as richness in expressiveness) is (or rather, was) one of the great strengths of dialects. Dialects have the edge on the standard language when they contain words for which the standard language has no equivalent. But this lasts only as long as certain (agricultural, artisan, culinary, domestic) techniques last – techniques whose terminology was created or deposited in the dialect rather than in the standard language. Nowadays, in lexical terms, dialects are like tributary states towards the standard language: all they do is give dialectal endings to words that start off in technical language. And even outside the terminology of trades, the rarer words become obsolete and are lost.

I remember that the old folk of San Remo knew dialects that represented a lexical wealth that was irreplaceable. For instance: *chintagna*, which means both the empty space that remains behind a house that has been built (as always in Liguria) up against terraced land, and also the empty space between the bed and the wall. I do not think an equivalent word exists in Italian; but nowadays the word does not exist even in dialect; who has heard of it or uses it now? Lexical impoverishment or homogenization is the first sign of a language's death.

4) My dialect is that of San Remo (now called *sanremese* but formerly known as *sanremasco*) which is one of the many Ligurian

dialects of the Western Riviera, in other words of an area very distinct, in terms of cadence and phonetics, from the Genoa area (which stretches up to and including Savona). I lived the first twenty-five years of my life there almost without interruption, in times when the indigenous population were still in the majority. I lived in an agricultural environment where it was mostly dialect that was used, and my father (about half a century older than me, having been born in 1875 into an old San Remo family) spoke a dialect that was much richer and more precise and expressive than that spoken by my contemporaries. Consequently I grew up steeped in dialect but without ever having learnt it, because the strongest influence on my upbringing was my mother, who was an enemy of dialect and a rigid upholder of the purity of the Italian language. (I have to say that I have never learnt to speak fluently in any language, not least because I have always been a man of few words: and quickly my expressive and communicative needs became focused on the written language.)

When I began to write seriously, I was obsessed with the idea that my Italian should be calqued on dialect, because as I sensed the fake quality of the language used by the majority of writers, the only guarantee of authenticity which I thought I could achieve was this closeness to the spoken usage of the people. This approach can be detected in my earliest books, whereas it becomes rare subsequently. A sensitive reader from San Remo and old connoisseur of its dialect (a lawyer whom Soldati turned into a character in one of his books) recognized and appreciated dialectal uses in my books even later on: now he is dead and I do not believe there is anyone any more who is capable of doing this.

The impact of dialect soon becomes adulterated in whoever moves away from the place and daily conversation there. After the war I moved to Turin, where at that time dialect was still very strong at all levels of society, and although I tried to resist changing my natural Ligurian dialect, the different linguistic atmosphere could not but rub off on the way I spoke, given these dialects' common Gallo–Italic roots.

Dialect

Nowadays my wife speaks to me in the Spanish of the River Plate, and my daughter in the French used by the school-kids of Paris: the language in which I write no longer has anything to do with any language spoken around me, except through my memory.

[Reply to a survey by Walter della Monica. Some of the points were published in *La Fiera Letteraria*, 9 May 1976. The questions were: 1) What weight can the knowledge and use of dialects have in contemporary culture? Could a renewal of interest in dialects typify a new culture? 2) Do dialects still have something to contribute to the Italian language? 3) Do you know a dialect? Has it impinged on the linguistic quality of your work? (Author's note.)]

The Situation in 1978

'The big secret is to hide, escape, cover your tracks.' Something you said to Arbasino,* at the start of the 'belle époque', as you called the 1960s. You've managed to do so. So much so that nowadays we wonder: is Calvino, like Astolfo, in the moon?

The moon would be a good vantage point from which to observe the earth from a certain distance. Finding the right distance to be present and at the same time detached: that was the problem of *The Baron in the Trees*. But twenty years have gone by, it is becoming more and more difficult for me to situate myself on the map that charts today's dominant mental attitudes. And every elsewhere is unsatisfying, you cannot find one. Nevertheless I still reject the role of the person chasing events. I prefer that of the person who continues his discourse, waiting for it to become topical again, like all things that have a sound basis.

'Discourse': you said it. Now you have to explain.

Perhaps it was only a certain number of Yeses and Noes and a huge number of Buts. Sure, I belong to the last generation to believe in a model of literature that could be part of a model of society. And both models have gone up in the air. My whole life

---

* Alberto Arbasino (1930–), journalist and avant-garde writer. He was a member of the Gruppo 63, and his most famous novel, *Fratelli d'Italia* (1963), articulated his critique of his own country and his delight in linguistic play and parody.

has been a process of recognizing the validity of things I said No to. But attributions of fundamental value remain, the more so the more you hear them being denied.

That model of society, your generation's Communist model, has burnt out. New ones have appeared, from the same source. Do you feel at home with any of them?
The workers' movement meant for me an ethic of work and productivity, which has faded in the last ten years. Today it is existential motivations that are in the foreground: everyone has the right to enjoy life just because they are in the world. This is a 'creaturalism' I do not share: I do not love people just because they are in the world. One has to earn the right to exist, and justify it with what you give to others. That is why the common ground which today unites Christian Democrat welfarism and the youth protest movement is foreign to me.

Every elsewhere, you said, is unsatisfying. Where would there be an elsewhere that would suit you?
For many writers, their own subjectivity is self-sufficient. That is where what counts happens. It is not even an elsewhere, basically what you live through is the totality of the world. Think of Henry Miller. Since I hate waste, I envy the writers for whom nothing is wasted, who use everything. Saul Bellow, Max Frisch: daily life as the constant nourishment for writing. I, on the other hand, feel that what happens to me cannot interest others. What I write I have to justify, even to myself, with something that is not just individual – perhaps because I come from a secular and intransigently scientific family, whose image of civilization was a human–vegetable symbiosis. Removing myself from that morality, from the duties of the agricultural smallholder, made me feel guilty. The world of my imagination did not seem important enough to be justifiable on its own. A general context was essential. It is no accident that I spent many years of my life banging my head against a brick wall, trying to square the circle that was

involved in living the life of literature and Communism at the same time. A false problem. But still better than no problem at all, because writing only makes sense if you are faced with a problem to solve.

Would you like something which allowed you once more to say Yeses and Noes? To go back to the beginning? Would you like to have the 'plan'?
Every time I try to write a book I have to justify it with a plan or programme, whose limits I quickly realize. So then I put it alongside another project, many other projects, and this ends up in writer's block. Every time I have to invent, alongside the book I have to write, the author who has to write it, a kind of writer that is different from me, and from all other writers, whose limitations I see only too clearly…

And what if among the victims of this epoch was the very concept of 'plan'? What if this was not a transition from a 'used' plan to a new one, but rather the death of the whole notion of 'plan'?
Your hypothesis is plausible, it could be that it is our need to work things out in advance that is disappearing, and that we are entering into the way of life of other civilizations, which do not have time to plan. But the good thing in writing is the happiness in doing something, the satisfaction of something that has been completed. If this happiness replaced the will power involved in plans, then, my goodness, I would sign up immediately.

In one of your early narratives there is a cannon shot which divides The Cloven Viscount *in two. For you then [1951] there were many possible divisions: subject/object, reason/fantasy, 'the outside road', as Vittorini called politics, and the inner road; Calvino the journalist on the Turin* l'Unità *and the writer who was already seeking images from the Middle Ages. For you, harmony was lost from the beginning. Have you ever found it again?*
That's true, there is laceration in *The Cloven Viscount* and perhaps

186

in everything I wrote. And the awareness of laceration carries with it the desire for harmony. But every illusion of harmony in contingent things is mystification, so you have to look for it on other levels. That's how I arrived at the cosmos. But the cosmos does not exist, not even for science, it is only the horizon of a consciousness that goes beyond the individual, where all chauvinistic and particularistic ideas of humanity are overcome, and one can perhaps attain a non-anthropomorphic perspective. I have never indulged in cosmic euphoria or contemplation in this 'ascent'. More a sense of responsibility towards the universe. We are part of a chain that starts at sub-atomic or pre-galactic level: giving our actions and thoughts the continuity with what came before us and what will come after is something I believe in. And I would want this to be something that could be gleaned from that collection of fragments that is my *oeuvre*.

In your search for harmony, you have focused on higher rationality. This is the mathematics of geometrical metaphors (in the Our Ancestors *trilogy), the combinatory calculus of structures (in* The Castle of Crossed Destinies *and* Invisible Cities*). Becoming more and more refined and perfect, forever upwards. At the top of this, will there not be just silence?*

Yes, and this is the anguish I have been living with for years, and I do not know if I will find a way out of it. Even calculus and geometry represent the need for something beyond the individual. I have already said that the fact of existing, my biography, what goes through my head, does not authorize my writing. However, for me the fantastic is the opposite of the arbitrary: it is a way of going back to the universals of mythical representation. I have to construct things that exist for themselves, things like crystals, which answer to an impersonal rationality. And in order for the result to be 'natural' I have to turn to extreme artifice. With the inevitable failure this involves, since in the finished work there is always something arbitrary and imprecise which leaves me dissatisfied.

Of your life in the 1950s, the militant years, you said: 'permanent profes-
sional (political) duty'. Of the 60s: 'belle époque'. What name do you
have in your calendar for the third decade that is now drawing to a close?
I would say: non-identification. There have been many things in
the air, I have experienced them while remaining open to how
they might develop, but always with reservations. In the final chapter of *The Castle of Crossed Destinies* I compare the figure of the
hermit with that of the knight who kills dragons. Well, in the 1970s
I have been, above all, the hermit. At a distance, yet not very far
away. In the paintings of Saint Jerome or Saint Anthony the city
is in the background. An image with which I identified. But in
that same chapter of *The Castle of Crossed Destinies* there is a sudden
switch, a revolt: I move towards the juggler, the *Bateleur* in the Tarot
cards. And I offer this as the final resolution. This conjurer and
charlatan, presenting himself openly as someone who does conjuring tricks, is deep down the one who is least mystificatory.

The Bateleur, *the Juggler: is that the only card the intellectual can play*
today?
You know that my method never leads me to put everything on
one single card. That is why I am remote from the hero-figures
of culture in this century. The final three cards in *The Castle of*
Crossed Destinies are three possible alternatives, united in their
combination. But if the *Bateleur* wins, I then feel within me the
need to undo all his tricks.

Paris, 'the metropolis that my long flight took me to'. What were you
fleeing, Calvino? And is Paris adequate for this flight?
The hermit has the city in the background, for me that city
remains Italy. Paris is more a symbol of somewhere else rather
than an actual elsewhere. And in any case is it true that I live in
Paris? I have never managed to put together a discourse on my
life in Paris, I've always said that instead of having a house in the
country, I had a house in a foreign city, where I could have no
function or role.

To stay in one place you stay away from it. In Paris, watching Italy. What sort of a trick is this?

Among the *Invisible Cities* there is one on stilts, and its inhabitants watch their own absence from on high. Maybe to understand who I am I have to observe a point where I could be but am not. Like an early photographer who poses in front of the camera and then runs to press the switch, photographing the spot where he could have been but isn't. Perhaps that is the way the dead observe the living, a mixture of interest and incomprehension. But I only think this when I am depressed. In my euphoric moments I think that that void which I do not occupy can be filled by another me, doing the things that I ought to have done but was not able to do. Another me that could emerge only from that void.

Great absence or great presence, a public personage plays on one or the other. For instance, Tommaso Landolfi won by playing the mystery card. Did you win by absence?

I certainly cannot compete with Landolfi's consistency. If in recent years I have even written lead articles for the *Corriere della sera*, that means that a part of me, which is the heir of a serious sounding voice and defined by Fortini as 'the noble father', is always on the public stage. It is not that I am very happy about this. I would rather pension off this noble father and use other images of myself. Perhaps that of the 'cynical child', to use another Fortini definition, from one of his epigrams.

Between laceration and harmony it is precisely the cynical child who is there, namely irony. What role does irony have for you: defence, attack, making the impossible possible?

Irony warns that what I write must be read with a distracted air, a mood of considerable lightness. And since I sometimes use other tones of voice, the things that count are particularly those I say with irony.

That is an irony for external use. What about inside?
With regard to laceration, irony is the announcement of a possible harmony; and with regard to harmony, it is the consciousness of the real laceration. Irony always warns of the other side of the coin.

We are what we do not throw away. Is that also what you wanted to say in your last story, 'La poubelle agréée' ('The Common Dustbin')? What elements in your intellectual journey have and have not ended up in the 'bin'?
Sometimes it seems to me that I have not thrown anything away, at others that I have not done anything but throw things out. In every experience what has to be looked for is the substance, which is then what remains. Here is a 'value': throwing much out in order to conserve what is essential.

With the passing of time the hand stiffens or becomes lighter. How do you come to write now compared with fifteen years ago?
I have learnt to discover the joys of writing to order, when I'm asked to do something for a definite destination, however humble. At least I know for certain that there is somebody for whom my writing serves a purpose. I feel freer, there is not that feeling of imposing on others a subjectivity that even I am not sure about. I believe in the absolute and necessary individualism of writing, but in order for it to work it has to be taken as contraband into something which denies it, or at least impedes it.

Calvino, I will not ask you what you are writing. I'll ask you what you will not write any more.
If you mean will I never write again what I have already written, there is nothing that I reject in any of my writing. Of course, some roads do close. What I keep open is fiction, a storytelling that is lively and inventive, as well as the more reflective kind of writing in which narrative and essay become one.

The Situation in 1978

[*Paese sera*, 7 January 1978. From an interview with Daniele Del Giudice. (Author's note.) On the original is a note by Calvino: 'Needs editing.']

Was I a Stalinist Too?

I was one of those who left the Communist party in 1956–57 because it did not de-Stalinize fast enough. But what did I say when Stalin was alive and Stalinism was accepted without question inside Communist parties? Was I or was I not a Stalinist too? I would like to be able to say: 'I was not'; or: 'I was, but I did not know what it meant'; or: 'I thought I was but in reality I wasn't.' I do not feel that any of these answers corresponds entirely to the truth, however much partial truth there may be in all of them. If I want to succeed in understanding and making others understand what I thought then (something that is not easy because we change over the years and we end up changing even our memories, our memories of how we were), I had better start by saying: 'Yes, I was a Stalinist', and then try to see more clearly what that might have meant.

I will not situate the problem in either its subjective context (how in the general upheaval of the war a young Italian, without any political experience or instruction, found that he was all of a sudden a Communist), or its objective context (Stalin meant then Stalingrad, Russia stopping Hitler's triumphant march and descending like an avalanche of fire and sword on Berlin), not because these are unimportant, but because we can take them as read. And let's come to the crucial point: who was Stalin for us, for me? (I had better speak in the singular, and then see whether this exploration of my individual memory yields any general consideration.) Who was Stalin between 1945 and 1953, here in this Western world which had taken its shape from the Allied victory and the Cold War? What image of him could be reconstructed from the official portraits which were all alike and from the almost total invisibility of his presence, from the written pages that descended every so often on to the world like oracles and from the tremendous silence that was his response to the endless choruses of praise?

The images of Stalin that one could generate from this distance of his (a fortunate distance, though not everyone realized it) were several: for many rank-and-file Communists waiting for the zero hour of the revolution, Stalin was the living guarantee that this revolution would happen. (And actually the opposite was true, since Stalin tended to rule out any revolution that could happen outside the Soviet Union's sphere of direct influence.) Then there was the Stalin who said that the proletariat had to pick up the flag of democratic liberties that had been dropped by the bourgeoisie, and this was the Stalin whose strategy offered support for Togliatti's party line, and seemed to suggest a perspective of historical continuity between the bourgeois revolution and that of the proletariat, a continuity which the alliance between the Three (or Five?) Great Powers against the Axis had sealed ... Was that what Stalin was for me? But how could this image be preserved given all the aspects which blatantly contradicted it? Let us try out a first formulation: *although Stalinism was very compact, it contained for Western Communists a range, however limited, of possibilities in politics, culture and behaviour which all differed to a certain extent. There were different ways of being a Stalinist, but the rules of the game were that whoever upheld one line was obliged not to present it as an alternative to the others.*

As far as I am concerned, Stalin had become a figure in my life only at the moment when he had had himself photographed with Roosevelt and Churchill in the wicker armchairs at Yalta. What had happened previously, the struggle against Trotsky, the great purges, were just that, things that had happened 'previously', when I did not feel directly involved. Of course, the mystery surrounding the incredible self-accusations in the Moscow trials continued to cast an icy shadow (all the more so when the same scene repeated itself in the trials of Budapest and Prague), but the huge pyres of the war seemed to have diminished all other pyres and to have absorbed them into one furnace, in the climate of imminent tragedy. Even the enormous trauma of those who had entered the political struggle before us – the German–Soviet pact of 1939 – was counterbalanced by the history of the subsequent years (as long as you did not look too closely into the details, which in any case were not very well known in Italy). What I wanted to identify with was the history that began with the rescue from Nazism and Fascism which then ruled Europe, and with everything else that had anticipated it in the past. Stalin seemed to represent the moment when Communism had become a huge river, now distant from the headlong and uneven course it began with, a river into which the currents of history flowed. I could, then, formulate my own position thus: *my Stalinism as much as my anti-Stalinism stemmed from the same nucleus of values.* For this reason, for me and for many others, the development of an anti-Stalinist conscience was not felt as a change, but as a fulfilment of one's own convictions.

Not that I did not believe there was *another* version of history, incompatible with that image. I would prefer to be taken for a supporter of the most cynical Machiavellian approach than for one of those who say: 'Stalin's atrocities? Who knew anything about them? I had no idea.' Of course no one suspected the extent of the massacres (and even now every new estimate of the number of millions of victims shows up the preceding estimate as too optimistic), nor did anyone know what the mechanism was that produced the grotesque confessions in the show trials (people sought sophisticated explanations in terms of revolutionary psychology, by which the disgraced leaders, now with no hope, calumnied themselves solely to collaborate in the development of socialism, even Koestler, who had written the most horrific book on the subject, was guilty of optimism), but the elements to make some sense of it all – or at least to understand that there were many grey areas – were in plentiful supply. You could take them into consideration or not: which was something different from believing in them or not. For instance, I was a friend of Franco Venturi,* who knew a lot of the things that had happened out there, and told me about them with all the sarcasm of the Enlightenment man he was. Did I not believe him? Of course I believed him. It was just that I thought that I, being a Communist, had to see those facts from a different perspective from his, weighing them in different scales of positive and negative. And moreover, to draw the logical conclusions would have meant detaching myself from the movement, the organization, the masses, etc., missing the chance to participate in something that at that time counted more for me … This incapacity to transmit experience, or let's say the lack of efficacy in communicating one's experience, continues to be one of the most depressing facts in the way history and society work: there is no way of preventing a generation from closing its ears, history continues to be propelled by urges that are not completely under control, by partial and unclear convictions, by choices that are not choices and by necessities that are not necessities.

At this point I can attempt to clarify my definition: *Stalinism relied on necessity, things could not happen any other way from the way they happened*, even though the face of that history had nothing pleasant about it. Only when I managed to understand that even inside the most iron necessity there is a point where choices are possible, and Stalin's choices had been largely disastrous, did any justification of Stalinism become unthinkable.

Naturally there was an area where I could not hide from myself

---

* Franco Venturi (1914–94), historian and key figure in the Einaudi publishing house. Brought up in exile in France, he later took part in the Resistance, lived in the USSR (1947–49) and became a famous historian of the Enlightenment as well as of Russian populism.

the negativity of Stalinism in any way, and this was in my very own field of work. Soviet art and literature – once the revolutionary period had burnt out – were grim and wretched, and official aesthetics consisted in crude, high-handed directives. Not having clear ideas on how the Soviet system of directives worked, I was not inclined to hold Stalin directly responsible (in his 'signed' interventions he seemed to be more open than his followers). This was how I explained the system to myself: in the years when in the USSR the Communist leadership had imposed itself on the various sectors of cultural and social life, some areas had been able to profit from the leadership of people who were creative in a genuinely Communist sense, whereas other fields – like literature and art, after the various deaths and notorious suicides – had fallen into the hands of crooks and opportunists. In short, I had understood something, but not the most important thing: that it was the Stalinist system of culture that of necessity imposed this predominance of crooks, and that this system was an absolute monarchy and not a collegiate leadership.

In order to bar the dishonest from the route to cultural power I thought it was necessary to undertake in one's own field practical and theoretical work that was unimpeachable from the political point of view and that would act as a model of values for the new society. For this reason one had to exclude many things from one's horizon; Communism was a narrow funnel one had to pass through in order to discover an unlimited universe on the other side. I can then add this corollary to the 'formulation' regarding the necessity of Stalinism I enounced previously: *Stalinism possessed the power and the limitations of all great simplifications. The vision of the world that it took into consideration was very compressed and schematic, but inside it there were choices and one could struggle to make one's choices prevail, choices which allowed back into play many values which one thought excluded.*

Behind this I could still see operating as a model that extraordinary combination of, on the one hand, intellectuals fired by a practical and inventive spirit and, on the other, the proletariat with its need for renewal, the combination that had been the miracle of revolutionary Russia. It was only later that I realized that this combination (perhaps a natural consequence of the Russian Socialist revolutionary tradition rather than the result of conscious intention by Lenin and the Bolsheviks) had lasted just a few years and had been dispersed by Stalin, depriving the workers of any power to claim rights and decimating the intellectuals in a reign of terror. So now I am able to introduce a formulation of wider import: *Stalinism presented itself as the conclusion of the Enlightenment project of placing the whole mechanism of society in the domain of the intellect. It was instead the most comprehensive (and perhaps inevitable) defeat of this project.*

To this picture I have to add a more personal detail: my utopian desire to attain a non-ideological conception of the world. The intellectual atmosphere of those years was certainly less ideological than it is now, but the world in which I moved was saturated with ideology. And I had convinced myself that every time Stalin spoke, the ideologues choked on their food. And this caused me great satisfaction. It seemed to me that Stalin was always on the side of common sense over ideology. My friends criticized me heavily for this attitude both then and later, but it met the need I felt to find my own position vis-à-vis the people I regularly debated with who were very much ideologists. I was wrong, at least as regards Stalin: because Stalin was not at all the end of ideology; because my superficiality led me to identify with the worst kind of ideologizing; and because when examples of openness of thought come from a single ruler, they count for nothing, except to show that he alone can afford to be like that because he is king. So I can add this to my series of conclusions: *Stalinism appeared to establish the primacy of practice over ideological principles, but in fact it twisted ideology in order to ideologize something that functioned only through force.*

I am only now beginning to understand how things stood. I mean things like me and Stalin, and me and Communism. The suffering of the Revolution, Red October, Lenin, were always distant ghosts for me, events that happened once upon a time, irrevocable events which would never happen again. I had become involved with the problematics of Communism during Stalin's time but for reasons that were to do with Italian history, and I had to make a constant effort to bring the Soviet Union into my frame of reference. As far as the popular democracies of Eastern Europe were concerned, I had pretty quickly come to the conclusion that this was simply a highly artificial and compulsory manoeuvre, imposed on them from outside and from on high. I thought things were different for the USSR, that Communism, after the years of the harshest struggles, had become a kind of natural state there, it had reached a spontaneity, a serenity, a mature wisdom. I projected on to reality the rudimentary simplification of my political ideas, whose ultimate aim was to rediscover, after all the distortions and injustices and massacres, a natural equilibrium beyond all history, beyond class struggle, beyond ideology, beyond Socialism and Communism.

This was why in my 'Diary of a Journey to the USSR', which I published in *l'Unità* in 1952, what I noted down was almost exclusively minimal observations of daily life, its heartening, reassuring, timeless and non-political aspects. This non-monumental way of presenting the USSR seemed to me the least conformist approach. But in fact the real Stalinist sin I was guilty of was precisely this: in order to defend myself from a reality which I did not know, but which in some way I sensed but did not want to articulate, I collaborated with this unofficial language of mine; it presented to official hypocrisy as a picture of serenity and smiles something that was trauma and tension and torture. *Stalinism was also the smooth-speaking and cheerful mask which concealed the historical tragedy taking place.*

The rumbles of thunder in 1956 swept away all the masks and screens. Many who come to self-awareness in that hour of truth went back to the revolutionary origins of Communism (and almost all of them accepted a new mythical image, one that looked different but was no less prone to mystification: Mao Tse Tung).

Others took the more practical road of recognizing what existed to try to reform it, some with rationalist optimism, others with a sense of limits, of avoiding the worst, of the relativity of the results. I followed neither of these paths: I lacked the temperament and conviction to be a revolutionary, and the modesty of the reformist aims (both in the Socialist and capitalist world) seemed incapable of curing me of the vertigo I suffered as a result of the abysses I had hovered over. So although I remained friendly with both groups, I gradually whittled down the room that politics occupied in my interior space. (Meanwhile politics gradually occupied more and more space in the world outside.)

Perhaps politics remains tied in my experience to that extreme situation: a sense of inflexible necessity and a search for the different and the multiple in a rigid world. So I will conclude by saying: if I have been (though very much in my own way) a Stalinist, this was not by chance. There are elements that characterize that epoch, which are part of me: I don't believe in anything that is easy, quick, spontaneous, improvised, rough and ready. I believe in the strength of what is slow, calm, obstinate, devoid of fanaticisms and enthusiasms. I do not believe in any liberation either individual or collective that can be obtained without the cost of self-discipline, of self-construction, of effort. If this way of thinking seems to some people Stalinist, well all right, I will have no difficulty in admitting that in this sense I am a bit Stalinist still.

[*La Repubblica*, 16 December 1979. Contribution to a supplement dedicated to Stalin, on the centenary of his birth. (Author's note.)]

The Summer of '56

That summer of '56 was full of tension and hope. The 20th Soviet Congress had taken place in Moscow, Khrushchev seemed the champion of a new phase in world Communism, and the first signs of thaw were in the air. We militant Communists were convinced that that process would be irreversible and also quite swift. Thinking back on it now, after twenty-four years and after all that has happened, confirms me in my view that history is not an easy work with a happy ending, but a long, tiring and slow process, devoid of any perceptible direction or meaning.

However, in those days, this was not what I felt. When I found out about the Khrushchev report which denounced Stalin's crimes, after an initial moment of astonishment I felt as though I had been set free. That was the reaction of all my comrades then. You ask whether there was in us, in the party, a sense of defeat or humiliation: no, as far as I know, there was not. I shall try to describe exactly my reaction, which was very similar to that of others: for me de-Stalinization and the bearing of witness to the truth emanating from Moscow represented the fulfilment of Socialism. For years the country of Socialism, the USSR, had also seemed to us a dark place, governed by iron rules, by an inflexible austerity, by terrible punishments and ruthless logic. We put all this on the side of the 'siege', of the revolutionary struggle. But when Khrushchev denounced Stalin before the Central

Committee and then to the Party Congress, we thought: right, peace is flourishing, now the fruits of Socialism will be delivered, and that oppression, the secret anguish we felt, will disappear.

In Poland the Stalinist group had been removed. Gomulka had been released. In Hungary the renewal of the party had been even more comprehensive and radical. In place of the old Stalinists were Communists who had suffered imprisonment and removal from all party office. In all this we saw the confirmation of our hopes, a genuine renewal, a turning-point of historic importance.

My idea was that after that regeneration and restructuring, the cause of Socialism would be strengthened enormously everywhere. In Italy I believed that many people who had remained distant from the Communist party because of the tragic and ferocious system we were an integral part of, would join us, would fight the same struggles as ourselves, and would share our ideals of humanity and equality.

I was part of the Federal Committee in Turin, I worked for the Einaudi publishing house, I frequented the intellectual cadres in Turin, Milan and Rome. But in those months of great creative fervour, the ruling group and the intellectuals met with the rank-and-file militants, something that had not happened with that intensity probably since the time of the Resistance and Liberation. Endless discussions, whole nights given over to assemblies, debates, in a word, tremendous political passion.

That summer Lukács came to Italy.* In Hungary he was once more a flag to rally round as well as a national hero. I met him with Cesare Cases who was accompanying him on his Italian trip. Lukács brought us confirmation of our hopes for a new kind of Communism. Almost in those very same days we had further confirmation, one that was even more important for those of us

---

* György Lukács (1885–1971), Hungarian literary critic and philosopher. His Marxist aesthetics, particularly as expounded in *The Historical Novel* (1955), were very influential in Italy.

in the PCI [Italian Communist Party]: the interview with Togliatti in *Nuovi Argomenti.** I recall very well the effect it had on me when I read it on the front page of *l'Unità*. He said, with intellectual depth, diplomatic finesse, but also (at last) with sincerity, the things I expected would be said. That morning I was in Rome. I had a rendezvous with Paolo Spriano at Villa Borghese.[†] We walked along the paths of the park for a long time until, near the pond beside the Avenue of Magnolias, we met Longo.[‡] He was holding the string of a wooden model motor-boat belonging to a child who was with him. All three of us spoke with great passion about what was happening. I remember that Longo told us about when he was in Moscow, so many years before, when he was secretary of the Communist Youth. He mentioned the dark air there was everywhere, the lack of freedom not just for the citizens but also for the party militants. In short, it seemed to him as well that a great weight had been lifted from his chest.

You ask me: if all of you, intellectuals, leaders, militants, had this weight on your chest, why on earth did you never think of removing it before this? Why had we had to wait for the signal from Moscow, from Khrushchev, from the Central Committee? And why then, despite everything, in that very year, 1956, did things end up as they did? Well. This was the reply that was given to you yourself, if I remember correctly, by Giancarlo Pajetta,[§] in a press conference after the 22nd Congress of the Soviet Union's Communist

---

* Togliatti gave a positive interview in spring 1956 regarding Khrushchev's moves towards de-Stalinization. However, he later toed the Moscow line over the uprisings in Poland and Hungary that year, thus causing many Italian intellectuals to leave the party.
† Paolo Spriano (1925–88), historian. Friend of Calvino before and after the latter's departure from the Communist party, he went on to write the definitive history of the party (1967–75).
‡ Luigi Longo (1900–80), politician. After fighting in the Resistance, he was a key figure in the PCI, eventually succeeding Togliatti as leader of the party (1964–72).
§ Giancarlo Pajetta (1911–90), politician. Leader of the Communist Youth, he was imprisoned under Fascism (1933–43). He went on to become editor of the Communist daily *l'Unità* several times, and was on the reformist wing of the party.

party. You asked him more or less the same question that you are now asking me and he told you that when it comes to a choice between the revolution and the truth a revolutionary always chooses revolution. Personally I do not think that things are like that and I do not feel that that answer was acceptable. But at that time, twenty-four years ago, our perspective on things was more or less that. We Italian Communists were schizophrenic. Yes, I really think that that is the correct term. One side of our minds was and wanted to be a witness to the truth, avenging the wrongs suffered by the weak and oppressed, and defending justice against every abuse. The other side justified those wrongs, the abuses, the tyrannies of the party, Stalin, all in the name of the Cause. Schizophrenic. Split. I recall very clearly that whenever I happened to travel to some Socialist country, I felt profoundly uncomfortable, foreign, hostile. But when the train brought me back to Italy, whenever I crossed back over the border, I would ask myself: but here, in Italy, in this Italy, what else could I be but a Communist? That is why the thaw, the end of Stalinism, took a terrible weight from our chest: because our moral standing, our split personality, could finally be put together again, revolution and truth finally went back to being the same thing. This was, in those days, the dream and hope of many of us.

In those days Vittorini came back to the party. He had left it a long time before and sympathized with radical, liberal-Socialist positions, but in 1956 he returned. He wanted to go to Budapest. He wanted to help with the reform and renewal. In Turin, the reform man, Celeste Negarville, had been sidelined for some time and the Federation was run by an old Stalinist, Antonio Roasio.* But we thought that the time had come for him too to stand aside. Renewal was in the air. We waited, day after day, for the hundred flowers of Socialism to bloom.

---

* Antonio Roasio (1902–), politician. Inter-regional head of the Communist Youth under Fascism, he lived in exile in France, the USSR and Spain (during the Civil War). After the war he became a Communist MP, head of the Turin Federation of Communists, and later a member of the Senate. His autobiography, *Figlio della classe operaia* (*Working-class Boy*), was published in 1977.

In those months I wrote for *Città Aperta* the story 'La gran bonaccia delle Antille' ('Becalmed in the Antilles'). I reread it just recently. It seems to me that it has not lost any of its meaning, if for no other reason than that it is evidence of a state of mind, and of a great opportunity missed. Those events estranged me from politics, in the sense that politics has since occupied in me a much smaller space than before. I think today that politics registers very late things which society manifests through other channels, and I feel that often politics distorts and mystifies reality.

Our hopes for renewal were concentrated on Giorgio Amendola.* He had taken the place of Pietro Secchia† at the head of the party's organization. He maintained that we had already had our own 20ᵗʰ Congress the day Secchia had been removed from office. Amendola was the image of what I thought a Communist ought to be if he was to further rigorously and humanely Socialist ideals in a country like ours. Instead he was a terrible disappointment Perhaps I had not understood Amendola's character properly. But whatever the case, he certainly was not the 'new Communist' we had in mind then. What was for me and for many of us an inner split that only brought suffering, was a natural state for him. Amendola was extremely rigorous, but at the same time he possessed all the wiles of a political man. And on that occasion it was the latter aspect that prevailed.

The evening that the news arrived of the invasion of Hungary by the Red Army and of the entry of Russian armoured cars into Budapest, I was at dinner with Amendola in Turin, in Luciano Barca's house: Barca was the editor of the Turin edition of *l'Unità*. Amendola has recalled this episode in one of his books. He had come to Turin to meet me and our other friends from Einaudi; to 'keep us good', because people realized that difficulties

---

* Giorgio Amendola (1907–80), politician and historian. Imprisoned under Fascism, he went on to become a key figure in the reformist wing of the PCI.
† Pietro Secchia (1903–73), politician and historian. Also imprisoned for leading Communist Youth activities under Fascism, he was later more hard-line than Amendola. Wrote histories of the Resistance and of the Italian Communist Party.

were on the way and we were showing signs of impatience. For me it was a decisive evening. While Amendola was talking, Gianni Rocca, editor-in-chief of *l'Unità*, phoned Barca. His voice was choked with tears. He told us: 'The armoured cars are entering Budapest, there is fighting in the streets.' I looked at Amendola: it was as if all three of us had been hit over the head. Then Amendola murmured: 'Togliatti says that there are times in history when you have to be on one side or the other. In any case Communism is like the Church, it takes centuries to change its position. And don't forget that Hungary was developing into a very dangerous situation . . ' I realized then that the time of the hundred flowers in the PCI was still far away, very far away . . .

One month later the 8ᵗʰ Congress of the PCI took place. Antonio Giolitti's speech denounced the closed position of the party on Hungary. He spoke quietly, amid a glacial atmosphere. Togliatti was seated beside the rostrum, ostentatiously dealing with correspondence. Giolitti left the party and along with him several others. I decided not to leave the party then, at that time of particular difficulty, but by then my mind was made up. I went without a fuss in the summer of 1957. Many other comrades did the same: some did not renew their membership, others were expelled from the party. The whole group of *Città Aperta*, which was edited by Tomaso Chiaretti, was expelled. So was Bruno Corbi, Furio Diaz, Fabrizio Onofri and Natalino Sapegno all left.

If the PCI had reacted differently in 1956, its 'legitimization' would have taken place twenty-four years ago. How much would that have changed the history of our country? Obviously this is a question to which the only answer is: it would have changed it enormously. But none of the leaders felt they could do it. In this sense Togliatti bears a huge responsibility. Togliatti, from the turning-point of Salerno 1944 onwards,* when he urged

---

* In 1944 Togliatti urged his party at the Salerno conference to put aside its hostility to the monarchy and to join the royal government in opposing the Nazis and Fascists: national liberation was to take priority over constitutional questions.

Communists to put national liberation first, always combined two positions: a broadly reformist policy as far as the PCI was concerned and loyalty to the USSR. That loyalty allowed him to be reformist. Had there been a break with the USSR then, PCI policy could have and probably would have had to be more incisive in internal policy. The problems of a left alternative would have arisen. Clearly the PCI leadership did not feel they could go down that road.

That is what happened then. Twelve years later, when it came to the invasion of Prague, its position was different, the PCI condemned the invasion, but even on that occasion there was no break with Moscow. Today, faced with the risks of the Polish situation, it seems to me that the Communist party has taken another step. And is in the right position. This long march has taken twenty-four years. I can't honestly say whether the bus we missed in November 1956 can ever be caught again.

[Interview by Eugenio Scalfari: '*Calvino e la storia del suo tempo*' ('Calvino and the History of his Time'), *La Repubblica*, 13 December 1980.]

The Duce's Portraits

You could say that I spent the first twenty years of my life with Mussolini's face always in view, in the sense that his portrait was hung in every classroom, as well as in every public building or office. I could, therefore, try to chart a history of the evolution of Mussolini's image through his official portraits as they have remained in my memory.

I went into the first year of primary school in 1929 and I have a very clear memory of the Mussolini portraits of that period, still dressed in civilian clothes, with a stiff turned-up collar, as important people commonly wore in those days (but this look was to become old-fashioned in the years immediately following). That is the way I remember him in the coloured lithograph hung up in our classroom (on a side-wall; above the teacher's desk there still hung the picture of the king) and in a black-and-white photograph at the back of our ancient spelling-book (a picture that looked as if it had been added on to the most recent editions).

In those years, then, there still persisted the first image Mussolini wanted to give of himself immediately on seizing power, which was meant to emphasize a certain continuity and respectability in the man who had restored order. The portrait did not go down below his tie, but probably the jacket worn by the head of government was a morning-coat (the black jacket with tails known in Italy – and only in Italy – as a 'tight') which he habitually wore in those days at official ceremonies.

In these portraits Mussolini still had black hair on his temples and maybe (I am not sure) in the middle of his balding head. The statesman's dress accentuated his youthfulness, because that was the real novelty that the images had to convey (though I was not to know that at six years of age), in the sense that no one had ever heard of a prime minister who was only forty. Nor had anyone ever seen in Italy a statesman without a beard or moustache, and this was in itself a sign of modernity. It was common practice to shave, but the most significant politicians at the time of the First World War and after it all still wore a beard or a moustache. This was true throughout the whole world, I would say (I'm writing this without consulting any books or encyclopaedias), with the sole exception of American presidents. Even the quadrumvirate who led the March on Rome had moustaches and two of the four had a beard.

(I don't think there are historians who emphasize the facial-hair dimension in various epochs; and yet these are certainly messages that have a meaning, especially in periods of transition.)

In short, Mussolini's image in those days was meant to express at the same time modernity, efficiency and a reassuring continuity, and all that with authoritarian severity. This was certainly to counter a previous image, one associated with the period of Fascist lynch-squads. Among my memories there is also a portrait that I would date to that violent period (it does not matter if I saw it a little later), a dramatic black-and-white photograph, with his signature with the strong-willed *M* which would become famous. His face, angled slightly sideways, jutted out from the black, which could have been his black shirt but also a dark background like that evoked by the words 'the Piazza Sansepolcro gang', with which – as we were taught – the new age had begun.

The climate of violence from the Fascist action squads was also recorded in my very first memories as a child (at least one of its last outbursts, dateable to 1926), but when I started to go to school the world seemed calm and ordered. Signs of a period of civil war emerged occasionally, endowed with a dark attraction for a child or boy at a time when the official portraits of the Duce were identified with a discipline that brooked no sudden demurral.

The other salient feature of these first official images of the dictator was the thoughtful pose, his prominent forehead seeming to underline his capacity for thought. Among the affectionate games people used to play at the time with children of one or two years old, was the habit of saying: 'Do Mussolini's face', and the child would adopt a furrowed expression and stick out angry lips. In a word, Italians of my generation began to carry Mussolini's portrait within themselves even before being of an age to recognize it on the walls, and this reveals that there was (also) something infantile in that image, that look of concentration that small children can have and which does not at all mean that they are thinking intensely about anything.

The rule I have imposed on myself in writing these pages is to talk only of portraits and photographs I saw during the twenty years of Fascism, leaving aside the enormous amount of documentation I came across subsequently, in the four decades or so of post-Fascism. So I will only talk of official images, since no others circulated then: official images in portraits, statues, films made by his Luce Cinema Institute (the cinema newsreels of the time), illustrated newspapers. The last category basically comprised two: the very popular *Domenica del Corriere* and *L'Illustrazione Italiana*, which was a fortnightly magazine for a more upmarket readership.

I remember having seen at the time the famous photo of Mussolini with his top hat going to sign the Concordat in the Lateran and I recall that I continued to remember it when, shortly afterwards, I heard the grown-ups saying that the Regime had abolished the 'stove-pipes' (as the top hat was called), the symbol of bourgeois traditionalism. Unaware of the dialectic of history, this seemed to me an inexplicable contradiction.

I don't know if that was the last time that Mussolini wore a top hat; it could well have been, because by now, having secured the Church's consensus, he could start putting Italy into uniform. This shift in Fascist style (at least as it might have been perceived in the provinces) I would date to the tenth anniversary of the Fascist revolution, 1932. A tenth anniversary which remains linked in my memory with the fortnight's holiday I had in the fourth year of primary school, and with the series of commemorative stamps.

At that stage Mussolini's iconography had taken an important step forward in its glorification of the Roman emperors; so much so that one of the stamps in this series portrayed the equestrian monument to the Duce at the stadium in Bologna, modelled on Verrocchio's statue of Colleoni, with the inscription underneath: *'Se avanzo seguitemi'* (If I advance, follow me). (There was a second part to this lapidary sentence: *'Se indietreggio uccidetemi'* (If I retreat, kill me), which would come true in due course.) It has to be said that this was one of the few stamps (now I could not tell you of any others) with Mussolini's effigy: stamps were one of the few domains where the sovereignty of the sovereign continued to be displayed: a Victor Emmanuel III whose bodiless head might have been that of an extremely tall man.

The equestrian-monument Duce appeared in profile; another important shift this, from the frontal image to the side-image, much exploited from that point on, in that it enhanced his perfectly spherical cranium (without which the great transformation of the dictator into a design object would not have been possible), the strength of his jaws (also emphasized in the three-quarters pose), the continuity of the back of his head with his neck, and the overall Romanness of the whole.

It was in those final years of primary school that my enrolment in the *Balilla* could not be postponed any longer because it became compulsory even in the private school which I attended. I remember very clearly the smell of musty material in the depot of the *Casa del Balilla* where you bought the uniforms; I remember the old storekeeper, a wounded war veteran; but what I want

210

to recall now is the badge with the pin showing the Duce in profile, which helped to keep our blue kerchief pinned on (the colour meant: Dalmatia; that was what was explained to us, following a logic whose connections mean nothing now). I remember this portrait in profile with his helmet, but the adoption of that helmet must be a few years later than the memory I am trying to focus on now; so, either the blue kerchief was initially tied without a badge, or there was a first version of the badge with his profile showing a bare head. What I wanted to get at was a dating of the moment when the Duce becomes a profile on a badge, like a Roman emperor (thus invading the numismatic field which was reserved for the king for more than one reason), but I do not have enough evidence available.

We are still in the years 1933–34. It was then that I saw a portrait (or sculpture) of Mussolini in the 'Cubist' style, in the sense that it was in the shape of a cube with geometrical features. This was in an exhibition of drawings put on by the local primary schools, where I had to sit the entrance exam for high school. The cube, with an inscription that said something like 'Portrait of the Duce as the Duce prefers', was displayed as a model for the children's drawings. For me this memory is the start of the notion of the existence of a 'Fascist style' based on the modernity of smooth, square surfaces, which would superimpose itself and in many cases become identical with a 'twentieth-century style', which was already widespread even in the provinces.

Conforming to this style is the inscription DVX, looking like a Roman numeral, on the bases of busts or columns, often symmetrically placed alongside the analogous word REX. (By this stage the effigies of king and Duce are always together, and if one is missing it is not the Duce's.) In a more neoclassical and sinuous 'twentieth-century' style was the bust by Wildt with the laurel crown, the toga and the empty eye-sockets: an image which appeared very different from the ones then current, but which nevertheless had all the stamp of its official nature, in that it appeared as the frontispiece to the edition of his *Scritti e discorsi (Writings and Speeches)*.

I would like also to recall here an image that was in all our reading books: the house where the Duce was born in Predappio. That too was given to school-children to copy; and here I have nothing to object to, because it was a very beautiful house to draw, an example of a traditional Italian house in the country, with an outside staircase, a very high ground floor, and walls with few windows.

The classical image of Mussolini was by now established and not destined to undergo changes throughout the period of the peak of his dictatorship (namely the best part of the 1930s). Radio and cinema were the principal media not only of the dissemination but also of the very formation of this image. I never went to any mass rallies where Mussolini was present, because I hardly ever moved from the provincial area I was brought up in, which he did not like and never came to, but I believe that in the cinema the leader's image was more effective and tangible than when it was seen directly by the crowd underneath that balcony; and in any case his voice was always transmitted via loudspeakers. The audio-visual media of the time were, in short, an essential component of Mussolini's Roman cult.

Another necessary component was of course the prohibition of any criticism or sarcasm. One of the first Mussolini speeches I remember was, I think, the one about '*libro e moschetto, fascista perfetto*' (book and rifle make the perfect Fascist); at the end of it the Duce brought out from beneath the window-sill a book and a rifle: a wonderful coup. I remember having heard previously at home an anti-Fascist uncle who had seen it in the cinema. (If it was not that speech, it must have been another from the same time, shortly after 1930; this can be checked on film.) I recall my uncle describing his gestures, his fists firmly on his hips, and at a certain point the gesture of blowing his nose with his hand. I remember my aunt's interjection: 'Well, what do you expect? He's a builder!' A few days later I saw this Luce film with the speech, and recognized the grimaces described by my uncle, and even the quick blow of his nose. The image of Mussolini came to me, then, filtered through the sarcastic discourse of adults (certain adults) which jarred with the chorus of praise. But that chorus was expressed in public, whereas reservations remained confined to private conversations and never dented the unanimity that the Regime made great show of.

Mussolini soon learnt that the camera mercilessly emphasized every grimace and tic in his gestures, and I think that if you went chronologically through the films of his speeches you would see how his control of every gesture and pause and acceleration in rhetorical rhythm became more and more effective. However, the style of his performances remained the same as it had been from the start. Nowadays when young people see Mussolini in old films they find him ridiculous and cannot understand how there were enormous crowds who praised him to the skies. And yet the Mussolini model of oratory has continued to find imitations and variations throughout the whole world down to our own time, especially under populist or third-world labels, still exploiting the same regressive techniques.

In an age when enormous possibilities for manipulating the masses and for using them to consolidate one's power opened up, Mussolini was one of the first to construct a personality which corresponded to this intention in every single thing. That image of his as a popular leader with all the attributes that were easiest to swallow by the masses of his day (energy, arrogance, bellicosity, posing like a Roman captain, a plebeian pride which contrasted with everything that had been up until then part of the image of a statesman), all this he communicated through the physical characteristics of his person, his military dress, his oratory punctuated by brief 'lapidary' phrases, the booming voice, even his very pronunciation (for instance, in the words '*Itaglia*' '*Itagliani*' the sounds of his Emilia-Romagna origins took on an assertive note). Once the idea had been planted in people's heads that a leader must be endowed with an image like his, it was implicit that whoever did not possess that image could not be a leader.

For Hitler, who physically was the complete opposite of

Mussolini, this must have been an enormous problem, in the period when Mussolini was his model. (The person who understood this point with supreme psychological sophistication was Charlie Chaplin in *The Great Dictator*.) Hitler managed to overcome his handicap by going in the opposite direction from the Italian dictator, emphasizing the nervous agitation of his looks (his face, his moustache, his quiff of hair), or of his voice, adopting his own style of gestures and rhetoric which were such as to unleash a fanatical energy that bordered on the hysterical. In his dress the Führer avoided showiness, preferring the most ordinary of uniforms (the opposite of his dauphin Goering who flaunted his corpulent body in a series of garish uniforms which were always different).

I am speaking of that period by going back to my boyhood memories when I got my idea of the world mostly through the newspaper illustrations that most struck my imagination. Thinking back to the personalities who dominated world news at the time, the one who stood out most from all the others in terms of his visual image was without a doubt Gandhi. Although he was one of the people who was most caricatured and about whom huge numbers of anecdotes circulated, his image managed to instil the idea that in him there was something serious and true, even though very remote from us.

In 1934 (I'm quoting dates based on my memory's outline of events: if I'm wrong, it will be easy to correct them) the Royal Italian Army changed its uniform, which up until then had been the one they had worn in the First World War. For the Italy of that time, when many people were in the army (in addition to lengthy military service, you could also be 'called back'), this new uniform (with the flat beret, the jacket with the collar open to show your tie, long trousers for officers in dress uniform) marked a turning-point which at the time was merely one of appearance, but which was to coincide with the entry into a decade of wars.

Along with the uniform the helmets also changed: instead of

the First World War helmet, evoking as it did the poor infantry in the trenches, there was the drooping dome-shaped helmet, which belonged to a new age of industrial design. (The 'aerodynamic' lines in car design belong to the same era: but in this case I would need to check dates and types of car.) For Mussolini's iconography this was a huge turning-point: the classic image of the Duce became the one with the helmet, which looked like a metallic extension of the smooth surface of his head.

Underneath the helmet his jaw stands out more, acquiring a decisive importance because of the disappearance of the upper part of his head (including his eyes). Since his lips were kept turned up (an unnatural position but one denoting the power of his will) his jaw stuck out in front as well as laterally. From that moment on, then, the Duce's head seems to be made up essentially of helmet and jawbones, whose volumes counterbalance each other and also counterbalance the curve of his stomach which was then just beginning to stand out. The uniform was that of Honorary Corporal of the Militia. Instead of his profile, which could look a bit squashed under the helmet, official photoportraits preferred an almost three-quarters angle which allowed them to catch a flashing glance beneath his helmet. What inevitably did get lost beneath the helmet was the emphasis on his thoughtful forehead, a key attribute of the Mussolini of the 1920s; his character was thus changed in a way: the Duce as thinker was replaced by the Duce as *condottiere*.

This is the portrait of Mussolini that could be considered canonical and which I had before my eyes for most of my time at school, at sports, before call-up, etc. Matching this effigy of the Duce there was nearly always a portrait of the king, in profile, complete with helmet, moustache and protruding chin. King Vittorio's head was certainly much smaller than the Duce's, but in these portraits it was enlarged so as to appear, thanks also to the angle, almost of the same volume as that of his irreplaceable prime minister. I think both of them wore round their neck the Collar of the Annunziata, which was a gold chain with a little plaque just where the knot of the tie would be.

Of course there were also portraits of the Duce bare-headed. Perhaps basing himself on Erich von Stroheim, Mussolini had been able to transform his bald head from physical defect (like the 'Before' photos in cure-for-baldness advertisements) into a symbol of virile strength. His stroke of genius, again in the 1930s, was to have the remaining hair on his temples and neck removed. Also very common were pictures of him in the fez with the Honorary Corporal's red braid; or in the party uniform, and on his beret the eagle with angular wings. Very frequent too were the images of him on horseback, among which one should recall the one where he holds the Sword of Islam, brandishing it towards the sky.

On the rare occasions when he was portrayed in civilian dress, he showed that he had adopted a less formal style than previously. One summer he was present at manoeuvres with a white yachtsman's beret, cavalry boots and trousers and a jacket that was sky-blue, I think. (What I am recalling here is a colour plate by Beltrame in the *Domenica del Corriere*: the Duce is helping artillerymen to drag a cannon up a slope.) Then there were the famous shots of him in the 'Battle for Grain': the Duce in his vest or bare-chested at the threshing machine, with his helmet and motorcyclist goggles, lifting sheaves of corn amid the farmworkers. (Farmworkers or Security Police? The common joke at the time was the Duce congratulating the man on his excellent threshing: 'Well done! What can I do to reward your labours?' 'Transfer me from the police station in Rome to the one in Palermo, Duce!')

The photos showing him in private life were more rare: there were a few family photos, others showing him skiing or swimming or flying an aeroplane. They were distributed – so they said – because some foreign newspaper had printed rumours about his illnesses.

With the Conquest of Ethiopia, the cult of the Head moved more and more towards his apotheosis. The formula used in ritual acclamations: 'Hail to the Duce! To us!' was turned into a lengthy

'Hail to the Duce Founder of the Empire!' Jokes of the time had it that Starace* was so stupid that he could not keep that phrase in his mind (even though he invented it) and every time he had to shout it he furtively had to consult the piece of paper he had written it on.

That was also the period of Starace and his anti-bourgeois 'dress revolution', which consisted mostly in providing new uniforms regularly for the party's *gerarchi*: Fascist jackets without lapels, and black, khaki and white Saharan uniforms … To return to our subject, this was the period when the Duce's appearance was multiplied in that of all the *gerarchi* who tried to imitate him: they shaved their heads and temples to simulate virile baldness, they stuck out their chins, and made their necks swell out. Others remained faithful to brilliantined hair, like Galeazzo Ciano, who on the other hand did try to imitate his father-in-law in his poses when making speeches. But he was not photogenic and his unpopularity was surpassed only by Starace's.

The war was approaching. I entered adolescence and it is as if my visual memory of those years becomes less receptive than my childhood memory when the way people looked was my main channel of contact with the world; now my mind started to fill nebulously with ideas, reasoning, value judgments, and not just the external aspects of people and environments.

At Munich in 1938 the two dictators played the last round in this game of images, their gutsy expressions (that word 'gutsy', which today is wasted emptily, would have been most appropriate then) contrasting with the thin, old-fashioned figure of Neville Chamberlain with his tails, stiff collar and umbrella. But at that point the message the masses picked up was what Chamberlain's umbrella conjured up, namely peace; and Mussolini, too, who at

* Achille Starace (1889–1945). Hard-line secretary of the Fascist party 1931–39, he was obsessed with external trappings such as Fascist uniforms, the Roman salute and the use of '*Voi*' instead of '*Lei*'. He was shot by partisans and his body was hung up alongside Mussolini's in Piazzale Loreto in Milan in April 1945.

that point presented himself as the saviour of peace, elicited the last spontaneous cheers of the crowd.

Then came the war. Mussolini now wore the uniform of the Royal Army (campaign dress with forage cap and boots): he had had the army confer on him the lofty title of Marshal of the Empire. On battle fronts that were still far away young men a little older than I began to die (those born around 1915, the year-groups that bore the brunt of the war). Mussolini's outline, which up until a little while before tended towards roundness, now began to thin, to look haggard and tense. His stomach ulcer intensified along with the inevitability of the catastrophe. Particularly striking were the photos of his meetings with Hitler who now had him in his hands and did not allow him to say a word. Mussolini's uniform now includes a huge coat and cap with a visor of distinctly Germanic style.

Faced with the reality of the military defeats, the choreography of the parades revealed their vanity even to those who had not had eyes to notice it before. The rumour that started after El Alamein (as rumours did circulate, spreading throughout Italy) that along with the Italian troops retreating through the desert was the white horse Mussolini wanted for his triumphal entry into Alexandria, marked the end of his *condottiere* iconography.

The day was approaching when the Duce's portraits which had multiplied over Italian walls would be removed from their immobility as symbols of the established order and would be brought out into the open air through the streets and piazzas, in a tumultuous saraband. This happened on 25 July 1943 (or to be more precise, a day or two later) when the crowd which could no longer be kept at bay invaded the Case del Fascio and flung the effigies of the overthrown dictator out of the windows; everywhere you could see his paternal image mocked and spat upon; the pyres with his military portrait on top of them; plaster or bronze busts dragged along the pavement, with his huge head which overnight had become a relic from another epoch and was now an object of fun.

Was that the end of the story I had been telling up till now? No, a month and a half later we saw the dramatic photos of a ghostly, badly shaven Mussolini, snatched from Campo Imperatore by Skorzeny and taken north of the Brenner back to Hitler. Mussolini was the ghost of himself but he had no choice but to continue putting forward his weary image in the midst of aerial bombardment and the rattle of machine-guns.

Of course the Social Republic had its new official portraits of the Duce, in his new uniform and with his thin face; but I cannot get them to emerge from my memory of that epoch which was so full of emotions and fears. It has to be said that at a certain point my life in our town came to a stop and I found myself cut off from the circulation of those images. Only by hearsay did I find out about a cinema newsreel made by Luce in which Mussolini made once more an unexpected 'crowd immersion' a few months before the end, with his speech at the Teatro Lirico in Milan, the city where his fame as a crowd-puller had been born.

At the beginning of April in a leaflet dropped from an Allied plane to the partisans (rare gifts rained down on us from the sky) there was a caricature of Mussolini (I think it was the first I had seen in my life) by the most famous English cartoonist of the time. (I am sorry that I cannot recall his name; I could go and look it up, because recently the papers mentioned him on the occasion of his death; but up until now I have respected my commitment to rely only on my memory, and I do not want to break this rule right at the end.) In the cartoon Benito and Adolf were trying on women's dresses preparing to escape to Argentina.

It didn't happen. Having been the origin of so many massacres that had no image to recall them, Mussolini's last images were those of his own massacre. Not nice to see or recall. However, I would want all dictators or would-be dictators presently in power, whether they are 'progressive' or reactionary, to keep them framed on their bedside table and to take a look at them every night.

[*La Repubblica*, 10–11 July 1983, originally entitled '*Cominciò con un cilindro*' ('It All Began with a Top Hat').]

Behind the Success

I began to write as a child, though I was very far from the world of literature: in San Remo my father and mother dealt with the acclimatization of exotic plants, with the cultivation of flowers and fruit, and with genetics. Those who frequented our house belonged primarily to the scientific and technical world, the world of agriculture and agricultural experimentation. Both my parents possessed a very strong personality, my father in his vigorous practicality, my mother in her rigour as a scholar, and both had great knowledge in their field, which always intimidated me and gave me a kind of psychological block which meant that I was never able to learn anything from them, something I bitterly regret. The result was I turned more to comics, radio plays and cinema: in short, I developed an imaginative sensibility, which might have been fulfilled by a literary vocation if my surroundings had offered any stimulus in that direction, or if I had been more ready to seize that stimulus. Perhaps I could have realized this earlier, that my vocation was literature, and oriented my relationship with the world better, but I was a bit slow, especially in getting to know myself.

San Remo between the wars was an unusual city, compared to the average in Italian society: at that time there were still plenty of foreigners, which gave a certain cosmopolitan air which I breathed in right from my childhood; but on the other hand it was very provincial, remote from what was happening in Italian culture at that time (which was in any case a rather enclosed period, even in the livelier centres). To be blunt, I had my first contact with literature when I went to school.

I went to high school without achieving particularly brilliant marks, except in Italian, a subject in which I succeeded easily, and these marks made me study it very seriously. Of course, I could also have learnt much more from school, if I had understood myself more and what my life would be like, but that is something that I suppose everyone can say. I could not admit at that time that literature was the thing that interested me most. That would have meant enrolling for a literature degree at university, but the only thing I knew about the Literature Faculty was that it was chosen by those who wanted to become secondary-school teachers, a career which held no fascination for me. I was very attracted by what I called in a rather vague way 'journalism', but at that time the world of newspapers was connected with Fascism (or so it appeared to me, even more so than was the case in reality, since I was not aware of everything that was brewing): by temperament and upbringing I was not a Fascist, which does not rule out that I might have become one out of opportunism, but even in that case I would have had to struggle to go against my nature: in short, I did not have a clue what I wanted to do in life.

I dwell on this moment of uncertainty because I believe that this insecurity, this perplexity about my vocation, also caused after-effects later in life, in the sense that I never decided to 'be a writer'. If I was at that stage already determined to write, to express myself in literature, I still felt that I should back this dicey activity with something else, with a profession which appeared, I'm not sure whether to my own or to others' eyes, as something useful, practical, secure.

So much so that after getting my school-leaving certificate I made a choice which might have seemed, and perhaps was, determined by my family background, and enrolled in the Agriculture Faculty of Turin University where my father had taught up until a few years previously (he had retired by now) courses on 'Tropical

222

cultivation' and 'Tree-growing'. What I had in mind was that for me writing could be a side-line to a 'serious' profession: the latter would keep me in touch with reality and let me travel the world, like my father who had spent nearly twenty years of his life in Central America, and had lived through the Mexican Revolution.

This attempt at realigning myself with a family tradition did not work, but the basic idea was not a bad one: if I had been able to remain faithful to my plan of pursuing a profession with writing as an activity that was on the margins of this life-experience, sooner or later I would have become a writer anyway, but with something extra.

The new climate after the Liberation allowed me to frequent journalist and literary circles. That was when I abandoned Agriculture and enrolled in the Arts Faculty, but to tell you the truth I did not go much to the new Faculty because I was too impatient to join political and cultural life. That was in fact the period when a new element became decisive in my choices: politics. Politics was to have a major influence on my life for ten years or so. The situation, in short, had changed considerably on the outside, but inside myself it was still obeying the same mechanism: I was still unsure of my vocation and my chances of becoming a writer, and I tried to put this vocation below a broader and more imperative duty: joining in the renewal of Italy from the ruins of war and dictatorship.

During the Resistance I had found myself with the Communists, as a simple partisan, and at the Liberation the PCI seemed to me the most realistic and efficient party for the immediate tasks we faced. I had no background in theory. Under Fascism the only clear idea I had was an aversion to totalitarianism and its propaganda; I had read Croce and De Ruggiero and for a while I had called myself a liberal. On the other hand, my family's traditions were a humanitarian Socialism, and before that Mazzinianism. The tragedies of the war, the need to think about world problems in relation to mass society, the role of the PCI in the struggle against Fascism were all elements that led me to become a member of the Communist party. The practical tasks of constructing basic democratic structures after the Liberation, and immediately afterwards the campaign for the Constituent Assembly absorbed me totally, and at that time the idea of deepening my ideological knowledge or reading classics of Marxist thought would have seemed to me a waste of time.

Alongside this life as a rank-and-file militant (which was based largely in my own town and the surrounding area), I began to work for the party press: I did surveys, reviews, short stories, initially for the Genoa edition of *l'Unità*, then the Turin one (at that time there were four editions of *l'Unità*, each of them quite autonomous). It was with the Turin edition that, once I had settled in that city, I had the closest links, working also for some time (between 1948 and '49) as editor of the cultural page. But later, too, in the very bitter years around 1950, *l'Unità* would send me every now and again to do articles on the factories during strikes, occupations, moments of crisis. It was in this capacity that I followed the occupation of the Fiat factory in July 1948, the suppression of the trade unions, the rice-workers' strikes in the Vercelli region.

My encounter with journalism, then, happened in a very different way from how I had imagined it as a boy. It also involved things which from a journalistic point of view constituted a terrible apprenticeship, for instance having to provide local colour when there was a conference or exhibition; this was a practice of newspapers at the time and which still continues to a certain extent today, but it is now done more broad-mindedly, whereas in those days it was a form of second-rate literature. I remember that initially the job of writing features for *l'Unità* fell to the poet Alfonso Gatto, then my dearest friend and mentor, but he knew how to enjoy himself doing it, for instance covering the Giro d'Italia.

But this political journalist phase was only a secondary element in those years of apprenticeship. In 1945 I had started to gravitate towards the Einaudi publishing house; while I was still living in San Remo, I would often go to Milan to see Elio Vittorini and the editors of *Il Politecnico*, and to Turin where the gruff Pavese welcomed me with a friendship which became more and more precious to me, in what were to be the last years of his life. My friendship with Giulio Einaudi, which has lasted almost forty years now, was to prove decisive for me, because I met him in Milan towards the end of 1945 and he immediately suggested some things I should do. At that stage Giulio was convinced that I also had practical, organizational and economic skills, in other words that I was one of the new type of intellectuals that he was trying to foster; at any rate Giulio always had the gift of managing to get people to do things they did not know how to do.

In that post-Liberation period, which for me was like coming back to life again, I began to carry out some small jobs for Einaudi, particularly publicity notices, articles to send to local newspapers promoting new books, brief accounts of foreign books and Italian manuscripts that had arrived. It was then that I realized that my working environment could not be anywhere but in publishing, in an avant-garde publishers, amid people of widely differing political opinions who engaged in heated debates, but who were all very friendly with each other. I would say to myself: whether or not I become a writer, I will have a job I am passionate about, and I will be working with interesting people. The balance I had sought up until then between a practical profession and literature I found in an area quite close to literature but which was not quite identical with it: Einaudi admittedly published literature, but above all they published history, politics, economics and science and this gave me the impression of being at the centre of so many things.

After a period of uncertainty as to whether to settle in Milan or Turin, I opted for Turin, becoming a friend and collaborator of Giulio Einaudi and the other people who worked with him and were older than me: Cesare Pavese, Felice Balbo, Natalia Ginzburg, Massimo Mila, Franco Venturi, Paolo Serini and all the others who throughout the rest of Italy worked directly or indirectly with Einaudi, and naturally I also became friendly with those of the new generation who like myself were just beginning to start working in publishing.

So for fifteen years my life was that of an editor in publishing, and in all that time I devoted much more work to other people's books than to my own. In short, I had succeeded only in erecting a barrier between myself and my vocation to be a writer, even though it might have appeared that I was in the most favourable environment.

My first book, *The Path to the Spiders' Nests*, came out in 1947, a novel based on my experience of the partisan war. For a first novel by an unknown writer, it enjoyed what could then have been considered success: it quickly sold more than 3,000 copies and there was an immediate reprint of another 2,000 copies. At that time nobody read Italian fiction, but Einaudi believed in my novel and launched it. He even distributed round the bookshops a poster with a photograph in which I am walking with my hands in my pockets: at that time these were things that had never been done before. In short, I was immediately 'successful', but I did not realize it, because we did not talk in those terms, that kind of terminology did not exist. In any case by nature I have never been someone who lets success go to his head: I had managed to write that book and get people to read it but who knew whether I could do the same with a second novel? I continued to believe that real writers were other people; as for me, God only knew.

In fact I tried for years to write a second novel without success; the friends I showed my efforts to were not impressed. In 1949 I published a book of short stories, which, as happens with books of short stories, had a limited run of 1,500 copies: just enough to ensure that it reached the critics and the small group of readers who looked out for new Italian fiction at that time.

I obtained a critical consensus (including some authoritative critics) right from those very first books. I can say that everything was quite easy for me from the start; except that I had to work all day in an office, even though I did not have to clock in, and in order to write I had to take days off, which was never denied me and that was already a stroke of luck.

The book that marked my presence in a more identifiable way was *The Cloven Viscount*, a story of about a hundred pages which Vittorini published in his experimental series, '*I Gettoni*', in 1951; this edition was practically only for the specialist, but it enjoyed a good critical success, being mentioned by Emilio Cecchi, at that time the arbiter of taste in Italian literature. From that point on, a particular direction was signposted for my literary work, namely what we could define as fantasy fiction, which I would continue to alternate with stories written in other, more realistic, keys.

In 1957 I published *The Baron in the Trees*, and just afterwards (or just before, I cannot remember) the *Italian Folktales* appeared, a huge work which I had carried out after being commissioned to do so by my publisher. In 1958 I published my collected *Racconti (Short Stories)*, a volume which contained all the shorter fiction I had written up until then; in short, by now I was able to afford to publish stories that were just called *Short Stories*.

Was that the point at which I could consider calling myself a 'professional' writer? Ten years had elapsed since my first book and I would say that ten years is the time it takes for someone who continues to publish with some regularity to know whether he is going to make it as a writer. By then I no longer asked myself the question 'Will I become a writer or not?' since it was other people who considered that I was. Even royalties, though by no means enough to live on, were beginning to become a significant item in my meagre income. So much so that, roughly just as I turned forty, I left full-time employment at Einaudi, but I stayed on as a consultant.

The screens I had erected around me to prevent me from considering writing as my main job were collapsing. I mentioned that my editorial work continued to interest me, but I was much more independent; the same could be said of politics: not that I was less interested in it, but I had gradually reached the point (better late than never) of wanting to state my own autonomous position against the all-powerful force of the ideological and party line. And in 1957 I declared my resignation from the Communist party with an open letter, after the debates and disagreements that had taken place in 1956.

From the beginning of my militancy it had been the political struggles in Italy that had kept me loyal to the party; but I had always had reservations about the 'Soviet model' and about the ways that had been imposed on the 'popular democracies', all of which were topics that a Communist could not discuss 'in case you played the enemy's game'. When finally there was open debate in Moscow, and Warsaw and Budapest rebelled, I was one of those who believed that the hour of truth had come. I tried to participate, with many friends also from Einaudi, in the debate that was engulfing the left in the West. And I did not feel I could go back to accepting the new clampdown.

This was a painless break in that it took place amid a general reshuffling of the Italian left, in which everyone felt the need to check their convictions and adopt a more precise political identity. At that point I was not yet able to say where I stood in this picture. Perhaps it was only then that we began to realize what Communism, Socialism, Marxism meant; previously, when I had joined the party, I had been more inclined to view problems on a day-by-day basis and leave general questions to one side. It was then that I saw taking shape the positions which, in their critique of official Communism, would be defined as 'reformist', and those which came from 'the left' and predicted an intensification of social conflict in Italy and the world. For a while I did not identify with one side or the other: reformism seemed to me to lead one to deal with the humdrum practicality of participating in political and administrative current affairs, which may be essential but which did not interest me at all (so that, after supporting Antonio Giolitti at the time of his removal from the PCI and in his first cultural initiatives after that, I did not follow him into the Socialist party); and as for the intransigent or revolutionary tendencies (whether they supported the workers, the Chinese model or called themselves 'third-worlders'), despite recognizing their idealizing thrust, my objections in principle against their doctrinaire approach, abstractions, blind faith, apocalypticism, their 'the worse it gets, the better' mentality, were such as to make me establish a very clear distance between myself and even friends whom I valued intellectually.

So within that world of the Italian left which was my natural habitat I found myself in a position of isolation, of politically 'not belonging', which would only become more pronounced with the passing of time and which would encourage my natural tendency to stay silent the more I heard the inflation of words and discourses around me.

Instead I deepened what had always been my conviction: that what counts is the complexity of a culture in developing its various concrete aspects, in the things produced by labour, in its technical methods for doing things, in experience and knowledge and morality, in the values which become defined through practical work. In short, my idea had always been to join in building a cultural context capable of meeting the needs of a modern Italy and in which literature constituted an innovative force and the repository of the deepest convictions. On this basis, I renewed and strengthened my friendship with Elio Vittorini and together we published *Il Menabò*, a journal which came out a couple of times a year, between 1959 and 1966, and which followed or predicted the changes taking place in Italian literature, in ideas and in practice.

Vittorini was a man who had always subordinated his own work to a broader battle to establish what the foundations of Italian culture and literature should be in the context of the whole cultural picture; so much so that he sacrificed for this battle his own creative activity, the books he could have written. He was a man of great decisiveness in the different ideas he championed and was very combative; these were all qualities I did not possess

229

and when Elio died in 1966 that was the end of that kind of activity for me. But the moral imperative of this writer who was so different from any other marked me deeply, in the sense that I always need to justify the fact of writing a book with the meaning that this book might take on as a new cultural operation in a wider context.

But now, once again, I have found a formula for putting something else before writing, namely my need for what I do to make sense as an innovative operation in the present cultural context, to be in some sense something that has never been attempted before, and which represents a further development of the possibilities of literary expression. I would very much like to be one of those writers who have something really clear in their head to say and throughout their life they promote this idea in their works. I would like to be like that, but I am not; my relationship with ideas is more complex and problematical; I always think of the pros and cons in everything and each time I have to construct a very complex picture. This is the reason why I can even go many years without publishing anything, working on projects which constantly end up in crisis.

So you see that coming to interview me on the subject of success is really barking up the wrong tree, because the successful writer is the one who believes strongly in himself, in his discourse, in the idea he has in his head, and he goes along his road certain that the world will follow after him. I, on the other hand, always feel the need to justify the fact that I write, that I impose on other people something that has come out of my head and which I am always unsure of and dissatisfied with. Now I am not making a moral distinction: even the writer who is sure of his own truth can be morally admirable and even heroic; the only thing that is not admirable is to exploit success by continuing to meet the public's expectations in the most obvious way. I have never done this, even though I knew that my innovations might cause consternation among my readership and I could lose part of it along the way.

Now that I am sixty, I have at last realized that the duty of the writer is simply to do what he knows how to do: storytellers have to tell stories, to portray, to invent. For many years I have given up laying down precepts about how one should write: what is the point of preaching one kind of literature or another, if then the things that you end up writing are maybe totally different? It took me a long time to realize that what counts is not your intention but what you actually achieve. So my literary work has become also a search for myself, an attempt to understand what I am.

I notice that up to now I have talked little about the pleasure you can enjoy when writing: if you don't experience at least a little bit of fun, you will never write anything good. For me doing things that give me pleasure means doing new things. Writing as such is a boring and solitary occupation; if you repeat yourself, an infinite sadness seizes hold of you. Certainly, it has to be said that even the page that I think I've written most spontaneously costs an awful lot of effort; a sense of relief, of satisfaction, only sets in afterwards, once the book is finished. But what is important is that my readers enjoy themselves, not me.

I think I can say that I have managed to keep on board at least a part of my readership, even when writing new things; I have accustomed my readers always to expect something new from me: they know that tried-and-tested recipes don't satisfy me and that I don't get any fun out of repeating myself.

My books do not belong to the category of best-sellers, books that sell tens of thousands of copies the minute they are published and then are already forgotten the following year. My greatest satisfaction is seeing my books being reprinted every year, some with print-runs of ten or fifteen thousand copies every time.

Up to now I have only been speaking about Italy, but under the subject of this interview it is also relevant to speak of how an Italian writer can also become known outside Italy. Of course, an author's image changes because in Italy he is seen for the ensemble of his activities, in the context of a culture consisting of many components, of many reference points, whereas abroad it is only the translations of your books that arrive, like meteorites, from which critics and readers have to develop an idea of the planet that they have come from. I began to be translated in major countries towards the end of the 1950s; it was a period when works were translated everywhere more perhaps than they are now; perhaps because there was a greater expectation for what might emerge. But being translated does not yet mean being read properly. It is a kind of routine: even abroad a novel in translation is published in a few thousand copies, polite reviews appear in the papers, the book stays in the bookshops a couple of weeks, then it disappears, only to reappear remaindered at half price, then it is pulped. International fame means mostly this; in my case too it was like this for a long time. The fact of 'existing' as an author abroad is something that I've only been aware of for the last ten years or so, and it relates particularly to two countries: France and the United States.

In France I began to 'exist' really when I was published in the *Livres de poche*, and subsequently in other paperback series by other publishers. Suddenly I began to meet French people who had read my books, something which had never happened before, even though many people had heard of me. Nowadays all my books are reprinted frequently and several are available in paperback: so I would say that in France my success is due more to anonymous readers than to critics.

In the United States you could say that what happened was the opposite: my name became established first thanks to some important 'opinion-maker' (such as Gore Vidal: you could say that it was he who really launched me) and the book of mine that became a hit was the one that you would have said was the furthest from American reading habits: *Invisible Cities*. Even today in the United States I am still considered above all as the author of *Invisible Cities*, a book that is apparently loved by poets, architects and in general by young students. All my books are reprinted in 'trade paperbacks' which is the mid-market category of quality paperbacks, which reaches out also to the vast student reading public. But when the *Italian Folktales* were translated unabridged (twenty-five years after the original Italian edition) the surprise success was considered almost a 'mass' phenomenon.

At this point I could start to create new problems for myself, in other words to think how to place myself in terms of world literature. But to tell you the truth, I have always considered literature in a context broader than the purely national one, so this could never be a problem for me. Just as the fact of being an Italian writer who has never indulged in any of the commonplaces that foreigners expect from Italians has never made me feel the need to explain how and why I could not be anything but an Italian writer. In short, perhaps the time has come for me to accept myself as I am, and to write just as it comes, for the remainder of life that is left to me, or even to give up there and then if I saw that I had nothing more to say.

[Interview with Felice Froio, published in his *Dietro il successo. Ricordi e testimonianze di alcuni protagonisti del nostro tempo: quale segreto dietro il loro successo? (Behind the Success. Memories and Declarations from Some of the Most Important People of Our Time: What is the Secret behind their Success?)* (Milan: Sugarco, 1984).]

I Would Like to be Mercutio ...

I would like to be Mercutio. Among his virtues, I admire above all his lightness, in a world full of brutality, his dreaming imagination – as the poet of Queen Mab – and at the same time his wisdom, as the voice of reason amid the fanatical hatreds of Capulets and Montagues. He sticks to the old code of chivalry at the price of his life perhaps just for the sake of style and yet he is a modern man, sceptical and ironic: a Don Quixote who knows very well what dreams are and what reality is, and he lives both with open eyes.

[The *New York Times Book Review*, 89:49 (2 December 1984) asked a certain number of celebrities what character from a novel or from a work of non-fiction they would like to be. This was Calvino's reply (in English).]

My City Is New York

In what way did your first contacts with American culture develop, and in particular your contacts with its literature, from Hemingway's novels to Faulkner's?

In terms of my own development, which took place in the 1940s, it was initially as a simple reader that I first discovered American fiction, which at that time represented a huge opening on the Italian horizon. For that reason, when I was young, American literature was very important and of course I read all the novels that reached Italy in those days. To begin with, however, I was a provincial: I lived in San Remo and had no literary background since I was a student in the Agriculture Faculty. Later I became a friend of Pavese and Vittorini; I never knew Pintòr* as he died during the war. I was a *homo novus*: I started to get around only after the war.

It is true that Hemingway was one of my models, perhaps because in terms of stylistic models he was easier than Faulkner, who is so much more complex. And also as far as my first writings are concerned, I was definitely influenced by Hemingway; in fact I even went to see him in a hotel in Stresa, in 1948, I think, and we went out fishing on a boat in the lake.

---

* Giaime Pintòr (1918–43), writer and Resistance leader. He took a heroic part in the defence of Rome against the Germans in September 1943; his *Sangue d'Europa (The Blood of Europe)* was published posthumously (1950).

Faced with a literary output as vast and heterogeneous as yours, it is not always easy to trace and focus on possible links and genuine influences which tie it to one writer or another; as far as American literature is concerned, which classic works do you appreciate and like the most?

I am a writer of short stories first and foremost more than a novelist, so one area of reading which has certainly influenced me, right from childhood, if you like, and not just in an American context but in absolute terms, I would say is Edgar Allan Poe, since he is a writer who knows how to do everything, in terms of the short story. Within its confines he is an author of limitless possibilities; and also because he seems to me to be a mythical figure, a hero of literature, a cultural hero, founder of all the narrative genres that would be developed after him.

For this reason one can trace lines which link Poe with, for instance, Borges or Kafka: you could trace extraordinary links like this that never end. Even a writer as unusual as Giorgio Manganelli – certainly one of the most notable Italian writers of recent years – he too, despite being so different from Poe, discovered him when he translated him, and he too has established a genuine rapport with Poe. For this reason also I think that Poe's presence is very much a contemporary one. Still on the subject of links with classic American writers, I could cite the names of Hawthorne or Mark Twain: the latter is a writer I certainly feel close to, particularly in what we could call his more ungainly and 'unsophisticated' aspects.

Let us continue following the evolution of this relationship of yours with a society and a literature which in turn was changing as new avenues, new experiences opened up, compared with those that had inspired the generation of the 1930s and 1940s.

Naturally American literature became different, around 1950, after Pavese's death; but already towards the end of the 1940s this change was in the air. I remember when Pavese began to read the new books that arrived here in the post-war period – there was Saul Bellow with his first novel, *Dangling Man* – and I remember

Vittorini too, who said: 'This lot are like European writers, they're more intellectual, we are not so interested in them.'

It was a completely different turn that American literature had taken, and when in 1959 I went to the United States for the first time as an adult, that mythical picture of the writers of the early post-war years, which was still that of the so-called Lost Generation, no longer held sway. This was the time when a figure like Henry Miller was much more important than Hemingway, whom nobody bothered about any more. Things, then, have changed radically: nowadays you would need to see what relations there have been between the writers of my generation, both in Italy and in America; you could make some comparisons. Who is the equivalent of Norman Mailer, for instance? For certain provocative aspects, Pasolini could be, even though Mailer is a character who still is much more like Hemingway, who was linked to that kind of writer.

We have come to the present situation, to the time when it is no longer possible to look at America in terms of the barbaric, nor at the American writer as the crude, violent, often unreflecting interpreter of that reality.
This is something that needs to be thought out fully: this image of an America that is barbaric and full of vital energy certainly no longer exists. The American writer, unlike what happens, or happened, in Italy – since even here we are moving in that direction – is someone who works in a university, who writes novels about campus life, about the gossip surrounding the adulterous affairs between lecturers, which is not the big wide world, not something genuinely exciting, but that is the way things are: life in American society is like that.

What aspects of the American literary world of today seem to you to be most significant, and who are the most important personages?
Nowadays, in American literature, sometimes I look with envy at those writers who know how to instantly catch something of contemporary life in their novels, who have a chatty and ironic

style, like Saul Bellow; I am certainly not good enough to do that kind of thing. American fiction has novelists capable of writing a novel a year and of giving the flavour of a period; I envy them enormously.

Among writers who are my contemporaries I would say that I lived through the discovery of a writer who had a genuinely beautiful style – I'm talking about John Updike – and that when he began writing he seemed a really important author. Later he also wrote a bit too much: he still remains an intelligent, brilliant person, but at times one notes a certain facileness in American writers of today. If I had to say who is the living author I like best, and who has also influenced me in some way, I would say it is Vladimir Nabokov: a great Russian writer and a great writer in English; he has invented an English which is of extraordinary richness. He truly is a great genius, one of the greatest writers of the century and one of the people with whom I identify most. Of course he is also someone of extraordinary cynicism, of formidable cruelty, but he is genuinely one of the great authors.

From the way your most recent fiction has developed – If on a Winter's Night a Traveller *and even more so* Mr Palomar *– one might think there was some link between you and the so-called initiators of the postmodern.*

Of course I also have links with what could be defined as the new American avant-garde: I am someone who goes to the United States every so often to do these creative writing courses, and I am a friend of John Barth, a writer who began with a very fine novel, *The End of the Road*. After this first book, which we could define as existentialist, Barth became more and more complicated, with works of more sophisticated structure; it is he who, despite not reading works in any other language than English, is to an extent the American ambassador to the new European literatures. Apart from Barth, Donald Barthelme and Thomas Pynchon, there are other writers whose works I follow and with whom I am also friends.

In conclusion, I would like to ask you what your encounter with America as a physical entity has meant for you in terms of personal sensations: city America, as it is portrayed in so many films as well as novels, and the real city, which is the symbol of today's America.

In terms of literature I am a bit of an autodidact, I was a late starter and naturally for many years I went to the cinema, when you could see two films a day, and these were American films. I had an intense rapport as a spectator with American cinema, so much so that for me cinema remains essentially American cinema.

My physical encounter with America was a truly marvellous experience: New York is one of my cities, and in fact, still in the 1960s, in *Cosmicomics*, and also in *Time and the Hunter*, there are stories that are set in New York. On the other side of the Atlantic I feel part of that majority of Italians who go to America with great ease – by now there are millions and millions of them – and not of that minority who stay in Italy; perhaps because the first time I went to America, with my parents, I was just one year old. When I went back for the first time as an adult to the USA, I had a grant from the Ford Foundation which entitled me to go round all the States, with no obligation: naturally I did this trip, travelling in the South, and also in California, but I felt I was a New Yorker: my city is New York.

[Interview by Ugo Rubeo, recorded in Palermo in September 1984; later published in *Mal d'America – da mito a realtà (The American Malaise – from Myth to Reality)* (Rome: Editori Riuniti, 1987). The title is not by Calvino.]

Interview with Maria Corti

Which authors had the greatest influence on your development as a writer? And is there a common element, something which unifies those that were your most genuine preferences in reading?

You would like me to mention some book I read as an adolescent and which subsequently made its influence felt in things I later wrote. I will say at once: Ippolito Nievo's *Le confessioni di un ottuagenario (Confessions of an Octogenarian)*, the only Italian nineteenth-century novel which had a novelistic charm that was comparable to that found so abundantly in foreign literatures. An episode in my first novel, *The Path to the Spiders' Nests*, was inspired by the meeting of Carlino and Spaccafumo. An atmosphere vaguely reminiscent of the Castello di Fratta is evoked in *The Cloven Viscount*. And *The Baron in the Trees* reworks Nievo's novel around the protagonist's entire life, and it covers the same historical period, straddling the eighteenth and nineteenth centuries, and the same social environments; moreover, the female character in my novel is modelled on Nievo's La Pisana.

When I began to write I was a young man who had read very little; so trying to reconstruct an 'influential' library means going immediately back to the books of my childhood: every such list, I believe, must begin with *Pinocchio* which I have always considered a model of narration, where every motif is presented and returns with an exemplary rhythm and clarity, every episode has a function and a necessity in the overall design of the plot, every character has a clarity of visual outline and an unmistakable way of speaking. If a continuity can be discerned in my earliest development – let's say from the age of six to twenty-three – it is one that goes from *Pinocchio* to Kafka's *Amerika*, another decisive book in my life, and one which I have always considered 'The Novel' *par excellence* in world literature in the twentieth century and perhaps not only in that century. The unifying element could be defined thus: the adventure and solitude of an individual lost in the vastness of the world, as he moves towards an internal initiation into the world and a construction of the self.

But the elements that go into the construction of a poetic world are many; for each one of them precise sources can be found in some of the things one reads when young. Recently, when rereading the hunting scene in *The Legend of St Julian the Hospitaller*, I relived with precise certainty the point when that taste for the Gothic and animalistic first took hold of me, the taste that emerges in a story like 'The Crow Comes Last' and in others of that period and afterwards.

In your creative career, as suggested by your works, one never finds repetition, which is an extremely positive thing. In this context do you prefer to pick out, in the history of your narrative works, a process of consistent development, of going forward in stages, or would you stress changes of route which were due to the fact that you had reached in each phase of your work the essential goal you had set yourself? Or, a third hypothesis, are you one of those writers who think they have continued to write only one book throughout their life?

I would opt for the second hypothesis: a change of direction in order to say something that I would not have been able to say with the previous approach. This does not mean that I regard the preceding line of research as coming to an end: it can happen that I continue for years to plan other texts to add to those I have already written, even though now I am busy with something completely different; in fact I do not consider any operation complete until I have given it a sense and a structure I can consider definitive.

Almost everything I write can be ideally fitted into 'macro-texts', a procedure that you, Maria Corti, studied with regard to the Marcovaldo stories. Even the Marcovaldo suite, which I consider closed, I could have continued further, applying that narrative mechanism to the technological and social changes in the city in subsequent years; but after a while, the spontaneity of a certain type of writing, as you noted in your analysis, runs out. Consequently there have been many series which I began but which I then abandoned without bringing them to a conclusion.

'A Plunge into Real Estate', 'The Watcher' and a third story of which I only wrote a few pages, '*Che spavento l'estate*' ('What a Fright that Summer'), were all conceived together around 1955 as a triptych with the overall title *Chronicle of the Fifties*, centring on the reaction of the intellectual to the negative reality around him. But by the time I managed to complete 'The Watcher' too much time had elapsed, we were already in the 1960s, I felt the need to search for new forms, and so that series remained unfinished.

In the meantime I had also written 'Smog', a story that at that time I considered very different because I had written it using a different method of transforming experience, whereas it could easily have become the third story in the planned triptych. Instead, it found its place as an accompaniment to 'The Argentine Ant', written ten years previously, in a diptych justified by structural and conceptual affinities.

The language of an artist, as Montale said, is 'a language that is historicized, that has a relationship. It is valid in as much as it opposes, or differs from, other languages.' How would you describe the identity of your language from this perspective?
This question ought to be turned back to you critics. I can only say that I try to counteract the mental laziness that is in evidence

in the works of so many of my fellow-novelists in their use of a language that is as predictable and insipid as can be. I believe that prose requires an investment of all one's verbal resources, just as poetry does: a spark and precision in the choice of words, economy and significance and inventiveness in their distribution and strategy, élan and mobility and tension in the sentence, and agility and ductility in shifting from one register to another, from one rhythm to another. For instance, writers who use too obvious or redundant adjectives or ones that are only there for an effect which they would be unable to achieve otherwise, can be considered in some cases as naïve, and in others as dishonest: in either case they are never people you can trust.

Having said that, I will add that I do not agree either that one should load the phrase with too many intentions, winks and grimaces to the reader, colouring, layers, blends, pirouettes. Yes of course, one must aim to obtain the maximum effect, but one must also take care that this result is achieved, if not with minimal means, then at least with means that are not disproportionate to the end one seeks to attain.

In the period when I began to ask myself the question of how to write, namely in the early 40s, there was an idea of a *morality* which had to give shape to the style, and this is perhaps the thing that has remained most with me from that climate in Italian literature, throughout all the distance that separates us from then. If I have to define with an example my ideal kind of writing, here is a book that I have to hand because it has just been published (1984) but it contains pages written in the 1940s: Giorgio Caproni's *Il labirinto (The Labyrinth)*.* I would choose this paragraph from p.17:

> On the bare slope of Grammondo we went out into the open air. And although the sky had turned filthy, and from

---

* Giorgio Caproni (1912–88), Ligurian poet, novelist and translator. Like Calvino, he fought in the Resistance, as this extract shows.

the West there blew an impetuous, rain-laden wind that was anything but gentle, the pleasure of giving our feet some air, feet still tender and burnt by that first forced march, prevented me from satisfying my overpowering desire to pitch camp and fling myself immediately under the covers. And yet there was still the odd rash person who, despite his tiredness, had the strength to try to be pointlessly clever, putting himself well on show on the crest of the mountain, right opposite the French, instead of staying with the rest of us a few metres below, under cover. Not courage at all: irresponsibility. And when an officer roared at him the rebuke he deserved, pointing out the danger he was exposing us to, I realized, or rather I felt, I was genuinely in line, and that the battle would be a question of hours, maybe minutes.

I will put two similar questions into one. Does the creative process behind your texts involve many phases of rewriting? It could be said that you attach great importance to the 'possible worlds' an author can invent, and therefore to the relationship between what you choose to actualize in the text, and what you are forced to exclude but continue to keep in mind. Would you like to say something about this?
Usually I carry an idea in my head for years before making up my mind to give it shape on the page, and on many occasions while waiting for this to happen I just let it die. The idea dies in any case, even when I decide to start writing: from that point there will exist only attempts to realize the idea, approximations, the struggle with my means of expression. Every time I start writing something, it requires an effort of will, because I know that what awaits me is the labour and dissatisfaction of trying and trying again, correcting, rewriting.

Spontaneity also has its moments: sometimes at the beginning – and in that case it does not usually last long – sometimes as a thrust you develop as you go along, sometimes as a final flourish. But is spontaneity something we should value? It certainly

Interview with Maria Corti

is for the writer, since it allows you to write with less effort, without going into crisis every minute; but it is not certain that the work always benefits from it. The important thing is spontaneity as an impression which the work conveys, but that does not mean that you can achieve this result by using spontaneity as a means: in many cases it is only patient elaboration that allows you to arrive at the most satisfying and apparently 'spontaneous' solution.

Every text has its own history, its own method. There are books which come to fruition by a process of exclusion: first you accumulate a mass of material, I mean written pages; then you make a selection, gradually realizing what it is that fits into that design, that programme, and what on the other hand remains extraneous. The book *Mr Palomar* is the result of many phases of this type of work, in which 'removing' played a much greater role than 'inserting'.

Have the natural and cultural environments in which you have lived – Turin, Rome, Paris – been congenial and stimulating for you, or did you preserve your solitude more strongly in some than in others?
The city which I have felt was my own city more than any other is New York. I once even wrote, imitating Stendhal, that I wanted 'New Yorker' to be engraved on my tombstone. That was in 1960. I have not changed my mind, even though I have lived most of the time since then in Paris, a city which I never leave except for brief periods and where perhaps, if I could choose, I will die. But every time I go to New York I find it more beautiful and closer to the shape of an ideal city. It may also be the fact that it is a geometric, crystalline city, without a past, without depth, apparently without secrets; therefore it is the city which intimidates me least, the city which I can have the illusion of possessing in my mind, of being able to think about in its entirety all in the same instant.

Despite all that, how much do you see New York in the stories I have written? Very little. Perhaps just a couple of stories from

Time and the Hunter or similar works, and the odd page here and there. (Look, I've just checked *The Castle of Crossed Destinies*: page 80.) And Paris? I certainly could not find many more examples. The fact is that many of my stories are not situated in any recognizable place. Perhaps that is why replying to this question is costing me so much effort: for me, the processes of the imagination follow paths that do not always coincide with the paths we follow in life.

As for a natural environment, the one you cannot reject or hide is the landscape of your birth, where you grew up; San Remo continues to pop up in my books, in the most varied panoramas and perspectives, especially seen from above, and it is particularly present in *Invisible Cities*. Naturally I am talking of San Remo as it was up until thirty or thirty-five years ago, and particularly as it was fifty or sixty years ago, when I was a child. Every investigation of this kind has to begin with that nucleus from which one's imagination, psychology and language develop; this attachment to San Remo is as strong in me now as the urge to stay close to my roots was in my youth, an urge which soon turned out to be pointless, since the places quickly ceased to exist.

After the war I could not wait to set against the fixity of that ancestral backdrop, from which I had never moved, the panorama of the big city; after some wavering between Milan and Turin, I ended up finding a job in Turin and also a certain number of reasons (that now it would take a real effort to dig up again) to justify my eventual place of residence as a cultural choice. Was I at that time trying to position myself in response to the Milan/Turin opposition? Probably I was, although I did have a strong tendency to try to link the two opposing terms. In fact for all the years I lived more or less definitively in Turin (and that was quite a few, fifteen or so years), I tried as far as possible to live in the two cities as though it were just one city, divided not so much by the 127 kilometres of motorway, as by the incompatibility between the grid pattern of one and the circular plan of the other, something which caused psycho-topographical difficulties for the person trying to live in both of them at the same time.

At the start of the post-war period, the general fervour of cultural productivity which took on different shapes in euphoric and extrovert Milan, as opposed to methodical and cautious Turin, shifted the magnetic pole of Italian literature to the North, which was a novelty by comparison with the geography of Italian literature between the wars, which had had Florence as its undisputed capital. However, even then defining a 'Northern' approach as opposed to a previous 'Florentine' approach would have been to force the terms, for the simple fact that the exponents of both traditions had been (at different times but without interruption) the same people.

Just as in later years it would have been difficult, when Rome became the residential centre of a large number of people who wrote, people from all over and from every literary tendency, to find a common denominator to define a 'Roman line' as opposed to any other line. In short, it seems to me that a map of Italian literature today is totally independent of the geographical map, and I leave the question open as to whether this is a good thing or a bad thing.

As for me, I am fine only when I do not have to ask myself 'Why am I here?', a question which you can forget about usually in cities which have such a rich and complex cultural texture, a bibliography so vast as to discourage anyone who was thinking of writing from adding anything else to it. For example, for the last two centuries writers from all over the world have lived in Rome, who have got no particular reason to be in Rome more than anywhere else, some of them curious explorers who found the city's spirit congenial to them (Gogol, more than anyone else), others profiting from the advantage of feeling like a foreigner.

Unlike other writers, in your case creative activity has never prevented you from producing parallel theoretical reflections, both metafictional and metapoetic. Just look, if we needed an example, at a very recent text, 'How I wrote one of my books', which came out in 'Actes sémiotiques. Documents', *6:51 (1984) ('Groupe de Recherches sémiolinguistiques' from the École des Hautes Études en Sciences Sociales). And confirmation would come from the powerful suggestions that semiologists and literary theorists have always derived from your oeuvre, even though you do not appear to be writing a programmatic work. How do you explain this sort of brilliant symbiosis?*

It is quite natural for ideas in general circulation to have influenced me, sometimes immediately, at other times with delayed action. The important thing would be to have thought in advance of something that was subsequently useful to others. The fact that I had dealt with popular folktales at a time when no one bothered about their mysterious mechanisms, made me particularly receptive to structuralist problems, as soon as they came to general attention about a decade later. However, I do not think I have a real theoretical vocation. One's pleasure in experimenting with a method of thought as though it were a gadget imposing demanding and complicated rules can coexist with a basic agnosticism and empiricism; the way poets and artists think, I believe, is like this. It is quite different from investing all your expectations of reaching a truth in a theory or a methodology (as one would in a philosophy or ideology). I have always greatly admired and loved the rigour of philosophy and science; but always from a bit of a distance.

How do you feel being part of Italian literature today? Can you glimpse anything in more recent times that goes beyond pure decorum? Moreover, does the question about the 'sense of literature', which has been asked by more than one journal, seem to you to have any sense?

To give an overview of Italian literature today – and to reconfigure in this light the literary history of the century – one must take account of various factors which were true forty years ago, at the time of my literary apprenticeship, and which have become clear again now, so they have always been true: a) the privileged position of poetry in verse, containing as it does values that prosewriters and storytellers also pursue, though by different means but with the same ends; b) in fiction the prevalence of the short story and other forms of creative writing, more than the novel, whose successes are rare and exceptional; c) the fact that unconventional, eccentric and atypical writers end up being the most representative figures of their time.

Bearing all this in mind, and going back over the totality of what I have done and said and thought, wrongly or rightly, I have to conclude that I feel perfectly at ease in Italian literature and that I could not imagine myself anywhere but in that context.

[First published in *Autografo*, 2:6 (October, 1985).]

Index

250

Index

251

Index

PML